# HOWARD MARKS
# HIS LIFE AND HIGH TIMES
## DAVID LEIGH

U
PA

LONDON SYDNEY WELLINGTON

First published as *High Time* in Great Britain by
William Heinemann Ltd, in 1984.
First published by Unwin ® Paperbacks, an imprint of
Unwin Hyman Ltd, in 1985.
Revised edition entitled *Howard Marks – His Life and High
Times*, published in 1988.

**Unwin Hyman Limited**
**15–17 Broadwick Street**
**London W1V 1FP**

Allen & Unwin Australia Pty Ltd,
8 Napier Street, North Sydney, NSW 2060, Australia

Allen & Unwin New Zealand Pty Ltd, with the Port Nicholson
Press
60 Cambridge Terrace, Wellington, New Zealand.

ISBN 0 04 3640 23 0

A CIP catalogue record is available from The British Library

Printed in Great Britain by Cox & Wyman Ltd, Reading.

# Contents

# Preface

In the summer of 1988, there was a worldwide sensation when the US Drug Enforcement Agency announced that they had arrested the planet's biggest, longest-practising and most-successful marijuana smuggler. They intended to extradite him from Spain to the US, they said, and put him on trial for having smuggled literally thousands of tons of dope in a professional career which had lasted the best part of eighteen years. The smuggler was British: his name was Howard Marks, and he was an outlaw – perhaps the last of the Sixties outlaws – who had already become a major celebrity, not least for his cheeky ability to outwit the law. This book is the true, and probably surprising, story of his life.

All the incidents described in this book actually occurred. In many cases, the dialogue is based on transcripts of tape-recordings, telephone taps, and court proceedings. Sometimes the dialogue has been reconstructed, either from the recollection of participants, or on the basis of facts contained in police reports, or authenticated by independent research. No facts have been invented and all the people who figure in this book are real.

Occasionally – and it will be obvious where – true names have not been given. This is to protect individuals who have so far managed to evade the law. This book is based on a great deal of documentary material, but also on many lengthy interviews with dope-smugglers and their friends. It is not possible to acknowledge them, because those who supplied me with tape-recordings made by HM Customs, and confidential police reports, would not appreciate being named. Nor would those who disclosed to me, more or less cheerfully, all kinds of conspiracy, aiding and abetting, perversion of justice, consumption of illicit drugs, and the harbouring of fugitives. Some of them are most respectable persons. They know who they are, and I would like to thank them.

This book sets out to be an uncharacteristically truthful account of a hitherto hidden social history, nurtured in the notorious 1960s, and flourishing to this day. It is not therefore written from the point of view either of an amateur moralist or a policeman. It is not a tract either for or against drugs in general, or cannabis in particular. If it seems outrageous or funny, that is because the events that occurred were really like that. But, because of the ambiguous attitude some people have towards cannabis, it is necessary to make one fact clear. Merely because someone's name appears in this book, unless explicitly stated otherwise, is not to suggest that they either approve of, or use, the substance.

# CHAPTER 1

# Effortless Superiority

When he saw them carrying the corpse of Harold Macmillan's grandson downstairs, Howard knew there was going to be trouble. He quietly shut his door as the inert form of Joshua Macmillan, still in his corduroy jacket and 'drainpipes', was lugged past him into the Balliol quadrangle. The next day, sure enough, there was a pencilled note in his pigeon-hole at the porter's lodge.

'Mr D. H. Marks. Will you please ring the dean as soon as possible.'

McCarthy peered at Howard over his half-moon spectacles, with all the resignation of an Irish Protestant landed gentleman who had been forced to change his name in order to inherit his mother's Worcestershire property. His name now was The Reverend Francis Leader McCarthy Willis-Bund. This talented young hooligan from a Welsh coalfield, who stood there shiftily with the Elvis Presley quiff, frayed jeans and 'winklepicker' shoes, was yet another cross McCarthy had to bear.

'Now, Howard. Joshua's death is, of course, causing concern. Harold Macmillan is Chancellor of this University and a personal acquaintance of the Master of Balliol. He is a frequent diner at our table. The death of his grandson under these circumstances is going to attract painful publicity. There will be a university inquiry by the Proctors. And a police inquiry, no doubt. It is my job to protect the interests of the College, and the welfare of all you young men. I need to know where we stand.'

He paused inquiringly.

'I saw him last night,' Howard said. 'We were in the pub with Andy Mowatt from Wadham. We live on the same staircase, so we go out together sometimes. He seemed very depressed: he kept playing "Cast

9

Your Fate to the Winds" on the jukebox. And he was drinking ever such a lot.'

'Which pub?'

'The Victoria Arms in Walton Street.'

'Howard, is there anything you want to tell me?'

'Well it's no secret about the heroin, is it? Everybody knew he went on a cure to Switzerland, and he was taking all that valium to try and get off it. But none of the rest of us shoot up on heroin. Wouldn't dare.'

'I know there has been a certain amount of drug-taking at Balliol. Young Dennis Irving and one or two of his friends had to be warned strongly last year. That was before he was rusticated. What I need to know is: How much is going on?'

'Yes um, there is a bit of pot smoked. I have smoked it. But not in college, only in people's digs. Josh and Andy Mowatt too.'

'It is not so much the consumption of marijuana that worries me, as the inevitable publicity that will follow this tragedy. If there is a disciplinary inquiry, the damnable pair of Proctors over there will want reprisals. I would advise you not to be quite as frank with them as you have with me.'

There was indeed a lot of publicity. It was 1965. The post-war rock-and-roll generation were just beginning to come into their own, and a good many social collisions were occurring. Dope hysteria was in the wings. Joshua Macmillan was also the kind of devil-may-care Etonian who excited the snobbery of newspaper gossip writers. His grandfather had been, until recently, Prime Minister. They wrote about his rock-and-rollers' suede shoes, his spells at the University of Mexico and in Morocco; his acquaintance with the jazz musicians and black men of Notting Hill in London, and his planned future as MP Maurice Macmillan's son in the wealthy Conservative family's publishing firm. He went to coffee bars. He knew 'beatniks'. And he had long hair. His death was clearly from an overdose of some kind.

Andy Mowatt, Howard's acquaintance from Bristol and Macmillan's closest friend, held forth after the inquest to reporters in his basement lodgings, with his Buddha statue, and the volumes of Sartre, De Quincey and William Burroughs on the shelves.

'Yeah, I smoked my first reefer three years ago. It was in Soho. And you get it from these clubs in Notting Hill. There's been a gradual escalation. When I first came up, only perhaps 10 people were seriously smoking pot. Now the hard core is about 30, with 200 on the fringe.

'Some students come up already initiated, but really it's an acquired taste. There's no real form to existence here: marijuana gives you this part of the day when you know you'll be happy, in the right room with the right people, listening to the right music. You don't have the usual feeling in Oxford, that something marvellous is happening round the corner.'

This was not playing the game. The ground rules for young gentlemen, by which Balliol and the other Oxbridge colleges operated, did not allow them to generate headlines like: 'Confessions of an Oxford Drug-Taker'. The Proctors set about a purge.

'The SENIOR PROCTOR requests Mr D. H. Marks of Balliol College to call upon him at 4.45 p.m. on Thursday the 27th of May 1965 at the Clarendon Building, Broad Street,' said the printed card. In the left-hand corner it said: 'CAP AND GOWN TO BE WORN'. And in fountain-pen had been added the words: 'In connection with a confidential matter'.

They wanted names. Howard fenced. 'If you do not co-operate and provide us with the identities of drug-takers, there may be disciplinary measures.' McCarthy Willis-Bund interceded on Howard's behalf with David Yardley, the Senior Proctor. Nothing bad happened to him. Andy Mowatt was suspended for a year, not for taking drugs, but for 'bringing the name of the university into disrepute'.

'Yeah,' said Howard to Julian Peto, one of his closer friends. 'It's all just a game. This place is just some idiotic playground for young gents. It's like forbidding you to have chicks in your room, unless you bribe your scout. They don't really *do* anything to you, whatever you do.'

It was his second major discovery about Balliol.

The first had been that it existed at all. When they sent him from school at the top of the slagheap-littered Pontcymer valley to sit the scholarship exam in Oxford, he was lost in every way.

'Where are you from?' said the boy sitting at the desk next to him, in crisp Home Counties tones.

'Garw Grammar School,' said Howard, in a thick Welsh accent.

'Oh. Where's that?'

'The Valleys. Near the Rhondda. Where are you from?'

'Eton, actually.'

'Where's *that*, then?'

If Howard had had an entry in *Who's Who*, all he would have been able to list under 'Clubs' would have been 'Van's Teen and Twenty,

Pyle, Glamorganshire'. His teachers did their best after discovering that, despite the mediocrity of his academic surroundings, and his lack of interest in much except beer and Chuck Berry, Howard was intelligent. They said 'Have a look at *Anatomy of Britain* by Anthony Sampson. That's got a bit about Balliol.'

He borrowed this fat, new book out of the public library. It said:

Oxbridge . . . In terms of sheer worldly success, the most formidable college is Balliol.

He read on, appalled:

A sense of Effortless Superiority . . . 'Life is one Balliol man after another', Lord Samuel said . . . Gives the impression of being more a cult than a college . . . since the war government grants for grammar school boys have enormously increased . . . but the quasi-aristocratic atmosphere of Oxbridge remains remarkably unchanged . . . Harold Macmillan (plus son and grandson): Ted Heath; Roy Jenkins; Aldous Huxley; Graham Greene; Dennis Healey; William Rees-Mogg; . . .

Howard did not know whether he could manage 'Effortless Superiority'. They did not have any of that in Kenfig Hill. He grew up in the shadow of the giant steelworks at Port Talbot, in a house crammed with oriental mementoes of the sea. His family had all been colliers in the Valleys, but his father rose to be a merchant navy captain, disappearing out of Swansea for endless voyages during the war. They did not let him come home to see his son until he was two years old. His mother was a schoolteacher, and nervously strict with Howard. It was no swimming in the sea, no bicycles, chapel on Sunday and no playing cards all that day, either. Howard was a polite, affectionate, very *Welsh* child. There is a certain celtic distaste for being lorded over, as they have been for 700 years, by forms of foreign authority. Yet, there is a certain passion for keeping up appearances. Englishmen would have perhaps called him 'sly'.

Howard, for example, had a period of detesting going to school. He was useless at rugby. He resolved the issue by announcing he was ill, and stayed in bed. When his mother took his temperature, he waved the thermometer in the coal fire, behind her back. He could not always manage the trick: sometimes his fever fell again. It was like many of

Howard's future scams which were to make him notorious: it got out of hand. The doctor pronounced the disease to be Undulant Fever: 'You see the way the temperature swings wildly throughout the day: quite characteristic.' Howard was removed to hospital for observation, for two weeks, terrified but at the same time exhilarated.

His heroes were rebels – his finest talent was for stealth. When his mother banned 'teddy-boy' clothes, Howard bought a second-hand drape jacket out of his dinner money and his after-school winnings at Three-Card Brag. He kept it at a friend's house – his first 'stash' of contraband. He was out at night, with his hair greased, his collar turned up, down to the dance-halls in Swansea or the villages round about, in somebody's father's old Hillman, as much beer as they could all manage before last admittance at 9.30 p.m.: under-age in the pub. He was the singer in a talentless group called The Strangers. He could imitate Elvis Presley, only less gracefully. He hung around with the toughest, least lawful kids he could find, and he took the precaution of making friends with the most ruffianly street-fighter in Kenfig Hill – Albert Hancock, James Dean lookalike, brawler, pillager of building sites, and unsuccessful burglar. He was invariably caught.

Howard did genuinely admire him. Hancock repaid the compliment by smashing a beer bottle on the pub counter and pointing it menacingly at the face of anyone who tried to take advantage of the gawky grammar-school kid.

'Howard. Is this your diary?'

'Yes, Dad.'

'Is this what you do when you go out at nights? "Drank 6 Pints" . . . "Shagged this chick". I see. From now on, you'll stay in in the evenings. You can do some schoolwork for a change.'

Howard could not bring himself to admit he had been making it all up. Stung, he did work. His 'O' level exam results were tremendous. Garw Grammar School suspected they might be on to something. In physics and chemistry, it did not matter that Howard was devoid of culture. He passed his 'A' level exams with three grade As. He was Brilliant but Bad. No public image could have given him greater pleasure.

'You know, Julian,' he said later to the blonde bespectacled grammar-school boy from Southampton as they sat drinking pints in Oxford, 'I was really depressed when I first got here. All these people talking about art and poetry and nobody understanding my accent.

You were the only bloke I could speak to, because you were the only one who was swearing! Like a normal person, I mean.' Julian Peto nodded sympathetically. He was later to be appointed to a Chair of Cancer Studies in London and avoided Howard's future world of crime. He was very idealistic, really. '. . . But I've cracked it, now. I've developed a system, and it works every time. Whenever one of those upper-class twits comes up to me and starts talking about Proust, or Thucydides, I give him a grin, and I say "How would you like to fuck a sheep?" '

It was this deliberate loutishness that made Howard popular. He was a character – although not with the other working-class grammar-school boys. They were all reading chemistry books in libraries like miniature Joe Lamptons, determined to pass exams and Make It. The Master of Balliol, Sir David Lindsay Keir, invited freshman Howard to sherry with him and his wife in the Master's Lodge. That was how Howard met one friend who was to have a great influence on his life. He was square, freckly, gingery and fleshy, with a fancy waistcoat, Edwardian mutton-chops, and a knowing manner.

'My name's McMillan: no relation to the PM's grandson. I just like to be called "Mac". Both my Christian names displease me. Which school were you at? It is apparent your name also begins with "M" or you wouldn't be here tonight.'

They liked each other. Howard was reassured by Mac McMillan's worldliness. He professed to regard Howard as a likeable throwback. Also, they both used to collect stamps.

They could be seen together at college drama productions. Howard, dressed as John the Baptist, pranced about the stage in a thigh-length floursack when they performed *Salome*. Mac McMillan lurked around the set, in the guise of a soldier. Much later, it was to be a game both of them would play again, in front of a much bigger audience. For the present, Howard made a cheerful pig of himself at the production party, where a group had been engaged to play music.

'What's this, Mac?'

'It's smoked salmon, you barbarian. And that stuff in your glass is what we call champagne.'

Later, mightily drunk, Howard stuffed two handkerchiefs down the fly of his trousers, grabbed the microphone from one of the musicians, and launched into a tuneless imitation of Elvis Presley, swivelling his hips in what he imagined was erotic frenzy. A number of the girls in the audience were, in fact, impressed. Howard discovered how easy it was to get laid in Oxford, and never really stopped. Howard had a Byronic sensuality in the right light; he was sharp and funny; and most irresistible of all, he never tried to be suave.

He could also be seen at the various exclusive 'Societies' which flourished in Balliol College. The members tended to spend a lot of money, wear dinner jackets, and throw bread rolls. One of the main purposes of their existence was to exclude those not invited. Howard and McMillan could be seen at the Grand Annual Dinner of the 'Victorian Society' along with the Dean. There were eight courses. It was Aloxe-Corton 1953 with the spitted guinea-fowl, Tokay with the 'Bombe Glacée Cheri Pom-Pom' and vintage port with the petit fours. They drank toasts to 'Queen Victoria' and 'The British Empire' and listened to comic Victorian monologues and recitations. After 'Polly Perkins' and 'My Baby has Gone Down the Plug-hole', it was 'Land of Hope and Glory' and the 'National Anthem'.

Mac McMillan stood rigidly to attention for this last.

'Ere!' hissed Howard. 'You don't take all this seriously, do you?'

'It's upholding British traditions.'

'Oh. I thought it was just getting pissed for nothing.'

McMillan invited him out to Germany in the summer vacation. It was his family home: 'Father runs the Chartered Bank in Hamburg. Just manifest yourself in August. We'll all be there.'

'Well, you come over afterwards and stay with me in South Wales for a bit. My father's in charge of the harbour now, at the Port Talbot steelworks.'

'Delighted. Splendid. They're all mad about rugby down there, aren't they?'

He made other friends. There was Henry Hodge, tall, and unconventional who always wore a tie – and jeans with it. He went on to become a well-known community lawyer. There was Steve Balogh, oddball son of one of the two Hungarian economic advisers to the current Wilson government, whose mother was a psychotherapist. There was also Mary Kaldor, daughter of the other Hungarian economic adviser to the Wilson government.

'You know what the treasury call them,' said Balogh: ' "Buda" and "Pest".'

Balogh was one of the friends of Howard Marks whose behaviour became decreasingly predictable. He was thrown into jail a few years

15

later by a dyspeptic judge, Melford Stevenson, for proposing to let off a cylinder of laughing gas in his courtroom during what Balogh considered, no doubt under the influence of the Sixties, an excessively boring pornography trial. Mary Kaldor, on the other hand, was a serious woman, who went on to write a number of influential books about the arms industry.

Invitations to tea from what he thought of incorrigibly as 'chicks' now landed frequently in Howard's pigeon-hole. One came from Kate Mortimer, daughter of the Bishop of Exeter and sister of Edward who was a fellow of All Souls and a leader writer on *The Times*; in later life, she herself became a member of the government's 'Think Tank' and then joined the Rothschild merchant bank. Indeed, another acquaintance was Emma Rothschild, Victor Rothschild's daughter, also a serious young woman. And there was Maria Aitken, daughter of a relation of Lord Beaverbrook, who went on to become a rather well-known actress.

'Yeah,' he said to Julian. 'I'm definitely becoming a Face. And I've worked out a scam for passing my exams. I bribe one of the porters to give me the key to my tutor's room, the night before he hands out the exam papers. It'll only cost 10 bob, and I'll get a copy of the key. Do you want to go in there and make a few free phone calls?'

By now, Howard was well into the embryonic dope scene. Dennis Irving, 6 foot 6, another public school boy from Dulwich, returned from his rustication, a hero to all his Oxford contemporaries. He wore a black leather jacket and black leather trousers. He was very cool.

'I've been on something of a world tour, man. It's not my best outfit. That's a suit all in silver. I wear it with high-heeled boots. Here you go.'

He fetched out of his cigarette packet a ready-rolled joint and lit it up. Trying to act as to the manner born, Howard and his friends inhaled the smoke, holding it in their lungs the way Dennis did, as they passed it round. This was fun. It was another exclusive Oxford society. They fell to giggling, and lay around on cushions listening to soul music.

'Oh no,' said Howard. 'They're putting Charlie Parker on again. I really can't cope with that stuff. But I love being stoned. You get such interesting ideas.'

Marijuana is a very humble drug that grows profuse as a weed in many countries of the world. The dried female top, or the crumbly resin the plant exudes, can be eaten. But it is much more practical to smoke it mixed with tobacco. You only need a little bit. Half an ounce of hashish resin will crumble into 20 cigarettes, and three or four people can generally get a lift off one fair-sized joint. It is a poor man's drug, not addictive, that black Africans and Lebanese and Indian peasants have used for hundreds, if not thousands, of years. It helps them work, it makes music more enjoyable, and it is a temporary escape from reality. Like liquor, but quieter.

Throughout history, those in authority have often tried to outlaw other people's drugs. In Britain and America, attempts to prohibit tobacco, addictive and dangerous as it is, were abandoned with King James I. The appalling miseries of over-reliance on alcohol by factory workers culminated in attempts to criminalise that too, in the early twentieth century. These were abandoned because there was a lot of money in brewing, and people simply would not stop drinking. It turned out, of course, that the problem was not caused by the alcohol – it was the poor and miserable conditions of the people who drank it.

Dope, being merely the pastime of uninfluential foreigners, was easier to stamp out in the West, like the San Francisco Chinaman's opium, and the South American native's coca-leaf. By 1928, it had been made illegal in Britain, and zealous US prohibitionists were following suit. The universal outlawing of marijuana has been one of the few more or less permanent triumphs of Western materialism. In fact, of course, most middle-aged people in America and Britain have never had any idea whether dope is bad for people or not. The atmosphere Howard Marks and his friends grew up in was one in which newspapers like *The Times* in 1957 could hire an anonymous lawyer to write:

## HAUNTS OF THE 'REEFER'
. . . Of the people convicted, seven out of eight are coloured men, mainly West Indians. The hemp problem has been with us now for about ten years. Will it become more serious? . . . The market in Great Britain will continue extremely tempting while it contains so many coloured people.

The Home Office and police tend to lump together . . . white offenders as band leaders who specialise in the more exotic types of dance music, or even as musicians who specialise in exceptionally 'hot' music at 'modern music clubs' in the West End of London . . .

White girls who become friendly with West Indians are from time

17

to time enticed to hemp smoking . . . this is an aspect of the hemp problem – the possibility of its spreading among irresponsible young white people – that causes greatest concern to the authorities. The potential moral danger is significant, since a principal motive of the coloured man in smoking hemp is to stimulate his sexual desires.

Bizarre stuff. When the energy of black music burst into white rock, marijuana was part of the cultural package which loosened everything up in the grey and rigid west. Dope was a fashionable way for Welsh nobodies like Howard to be somebodies and for all kinds of well-heeled somebodies to make friends. It started to become the badge of an international underground brotherhood.

Of course, everything got out of hand. The 'Beat' intellectuals – and these ranged from Jack Kerouac to Aldous Huxley – appeared to reason thus: 'Drugs change your consciousness. For the Better. Therefore, the more Drugs the Better.' The 'Drug Culture' reared its gaudy umbrella above ground, like some brief, highly coloured Magic Mushroom, not all of whose parts would turn out to be good to eat.

As far as the young Howard was concerned, however, life was pure pleasure.

That June he went to the Albert Hall, staying in the Balogh London home, for the Beat Poetry Happening 'Wholly Communion': A New Zealand poet called John Esam organised it in one week – he was shortly to re-enter Howard's life – and a young film-maker called Peter Whitehead was hopping about on stage with a single camera. Fifteen years later Howard was to be best man at his wedding, and Whitehead was to testify against him at the Old Bailey. Right now, Whitehead was trying to film, over a pall of pot-smoke and the surging of 7,000 more or less disorganised people, some key beatniks. Allen Ginsberg, the great bearded American bear, sang to his finger cymbals, and declaimed:

Be kind to yourself because the bliss of your own kindness will flood the police tomorrow . . .
   The soft vibrations of desire given with meat hand and cock, desire taken with mouth and ass, desire returned to the last sight and the happy laugh of innocent babies! –
   Tonite let's all make love in London as if it were 2001 the years of thrilling God –

18

Alex Trocchi hissed:

Revolt my child, revolt is a quick axe cleaving dead wood in the forest, by night. The woodsman of the day is the executioner.

The Briton, Adrian Mitchell, was politically impassioned:

You put your bombers in, you put your conscience out
You take the human being and you twist it all about
. . . Stick my legs in plaster
Tell me lies about Vietnam.

And the poet Harry Fainlight baffled most of the audience, including Howard, with his LSD trip:

Until suddenly I am shaking with it – the whole voltage of the city running through my mind! POWERRRRR – billioning itself with horrific catacombs – electronic scales assembling an organ dragon – THE SPIDER IN FULL ARMOR . . .

That summer, Howard rather enjoyed the fact that elderly Germans shook their fists at him on buses as he made his denim-clad long-haired way across the Baltic from Malmo, where he had been singing with a local group called 'Hithouse' to raise the fare on to Hamburg. He sauntered incongruously down the suburban Wohltorferstrasse to the heavily prosperous house on the Reinbeck outskirts, surrounded by woodland. There were three Mercedes cars in the garage, and a croquet lawn.

'How on earth can you go around looking like that?' said Mac McMillan's father in stunned tones. He was a sober-suited Scot.

'It's all right,' said Mac. 'Perhaps now you'll stop getting bothered about my side-whiskers.'

Mac's parents fed and entertained their son's friend, and he wandered round the big house with its live-in maid and enormous picture windows.

'Hey Mac. Your parents have got a phone by their bed.'

'It's an extension. Don't your people have one of those?'

'They haven't even got a phone at all.'

But Mac's return visit to Kenfig Hill went well enough. He muted his anti-socialist observations, in deference to the *Daily Herald*-reading world of the Welsh Valleys, and the Welsh Labour establishment, a back-scratching environment which perhaps explained Howard's anarchistic contempt for all politics. Mac went to rugby matches with Howard's grandfather. He was a big success. Howard took him out drinking with his Valley friends: shy Marty Langford, now working in a shoe factory, burly Mike Clarke, and Little Pete.

They gathered at opening time and, as Big Ben struck six on the radio, ceremoniously demonstrated the trick.

'. . . BONG! – Glug. BONG! – Glug!'

'That's six pints, Howard!'

'Sure is.'

He snickered with the others when the local policeman tried to throw them out.

'Come on now! I've got a Black Maria outside.'

'Bring 'er in!' shouted Howard. 'There's no colour bar 'ere!'

It was when they went out the following night, that Mac said: 'Allow me, Howard, to purchase this round. BARMAN!' The whole pub froze. Howard winced. 'Um, no, Mac, don't say that. Don't say "Barman!" Just go up there with the glasses, eh?'

Howard concluded that Balliol and the Valleys did not altogether mix.


By the time the poet John Esam came up from London the following autumn and banged on Howard's door at the top of a Balliol stairway, his new and luxurious set of rooms was quite a sight. The lights were blacked out, there were cushions on the floor and the Pink Floyd playing incessantly. Across the ceiling hung a large net: someone had thrown an empty milk carton and a cigarette packet into it. There were some odd people sprawled on the cushions; there always were these days. Terry Deakin, Dennis Irving's Egyptologist schoolmate, had virtually moved in. Tiny Bennie Fisher from Corpus Christi College would come over and offer opium around in his squeaky voice. He probably had heroin too, but he was not proposing to share it. Taciturn young Graham Plinston, in his first year at St Edmund Hall, began to appear regularly. He always had large supplies of dope of his own.

'Morocco,' he would say smugly. 'I've got a lot of connections. Brought back a pound of "Kif" last summer.'

'Townies' would drop by, say 'Got any dope?' and stay on for hours.

Whenever anyone made an expedition to London to the Flamingo or the Marquee Club, or to 'score' off the Notting Hill West Indians in All Saints Road, they would pass the hat round first, and come back to distribute as much hash as they could find. Howard was getting through 12 joints a day. He started when he woke. It was cheap – £6 an ounce in those days – but scarce. Selling hash was inseparable from smoking it – it was always a friendly act to sell. Deakin composed a poem and dedicated it to Howard on the subject of his celebrated druggy pad. It was called 'The net':

How often have we lain, my friend, under this net which watches
  us
Through spaces in infinity? The net sees all we do: laughter;
a passing hang up; chocolate scoffed; 'Who is to roll the next?';
Girls immolated on your manhood; a little work; drumming of
  stoned fingers
The net embraces you and me, Steve, Julian, other drunkards
  of transcendence


. . . Under the net we pick up fragments of truth and try to live
Each day as if it were our last. We fail and we succeed,
In psychedelic paradoxes. And we, Howard, hold knowledge
As our net holds in the rain. By this net which has seen us well
Delighted us and hung us in its spell
Friend, we must live till all our dues are paid
Knowing ourselves, receptive, unafraid.


So Esam banged on the door: 'Hi, we've been told you're a groove.' His project was to sell Howard some acid. He had a pocketful of sugar-cubes at £3 each.

'What is it?'

'LSD. It's much stronger than hash. Impossible to describe. Like a weekend in Paris, but cheaper. I can get you as much as you like. I'm making it at home in the kitchen.'

Howard liked the idea of a new high. He took a cube and went off to keep an invitation to tea with a girl in Somerville College. Then the face of a painting on the wall began to animate. The shadows started to breathe. Waves of delicious physical sensation swept over him. When he urinated, it felt like an orgasm. Time melted. Howard liked it. The next time he took LSD, in his familiar room with the net, he got the horrors. Julian and Terry Deakin, who were with him, spent hours trying to reassure him.

'It's OK, it's just the other side of the coin. Hold on, Howard.'

'I don't know who I am! I don't know my name! I think I've died! There isn't any difference between being alive and being dead. It's the ultimate reality! This horror!' He was screaming, and crying and whimpering.

Curiously enough, this confrontation with his own nihilism made Howard, for the first time, start to read books. He was troubled by the meaning of existence. He toiled through drug literature; the *Bhagavad Gita* and other Eastern works; and read Aldous Huxley's *Doors of Perception* about the mescaline cactus experiments. He studied Huxley's 1962 novel *Island*, in which Huxley imagines a utopia of brotherhood and love, nourished by doses of the psychedelic mushroom 'moksha medicine'. And he kept buying Esam's sugar cubes, and pushing them hard round Oxford. LSD was still legal in 1966, but Howard's impulse in 'turning on' everyone he met was a dark one. He wanted others to see the depths of meaningless with which he had been confronted. The ideology of 'inner space' had started with Huxley's California experiments six years earlier, made an evangelist of the Harvard Professor Tim Leary, and had arrived in 'Swinging London' in diluted form that very summer, via Michael Hollingshead and the 'World Psychedelic Centre' of Pont Street, Chelsea: chief officers two Old Etonians, Desmond O'Brien and Joey Mellon. Mellon was, as Hollingshead recalled in his autobiography written later in retreat in a Franciscan monastery, one of the first people to trepan himself, by drilling a hole in his head to release the mystic 'third eye'. An interest in LSD phenomena united Alex Trocchi, Feliks Topolski, Roman Polanski, Esam himself, the painter Nik Douglas, and Paul McCartney of the Beatles. It was what Hollingshead, despatched across the Atlantic from Leary's seminary at Millbrook in New York State, called 'a select group of young aristocrats and artists and musicians and writers, responsible for influencing sharply the patterns of the New Vanguard of British culture and intellectual life.'

While Howard was being influenced by the New Vanguard, he was not, of course, doing any physics. Eventually he was called up before McCarthy Willis-Bund, the long-suffering Dean.

'Howard, there have been complaints about you this term of interminable loud music; of flinging a shower of bottles out of your window into the street; and of offering to shoot a passer-by with an air rifle. Nor do you appear to be doing any work whatsoever.'

'I think I'm unhappy with physics. I'm not interested in it.'

'Yes, but we have explored the idea of you changing to read philosophy.'

'Yeah, I know. I can't understand it. And I've been to see that psychiatrist, and that didn't help. All he wanted to know was whether I walked on cracks on pavements!'

'Oh dear. I propose you do no work whatever for a bit. Resume your acting. I fear these experiments with LSD, of which you speak, are not assisting you, Howard.'

Eventually, in his third year, Howard got busted. He was living out of college in a flat in Paradise Square. The Thames Valley drug squad poured in. William Burroughs, the drug poet, had been briefly a tenant there. Those the police arrested included Howard, after a 'roach' had been found in his room in the house, and Steve Balogh, on the grounds he had two sugar-lumps in his pocket. The Dean, once more, intervened. They went down to see the drug squad:

'That bit of a joint couldn't have been mine,' said Howard in a saintly tone. 'I never touch the stuff.'

'Those sugar-lumps . . .' said Balogh.

'Yeah, we know. You were going to feed some horses. Well, it turns out they were just sugar-lumps, like you say. In view of the Dean's speaking up for you, we've decided not to press charges.'

It was just a little thing for Howard, who was eventually to break the drug laws of at least fourteen countries. But that was the great year for the police hounding of the 'dirty hippies' and their heroes. The Rolling Stones were raided after Mick Jagger tried to sue the *News of the World* for libel when it alleged he was a drug-taker. He was charged with possessing four benzedrine pills, and Keith Richard with allowing cannabis to be smoked, on the tenuous grounds that Marianne Faithful, present at the time, must have been under the influence because she was dressed in nothing but a 'skin rug around her shoulders'. The fur rug was produced and seen to be at least 8 feet long and 5 feet wide. Mick Jagger also produced his doctor who said he had authorised Jagger to have his Italian pep pills. Judge Block of West Sussex Quarter Sessions sent Jagger to jail for three months and Richard for a year. This was so obviously vindictive that the editor of *The Times*, William Rees-Mogg, wrote a famous leader headed 'Who breaks a Butterfly Upon a Wheel?' He said the 'new hedonism' could only be fought by the 'traditional values' of tolerance and equity. After the Appeal Court very sensibly quashed the sentences, Judge Block rather gave the game away by telling a public dinner of the Horsham Ploughing and Agricultural Society in Sussex: 'We did our best, your fellow countrymen, I and my fellow magistrates, to cut those Stones down to size, but alas it was not to be, because the court of Criminal Appeal let them roll free.'

Plinston soon materialised, talkative for once.

'I've been busted too, Howard. They raided this pad at Watereaton where we were all staying. And you know Stephanie Sweet, the teacher we rented it off?'

'Yeah, vaguely.'

'They're doing her for managing the premises.'

'But she didn't have anything to do with it? She wasn't even living there.'

'Doesn't matter.'

He turned out to be right. Plinston himself was fined £50 for possession of LSD, and was thrown out of St Edmund Hall for a year. His landlady was fined £25 by the Woodstock magistrates for being the innocent manager of premises where cannabis was smoked. She said wryly: 'I only had mini-skirts in my wardrobe, but I went out and bought a respectable knee-length black and white dress. I even put my hair up, but it didn't work.'

It appeared that, like Oedipus sleeping with his mother, she had committed an absolute crime from which there was no escape. Lord Chief Justice Parker fatuously said on appeal that she should have made it a term of the lease that there should be no dope-smoking. It was not a joke: she now had a criminal record. She was unable to get a visa to enter the US. The Department of Education and Science threatened her with dismissal as an unfit person to teach.

There was a tremendous row. Robert Graves, the poet, was a friend of the family and wrote a long, denunciatory article in the *Sunday Times*.

An honours graduate of St Annes', who sub-lets to a group of easy-going students she had casually met, because her car has broken down and she is no longer able to commute from the country, is arrested by Sergeant Parsley of the Woodstock Police – a bucolic character. She is stripped to the skin and searched for needle-marks. Her handbag is searched. She is interrogated for four hours.

The Labour MP Russell Kerr demanded a parliamentary debate. Michael Foot, the distinguished Labour left-winger, also took up the affair and so did the National Council for Civil Liberties.

The case of *Sweet* v. *Parsley* ended with the House of Lords unanimously clearing her name, saying the decision was 'obviously unjust'. Obvious injustice seemed to be a remarkably regular occurrence. A full-page advert, with financial backing from the Beatles, appeared in *The Times* calling for the legalisation of dope.

'The law against marijuana is immoral in principle and unworkable in practice,' it declared, going on to quote a remark of Spinoza's, the accuracy of which Howard Marks was later to demonstrate with great thoroughness:

All laws which can be violated without doing anyone any injury are laughed at . . . and men of leisure are never deficient of the ingenuity needed, to enable them to outwit laws framed to regulate things which cannot entirely be forbidden.

With 65 signatories, ranging from the gay Labour MP Tom Driberg to the heterosexual Tory Jonathan Aitken, the advert was put together by the Oxford American Steve Abrams, who had already volunteered to the public the disclosure that at least 500 Oxford students and 'several dons' were by now smoking dope. The text said:

Cannabis is usually taken by normal persons for the purpose of enhancing sensory experience. Heroin is taken almost exclusively by weak and disturbed individuals for the purpose of withdrawing from reality. By prohibiting cannabis, Parliament has created a black market where heroin could occasionally be offered to persons who would not otherwise have had access to it . . . in recent months, the persecution of cannabis smokers has been intensified . . . the crime at issue is not so much drug abuse as Heresy.

The Recorder of Birmingham, the relatively junior judge Michael Argyle, shortly to be promoted to the Old Bailey, at once announced that 69 of Birmingham's 'hard' drug addicts had, in his view, become addicted via marijuana. There was really no reason why Howard or any of his friends should have deferred to policemen and judges who said things like this: they thought they were ridiculous.

Howard eventually graduated, with a perfectly good physics degree.

Characteristically, he forged the dockets certifying he had carried out the necessary laboratory experiments. No one noticed. He had abandoned LSD, and temporarily even stopped smoking dope. But he was so completely lost when he left Oxford that he did two very conventional things. The first was to enrol in a teacher training course in London, and the second was to get married.

Ilse Kadegis, from St Anne's, was the first of the three important women in his life. She lasted three years. A tall, high-spirited, golden-haired girl, she was the daughter of a refugee Latvian landowner. The fortunes of war saw her father thrown into a Polish jail while trying to escape the Russians; then employed by the Gestapo as a reluctant translator; and eventually admitted by the British as a refugee to work in the steel town of Corby. Ilse was born in a European 'Displaced persons' camp. Her family never stopped being cultivated although they were poor and forced to live in Corby: her father would give his two 14-year-old daughters the fare to London and say: 'Go to Covent Garden! See Nureyev! Be Europeans!'

Ilse was sophisticated about dope – she had already made the hippy trip to the Balearic island of Ibiza. She was playing around like a puppy with all sorts of diversions; and few men were more diverting at Oxford than the notorious Welsh sex-pot, Howard Marks. They lived together in Notting Hill. Ilse too was training to be a teacher. But she was serious about it, and Howard was not.

' 'Ere,' said Howard. 'Let's get married. We could have a big party and get lots of wedding presents.'

Later, he said, 'Stuff this teacher-training. They make you wear a suit to do teaching practice. I won't do it.'

He kicked around, selling private chemistry coaching, and pining for Oxford. He bought half a pound or even an ounce of dope at a time from Plinston, and sold it around the streets of the Portobello Road, which seethed with bangles and beads and shoulder-bags and patchouli and incense. It was a very long-haired scene. One of his wedding presents was a board for the Japanese game 'Go'. It involves surrounding squares with counters or stones: it is a game rather like chess but more fluid and obsessional. The outcome of moves and positions can only be predicted in a general kind of way, according to the patterns of play that develop.

'Howard, you're not going round to play Go with Graham Plinston *again*?'

'Well he's got to do something while he's rusticated, hasn't he?'

'I'd have thought it was only too clear what he did: creepy little dope-head.'

'I didn't know you didn't like him.'

'Well, I don't much like the way that couple live. It seems so neglectful. And he always has this air: you know: "My thoughts are too important to divulge".'

'Yeah. Did you know it's the oldest board game in the world. There's an ancient Japanese proverb: "A man who plays Go will not desist even on the deathbed of his grandmother." Anyway, it's the only game you can really play when you're stoned.'

The following year, Howard managed to sidle back to Oxford. His uncle Mostyn, a Labour County Councillor, helped discover a local scholarship which would finance a one-year Philosophy of Science diploma. It was Howard's attempt to get away from the world of physics. His father bought him an old Hillman for £100. Howard and Ilse shared a picturesque cottage in the village of Garsington with Bill Parkinson, another Balliol man, who spent his time arranging 'Beat' poetry sessions and was proposing to marry the daughter of the governor of Anguilla. Howard would drive Ilse to the station in the morning, spend all day in the libraries, and drive back in the evenings.

'Are you happier now, Howard?'

'Well it's pretty borin', isn't it? There's nobody here in Oxford any more. All these little cliques. It's true what they say, isn't it? You're only famous for 10 minutes.'

'Well, what do you want to do?'

'I don't know. Make a million pounds. Be famous. Get somewhere.'

Like so many young persons who tumbled out of Oxbridge, ungrateful to the post-war welfare state, Howard was completely disoriented. It was only later that he realised that the thing about Oxbridge was the friends. They stayed with you all your life. It was like a freemasonry. Howard was good at friends. He made a lot more. Fanny Stein, for example, daughter of the new Master of Balliol, the famous Marxist historian of the seventeenth century, Christopher Hill. Fanny was married and pregnant. Christopher Hill would invite both Fanny and Howard to parties: he rather took to the young Welsh proletarian with the wicked sense of humour and the obvious lack of an aim in life. Hill and his wife visited Garsington where Howard cooked them an Indian curry. As an old Communist – he left the party over Hungary in 1957 – Hill perhaps saw Howard through somewhat idealistic eyes. Fanny's relationship with him was less complex:

'Do you like Elvis Presley?'

'Yes.'

'So do I. Let's do some jiving.'

Through Plinston, now allowed back to Oxford to finish his degree, he met skinny, blonde Charlie Radcliffe:

'Would you believe Charles Jeremy St John Radcliffe? I'm a descendant of Nell Gwynne. The family's got lots of land in Hampshire. Harold Macmillan comes down to fish.'

'Do you want to do some dope?'

'Sure do. I'm in left-wing publishing. Work at Robert Maxwell's place, Pergamon Press. But I'm down in London a lot. Committee of 100. Here, look at this.'

He showed Howard a dollar bill, quite reasonably forged, with the legend 'In God We Trust' changed to 'Stop the Torture in Vietnam'.

'It's all getting very borin' round here,' Howard said to Ilse. 'All anybody talks about is politics. Vietnam. The invasion of Czechoslovakia by the Russians. Karl bleeding Marx. Your revolting students in Paris. You look out the window, and it's crowds of kids rushing off to watch *Battleship Potemkin*, waving red flats . . .'

'I thought you were a revolutionary, Howard.'

'Naa, this is all phoney. I just want to get really stoned and smash the system. I'm a Hedonist.'

Christopher Hill was very astute. He enrolled Howard in a Balliol scheme to provide a summer school for proletarian 16-year-olds, in the hope they might overcome some of the barriers that discouraged them from going to the posh universities. Howard was good at it, of course – he was genuinely friendly with the teenagers, and bought them under-age half-pints round the pubs. But the experience never tapped the channels of altruism in Howard. He wanted excitement. Like the smart iconoclasts fizzing all around him, Howard, the archetypal Sixties youngster, wanted to do something *extraordinary*.

Howard and Ilse drifted to the dank and modernistic University of Sussex, at Brighton. Ilse got a job as head of department in a Worthing convent school, teaching English. She would show Howard her pupils' poetry.

'Bloody rubbish,' he said sourly. 'And your opera. That's bloody rubbish, too.'

Howard was supposed to be doing a PhD. He could be seen in the

'Star and Garter': '. . . a stuntman, eh? That's really interesting. Let's have another pint.'

'Well, you know, in work and out of it. The film business . . . cheers!'

'Cheers! . . .'

That lunchtime, he and the stuntman ended up after closing time, tiptoeing through Tesco's supermarket with their pockets full of rice and minced beef. Devoid of cash, they were shoplifting a curry. When the manager caught them, he locked them in an upstairs room.

'Come on mate, through the window!'

'It's all right for you, you're a STUNTMAN! Hang on, I think I've twisted my ankle. Hang on, I'm coming . . .'

He met lots of new friends. He spent days playing Go, taking more acid, drunk, or stoned. Finally, he left for London with the beautiful and idealistic middle-class wife of a maths lecturer, Rosie Brindley. She was the second woman of significance to him.

'We can do it together, Howard! You're the man I've really wanted all my life. I can grow! You've been dealing dope for Graham down here in Brighton. Well, we'll go back to Notting Hill and you can do the same there. It's the great liberating drug. Selling it isn't a business. It's more like a crusade!'

'I can't break up my marriage, can I? I can't stop doing my PhD, can I?'

'Oh Howard. You've had such a narrow life, haven't you? You can do anything you want to. Didn't you know that?'

Howard went into the dope trade, full-time.

# CHAPTER 2

# Ballinskelligs 1

Graham Plinston supplied all the hash. He was colourless, capable and ambitious. His father, Horace Plinston, was the town clerk of Letchworth, a small south of England town. None of Howard's 'straight' friends ever took to Plinston. He was not pretty, not witty, not left-wing and not charming. His personality was less interesting than were his achievements in the vast and blossoming dope market: in less than five years, smoking joints had moved from a chic little vogue to a great big fashion. Plinston had voyaged to Morocco, just the other side of the Straits of Gibraltar, and the nearest source for English supplies. (The American dope market was supplied quite differently – most of it came across the border from Mexico.) There he met a man whose mother was an opera singer in Beirut who knew a man who knew businessmen in Dubai on the Persian Gulf, the great Middle East smuggling entrepôt. Plinston seemed too have some sort of pipeline going. Every couple of months, 100 lb or so of black Pakistani hashish would materialise. It was unmistakable, reliable, commercial stuff, machine-pressed into half-pound slabs and reeking of the linseed oil that lubricated the presses. He was getting rather rich, as could be seen by his sophisticated stereo system; his rows of LPs, many clearly never taken out of their sleeves; his new cars; and the way he ostentatiously picked up the tab in restaurants. Howard himself was clearing £40 a week and all the dope he could smoke while selling Graham's supplies round Brighton. He felt tremendously affluent after living on a student grant for years. But Graham was probably making at the rate of £25,000 a year, tax-free, with his only expenses a heavy phone bill and a few plane tickets. For a young person of 21, in 1970, these were fabulous sums.

That spring, Howard's phone rang. He was moving to a bijou mews at the smart end of Ladbroke Grove. The £35-a-week Hillsleigh Road apartment was paid for by the affluent Brindley family: Rosie, separated as she was from her husband, was bringing up her one-year-old daughter there. It was generally stacked with pounds of dope, for Plinston and his friends were in the habit of using it as a 'stash': 'No hippies in this street man: it's a cool place to visit.'

On the phone was Plinston's girl.

'Howard, he's disappeared. There's something wrong. I think he must have been busted. If I give you a few hundred pounds, will you go and find out?'

'Where is he?'

'He's supposed to be in Germany.'

Howard had never been on a plane before.

'Why me?'

'You're the straightest of Graham's friends – you won't have a Customs file or anything.'

'Me, straight?'

'Well, at least you've got an occupation. You're still officially a PhD student. You should see the others.'

Howard thought of the mixture of Oxford men and hippy low-lifers who drifted through his living-room. Dave Pollard was Plinston's biggest dealer. He too was an Oxford physics graduate. He marketed 'Esmerelda' cigarette papers for joints. His flat in north Kensington was a mass of wiring: he was designing psychedelic lighting systems as a 'front', and couldn't stop inventing things. He had never been the same since earlier that year his girlfriend Barbara Mayo had gone hitch-hiking on the M6. She was raped and murdered. The police never found the killer; they merely grilled Pollard for hours as the chief suspect. The next day, Pollard heaved his LSD tableting machine, which the police had never noticed, into the Thames. He used to babble about it being a judgment on him, for all the LSD trippers who thought they could fly and had dived off high buildings.

'All right,' Howard said. 'I'll go.'

He went to an address in Frankfurt.

'Ja. We were indeed expecting him. With a car. Let us look through the newspapers.'

They found it soon enough. Plinston had been picked up in the border town of Lörrach. He was driving a Mercedes across the

31

Swiss border from Geneva with 100 lb of hash stuffed under the back seat and into door panels. He was in a German jail.

When Howard arrived back in London, with a lawyer organised as best he could, Plinston's girl had a second job for him:

'Just go and see these people – it's a flat in Mayfair, Curzon Street. It's got to be done.'

They were awesome. It was the air of power and money. These people were real smugglers. 'Mike' Durrani had a brown, hawk-like face, a Saville Row suit, beautiful fingernails, and a gold cigarette lighter. He was pouring drinks from a bottle of Johnny Walker Black Label. Nobody was smoking dope.

'Howard, what a pleasure it is to meet you. Please let me offer you a drink. It is kind of you to come. These are my friends – Sam from Beirut, and Nick from Amsterdam. Sam and I have a textile business in Dubai, and various other interests. I also have this residence here in London. I am in fact an Afghani by nationality: my grandfather's brother was king. We have been able to get a certain amount of hashish through Europe from time to time, for your friend Graham. How is he managing?'

It was a practical meeting. Did he think Graham had named them in his statements? Was the car-route 'blown'? Was Graham going to be convicted and permanently out of action? If that was to be the case, and in view of the unstable condition of Dave Pollard, would Howard ever think of taking over Plinston's smuggling work?

'Yes, please,' said Howard. Pound signs with rows of noughts after them flashed before his eyes. He very much wanted to be a smuggler.

Later, pulling his socks off in front of a grim-faced Customs Officer at Heathrow Airport's Terminal One, he wondered whether he hadn't been wrong. Plinston had done a short sentence after a lean six months for all concerned. With no stock, Howard had been once again reduced to coaching 17-year-old girls for Davies, Laing & Dick, the 'A'-Level exam crammers in Bayswater. Freed, Graham said, 'I shall never place myself in physical proximity to a slab of hash ever again.'

He had slipped out of the country without paying a £700 fine also imposed by the Germans.

'Just slip over there with this two grand, Howard. Pay the fine, so I can go back in the future, and give the balance to Lebanese Sam. He's in Frankfurt and funds are required.'

'Is it illegal?' said Howard.

'Definitely. You're not allowed to export sterling. Exchange controls. But nobody'll bother you.'

On the way out, he had stood in line while bored police did an unscheduled anti-terrorist pat-down of the German passengers. He was mentally rehearsing what he would say when he was discovered with the cash and feeling sweat trickle down both palms. On the way back, an alert Customs man gave the shifty-looking hippy an impulsive pull.

'Where did you buy this perfume?'

'In Germany. It's from the duty-free shop.'

'How long have you been away? What was the purpose of your trip?'

'A couple of days. Er, business.'

'Let me see your ticket, please. It appears you have been away less than 24 hours. Do you know you are not allowed to bring in duty-free goods under those circumstances? Would you step this way please?'

Inside his left sock, they found the receipt from a Frankfurt bank for Graham's £700 fine, and three ten-pound notes. Howard explained: '. . . so I went to pay his fine. No, of course I didn't take it out of Britain. I collected it from Plinston's friend out there, a bloke called Sol. Can't recall the address. I was just doing him a favour.'

HM Customs charged Howard duty on his cigarettes and perfume, and they opened a file:

| | |
|---|---|
| Name: | MARKS Dennis Howard |
| Date of birth: | 13.8.1945 |
| Also known as: | no aliases known |
| Came to notice: | Heathrow Airport 19.9.70 |
| CRO Number: | No previous record. |

Close associate of PLINSTON Graham, convicted Lörrach, Federal Republic of Germany, cannabis importation, 7.3.70.

'Yeah,' said Plinston, afterwards. 'Duncan Lowry, the one with the "Forbidden Fruit" Afghan shop in Portobello Road, did a kamikaze run from the Lebanon last month. He was so scared, he crapped in his trousers at Heathrow. They're bad bastards there.'

Plinston's future nervousness was Howard's opportunity. Soon the phone rang again. 'Howard. I'm in Geneva. How would you like to drive a load of hash from here to Germany? And I'll let you have the eventual selling of it, when it gets to London?'

In those days, the dope smugglers used to chat quite freely on telephones. Barring accidents like Lörrach, they did not imagine there was any great interest in their little illegalities. But Howard had a secret problem, for whom he could scarcely go to anyone for advice. He had never driven a car abroad, and was scared to be on the wrong side of the road. He approached a New Zealander, who was passing through.

'Pete, you've driven all over Europe, haven't you?'

'Yeah, drove back from Afghanistan, didn't I?'

'I'll go halves in this deal with you.'

Up in the hygienic Alps, in a Geneva hotel, Plinston rattled out their instructions.

'It's not here. It's in a town called Lausanne, just around the lake. Here's the keys. It's a light brown Opel. All you do is pick it up, and park it somewhere in Frankfurt. We'll arrange for German Klaus and Bob to meet you in the foyer of the Intercontinental Hotel, to hand the keys over. It's going through to Holland in a different car. Then get a cab to the airport and go home.'

Waved through the German border at Basle, Howard felt a rush. It was like a flash of chemicals racing through his body. It was what he imagined a religious ecstasy might be like. He had just smuggled.

'Nothing is it?' said Pete.

'Naa, never is,' said Howard as coolly as he could manage. 'Money for old rope. That's what hemp is, isn't it? Old rope!'

In the bijou residence at Hillsleigh Road, there was a rapid series of half a dozen phone calls.

'It's in. Really has arrived, for once. No, Graham wants me to do the sales from now on. He's going to stay in the background. Come on, man, what's another £10 a lb?'

He drove off on his calls round London, in his second-hand Corsair.

Putney, Wandsworth, Shepherd's Bush, Highgate – Charlie Radcliffe; Dave Pollard; and Vera, the north London hooker, the only female dope-dealer in the business, who sold it off through the black pimps she employed.

'Here's your sample ounce. Yeah, let's have a joint. Not bad, is it? I'll park the car somewhere round here tonight with a suitcase in the boot and call you. Pay me soon. Stay cool. And don't try to give me that old tenner again with "TAKE YOUR KNICKERS OFF" on it. *I'm* not putting it in the bank either.'

Back would come the grubby £5 and £10 notes within days, as the shipment cascaded out to the down-the-line dealers who handled 5 lb or so at a time, and drove up to town from the provinces. Howard made £2,000.

'Look at this!' He exulted to Rosie: 'Cardboard boxes full of money. It's the victimless crime!'

As spring blossomed in Notting Hill, there were more exotic phone calls from Plinston. Howard could be seen in Bonn, the diplomatic capital of Germany, struggling and grimacing while he hauled heavy tin trunks full of a Pakistani diplomat's 'personal effects' down the neat driveway and into a white Volkswagen camper. As night fell, he pulled up in a nearby disused gravel-pit. Five Dutchmen were waiting, with Volvos. Their job was to drive the load across to England on the Harwich ferry.

And Howard could have been next seen staring, awestruck, at a six-foot-high stack of crates in a Frankfurt garage, marked 'Streptomycin, Karachi'.

'I've never seen a ton of hash before,' he said. He tried to follow Plinston's instructions carefully.

'Be punctual. Lots of deals go down because one guy's late and the other's paranoid. Ferry quarter of a ton over to this layby. Two Americans will meet you there in their own car, and collect the boxes. They're going off on their own little importing trail. Then load up half the rest . . .'

'Graham, we can't do any more driving for a couple of days. It's these Nazis. This guy in a car nearly knocked Pete down while he was crossing the road in Frankfurt. So he bangs on the back window with a rolled up newspaper. You know? And this huge German gets out and comes round and just knocks him down. Splat! He broke his glasses. Got to get them fixed.'

'Good grief. Can't you drive?'

'Yeah, well, I'm not so good at it . . .'

'Oh shit. Well, go down the Rhine. Book into a nice hotel. Have a look at the castles and the barges and stuff. Let me know when we can start again.'

Back in action, Howard and Pete left the 'Swan' at Österreich and scoured the Rhineland countryside. Up a cart-track, they found a clearing in a wood. They handed over more crates and directed there the Dutchman sent by Graham.

'Doesn't it make you nervous, stashing up in the open air?'

'No, no. I get out the picnic table, the radio, perhaps I have the back seat out and I lie on it. Or I jack up one of the wheels. One door, then the other. Little bit at a time. Three, four hours, It's done. Easy.'

And back to Frankfurt to hand over the last consignment to the Germans, Bob and Klaus.

'Very good,' said Plinston, flourishing a huge wad of notes. 'The Americans and the Germans have paid me off for their supplies, so let's all drive to Switzerland, shall we?'

'This your BMW, Graham? Didn't know you had one.'

'This is just the one I keep in Europe.'

'Uh-huh.'

Across the border into Geneva, Plinston carrying nothing more incriminating than money, in his Delsey briefcase. 'Always buy these. French. It's hip. They have the best locks.'

'Anything to declare?'

'No.'

'OK.'

'The Swiss don't mind if you come in across the border with lots of other people's currencies. They *like* it.'

He disappeared into his Swiss bank with the Delsey swag-bag.

'OK gents. Here you are. £2,500 each, in marks. You'll have no trouble taking those back into Britain. I'm glad to be able to do you the favour. Stay cool.'


Later, much later, Durrani told Howard the real reason why Graham had let him in on the big one-ton deal.

'Graham, that garage was hot! You knew it might be watched. I was going blind into all that heat!'

'Oh come, come, Howard. We were following you all the time, you know. That was the idea. If the Polizei were on your tail, we would have rammed them.'

Howard stared at him. He really wanted to believe him.


The money was flooding in. Plinston bought a big house in Marylands Road near Warwick Avenue tube station in Maida Vale, and started making extensive renovations.

'Just soaks up money, Howard. Who knows what you've paid for and what you've done yourself? And builders always take cash. Think I might open up a property company. And an Eastern carpet shop. Imports. Bit of a front. You want to come round the Hilton with me? My friend Tony knows a Lebanese countess who's got some black

Nigerian money he says we might launder on commission.'

'How much?'

'Oh, about 11 million Nigerian pounds.'

'Shee-it!'

Howard went down to Port Talbot in South Wales and saw the local manager of a bank his Welsh relations had always found accommodating over matters of income tax.

'I might have some cash coming in, put in a deposit account. I'm doing a lot in the money business since I left Oxford, you know. For example, do you know whether I could process some Nigerian pounds through the bank? I know there's strict Nigerian currency control, but it's not illegal to have it here . . .?'

'Oh no. No problem. What did you have in mind? Couple of thousand?'

'11 Million pounds.'

Later, when he had given the bank manager a glass of water, and explained it was nothing to do with drugs, Howard produced just £3000 cash and said it was from money-dealing. His attempt to find a crooked bank manager had failed. He really didn't know what to do with all this bread. There were only so many records you could buy. There were only so many decent tandooris you could eat at the Standard in Westbourne Grove; only so many plates of lasagne at Bertorelli's in Charlotte Street. He rented an elegant flat for the summer back in Brighton, in Lewes Crescent. He experimentally bought a case of vintage champagne and drank a bottle a night for a fortnight.

Then the blow struck. They ran out of dope. By this time, Graham had purchased his carpet shop 'Hamdullah' at 3 Warwick Place, near the new flat and just on the corner of Little Venice. It was the smart part of Paddington, alongside the Regents Park Canal. He was to the north of the sleazy purlieus of Notting Hill and Ladbroke Grove. Howard, in Holland Park, was comfortably to the south. The Portobello Road, with its antique shops, blacks and street hippies, more or less connected the two fashionable districts. It was a territory decorated with slogans –

'END POLICE OPPRESSION!'

'I AM AN ANGRY TORMENTED SOUL SCREAMING OUT
IN THIS TORTUROUS MEDIOCRITY!'

'IF VOTING CHANGED ANYTHING,
THEY'D MAKE IT ILLEGAL.'

Plinston held court in the Warwick Castle, next door to the carpet shop. The raffish little pub was surrounded by smart houses with steel grilles behind the windows and conspicuous burglar alarm housings.

It was that sort of district.

'The position is this,' he said. 'It's very serious. The stuff all came in through diplomats, in their baggage. It was immune. But Durrani says he simply can't do it any more. It's got too dangerous. There's a bit of pressure on them all. That's the bad news. This is the good news. Durrani and I have a new contact in Karachi. He is a very, very powerful man. Big in the Film industry over there. And he controls Karachi Airport. Does watches, gold . . . He can get any quantity on to the planes there. But how do we get it down again?'

Howard and Plinston, living disproof of the theory that smoking hashish destroys the will, set about cracking the problem.

'Look at this. Once we're in Europe we've made it,' said Graham, waving a copy of the *ABC World Airways Guide*: 'I knew there had to be a flight like this. I've flown in and out of Switzerland a lot, and they have this fantastic Customs loophole. You go through Customs, they say, "Where are you from?" and *then* let you pick up your baggage and walk off . . .'

A week or two later, a middle-aged traveller – he was one of Plinston's older acquaintances – queued up at the Zurich Customs. 'No, nothing to declare.' He showed his internal Swissair ticket from Geneva to Zurich. They waved him through, and he went to the baggage carousel, picked up his suitcase and walked off. What Plinston had found was a Swissair flight which made two stops inside Switzerland. But it started its flight in Karachi, and so did the suitcase.

'Pretty idea,' said Howard. 'It's extremely pretty. But it's only a suitcase. If we can't import in bulk, we might as well not bother.'

They were sunk in gloom.

Moaning about this recession in their careers as dope tycoons, Plinston unburdened himself in the Warwick Castle to blond Charlie Radcliffe. Charlie was not only a revolutionary, but a writer. He had connections with the 'Underground Press', then spawning sheets all over London of anarchistic sentiment and even wilder graphics. They printed dense-packed type in such colour combinations as white on yellow or pink on purple. These were hard on the eyes, although designed to hint at grand psychedelic experiences.

Naturally enough, 'straight' society in Britain always rose to the bait. *Oz*, the most well-known underground magazine, was being run by the expatriate Australian Richard Neville, condemned as obscene by his own decent, beerswilling countrymen. Another one, *International Times*, was forced to change its name to '*IT*' after copyright protests from the London *Times*, which feared confusion between the upright Tory work of its editor William Rees-Mogg and the underground press's cheerful slogan:

'Dope, Rock 'n Roll, and fucking in the streets.'

This slogan got Richard Neville into the most terrible trouble. The Metropolitan plain clothes detective force was, in the words of its own Commissioner, Robert Mark, 'routinely corrupt'. But the police spent a lot of energy publicly rooting out the London literary hippies and prosecuting them for depravity.

*Oz* was raided several times, and finally the police came up with a winner. Neville organised a 'Schoolkids Issue' in which some high-spirited and progressively educated teenagers were given a more or less free hand to compile their own edition of poems, items, jokes and pictures. To the surprise of no one, and the delight of Neville, its general themes were rude. There were drawings of slobbering schoolmasters interfering with the backsides of schoolboys. Rupert Bear, traditional picture strip of that lust-free newspaper the *Daily Express*, was cartooned with an enormous penis, with which he was attempting to penetrate another cartoon character, Gypsy Granny. Dirty fun; and no doubt a mighty blow against hypocrisy in British life.

Certainly the official representative of hypocrisy in British life, the Director of Public Prosecutions, Sir Norman Skelhorn, could not live with this at all. The police bore off the reeking sheets to his Queen Anne's Gate office, and there he authorised a prosecution at the Old Bailey.

'It seemed perfectly apparent that it contained obscene material,' he recorded. 'The lovable Rupert Bear was assaulting an elderly lady!'

A massive trial ensued, followed with interest by among others, Howard Marks, Rosie Brindley, the libertarian left, the rock music fans, the dope-smokers, and the revolting students. Decent, short-haired bullies in uniform everywhere looked forward in some anticipation to the jail sentence and ceremonial haircut or castration it was envisaged to be the due of the noxious Neville.

Sir Norman jotted down for his memoirs: 'One would not wish to emulate the wider vagaries of the Victorian age, but it is another matter deliberately to advocate and set out as attractive a policy that cannot but strike at the roots of human society.'

What an honour for *Oz*! – Sir Norman cast himself in the heroic mould of those doughty men who had prosecuted Flaubert for writing *Madame Bovary* and banned James Joyce for *Ulysses*. It was to be a struggle of the Titans.

This ludicrous atmosphere was nice for the young dope-dealers. Their elders and betters were becoming more apoplectic by the minute. The barricades were being thrown up, and, by luck and temperament, they had found themselves on the right side of them, admired by their peers. Also, they were making a lot of money. Or at least, there was a lot more money to be made if only they could work out a steady way of getting those tons of Pakistani hashish down out of the air . . .

The underground magazine for which Charlie Radcliffe wrote was called *Friends*, He shared the Belsize Park flat of its editor and financier, another expatriate, the young South African Alan Marcuson. Marcuson ran it out of chaotic offices at the north end – the sleaziest, blackest, most druggy end – of the Portobello Road. Marcuson dealt some of Charlie's dope for him and quietly kept *Friends* afloat with the cash – his lean, bearded figure was occasionally to be seen in the Warwick Castle. Could the *Friends* connection rescue the Plinston organisation from the doldrums? It was in the end to send them plunging off on one of the biggest and most extraordinary secret smuggling adventures of the 1970s.

By 1971, his friends at the Warwick Castle noticed a growing preoccupation with Irish affairs in Marcuson's life. The ancient 'troubles' had burst out in 1969, and as the British authorities struggled to put down the ferment and the bullets began to fly, excitement swept over many of the would-be revolutionaries in the 'counter-culture'. They knew they were indeed revolutionaries in their hearts – even the most stupefied hedonists among them – but where was their revolution? In the 1930s, they could have enlisted in the International Brigades and fought for Spain, the Americans had been drafted to fight in Vietnam and could signal their loathing of the buttoned-down murderousness of their parents by shouting 'Hell, no, we won't go!' or 'Hey, hey LBJ! How many kids did you kill today?' In San Francisco, there was more than long hair, dope and LSD to talk about – there was the Vietcong, and the Black Panthers, and the Weathermen. In Britain, there were many innocent and well-fed youngsters longing for the sound of gunfire.

So no one was particularly surprised to see Marcuson's magazine running the bold streamer:

### 'IRELAND – BRITAIN'S VIETNAM'

Nor was it unexpected when he started to publish long interviews with Irish 'revolutionaries'. It was, however, the occasion of some remark when numbers of his friends were arrested along with an Irishman in Belfast and Marcuson began heatedly organising a 'Defence Committee' for the 'Belfast Four', accused of a petrol-bombing outrage.

Even to such busy men as Howard and Graham Plinston, absorbed in the logistics of dope deals, playing 'Go' for hours on end, skimming accounts of the drawn-out and increasingly grotesque *Oz* trial at the Old Bailey, Marcuson could be seen to be at the heart of strange events. Ireland was becoming a vortex: internment of IRA families was introduced, the British army were moving in in strength and brutalising suspects; virtually every week brought lurid accounts of soldiers being shot, of jail-breaks, and of machine-gun battles across the Irish border. Marcuson began to spend more and more time out of town, returning sporadically and excitedly to hustle for money. The magazine *Friends*, which never sold more than about 5,000 copies of an issue, was beginning to run out of focus, which did not really matter, and out of cash, which did.

Marcuson finally dropped his sensational bomb-shell at the Warwick Castle. The Plinston crowd needed a way of getting dope down out of the air and into Britain. Right? Preferably by the truckload. Right? Well, he knew a connection who could do it for them.

'This boy,' he said emphatically, 'can do *anything*.'

'Who is he?'

'His name is Jim McCann.'

'Where is he?'

'Ballinskelligs.'

'Where's that?'

'Ireland.'

And Marcuson proceeded to unfold to them a truly amazing story.

One afternoon at the end of February 1971, shortly after his 'Britain's Vietnam' issue, Marcuson and his friends were sitting peacefully in their office awaiting the arrival of the American 'Yippie' Abbie Hoffman – one of a stream of US pilgrims who were arriving with gratifying frequency to observe the progress of the Irish 'revolution'.

The door burst open. An alarming apparition manifested itself. It was a plumpish Irishman in his early thirties, with a thick Belfast accent, a pointed nose, and – hidden at first under his cheap leather jacket and then not merely revealed but waved terrifyingly around – a real gun. It was a sawn-off shotgun of the kind used by bank robbers. It looked as though it might be loaded. With real bullets. Looking round at the aghast expressions of the faces of these hippy journalists, it was clear to McCann that his instinctive approach to any new situation had, as usual, succeeded. His audience were off-balance.

'I'm Jim McCann,' he told Marcuson. 'And what you wrote about the Irish struggle was all shit. Now I'll tell you the real truth.'

He unfolded a marvellous tale. Marcuson, enraptured, fumbled for his tape-recorder.

'Every Irishman considers himself a keeper of the Holy Grail,' McCann said. 'I hate all that fucking linguistic froth they use in the pop culture over here. I fucking detest it.'

'Well what movement are you a member of?'

'Nobody's a member. You don't go and sign here. A group of us were totally disenchanted with fucking politicians and fucking structures . . . Sartre . . . We originally called ourselves the Belfast Liberation Front, but now we call ourselves Free Belfast. We only interact with the people when they're ready to be interacted with. In our group there are about 100 people to be called on. There's about 9 in jail at the moment. Pigs, Priests and Politicians, that unholy trinity, are totally barred. We refuse to negotiate on any terms with them. Belfast is like a stunted pygmy wandering in the mist, searching for an awakening . . .'

'Uh. Are they Maoists?'

'They're not even Maoists: they don't know what they are. They're situationists cum Maoists, cum freaks, cum many, many things. It's a sort of free-wheeling, open-handed situation. British imperialism is trying to shit over the Irish, and the Irish are sticking the big dick of their historical neuroses right up their ass-hole, and they're screaming.'

'Well, right on! Is there a, er, heavy criminal element involved in the struggle?'

'No. It's under control. And all the fucking John Genets who think stealing's a religious and sacred act. I'm saying to them: "Don't steal off me! I ain't got nothing! What's mine is yours!" '

'Yeah, um, to what extent do street committees run Free Belfast?'

'They police it, and they defend it. Their main influence comes from the people. You can't say: "This comes from Che Guevara, and this is the way to dig it, man" and "This is the way it was done in Chicago." This guy has a donkey, wouldn't conform; he brings in the best donkey trainer in Ireland, says "Listen man, I've spent a lot of bread, can you cure it and educate it?" He says "Of course I can." So he picks up a big hammer and hits it right between the eyes. And the guy said "I asked you to fucking cure it, not kill it!" So the trainer says "Before I can fucking cure it, I've got to get its attention first!" There you go . . . We've had to take to the sewers in certain parts. *Kanal*. You know. *Ashes and Diamonds* type. "Kanal" scene . . . The fucking movies. We're gonna have Great Britain's Sharpeville.'

'Wow,' Marcuson said.

This rough, bold, instinctively revolutionary account of the Belfast struggle warmed his heart. He published it word-for-anonymous-word in the next issue of *Friends*, under the headline drawn from the Rolling Stones' 1968 hit single:

'Interview with a Belfast Street Fighting Man.'

Actually the whole story was a fabrication from beginning to end, apart from the circumstance that McCann was indeed from Belfast. A tremendous liar, Jim McCann had simply made the whole thing up. Marcuson was not to discover this until much later, by which time McCann had done such genuinely astonishing things that he had almost parlayed himself into the position of being a genuine IRA folk hero.

As it was, in his innocence, Marcuson ignored the hoarse telephone call which came from Ireland a few days after publication. The voice croaked indignantly: 'Dis guy is all bullshit.' And it was too late when he got the letter signed 'John Belfast' which said:

The notorious and ludicrous load of drivel written by James McCann, who doesn't have the first idea as to the geography of Belfast . . . is a string of lies, distortions and fictions, such as the invention of the non-existent 'Belfast Liberation Front'. The Belfast sewers are 4 feet high – just the setting for a running gun battle!

Jim McCann was in fact currently on the run for burglary from the

Wiltshire police. He had done time in Parkhurst for fraud where he had a psychotic breakdown he was later to describe, characteristically, as 'a mystical experience'. His experience of psychiatry somehow led to a poem of his own creation being printed in a little radical medicine magazine called *Fire*. These were his sole hippy credentials. But McCann sensed that a number of rock stars with perhaps much more money than brains were vaguely sympathetic to the Irish revolutionary cause. His instincts told him to get in with the hippies and 'play the Green card'. That was what he would call it in relaxed moments. It was all part of what he explained to Marcuson as 'life in the fast lane'.

McCann was anxious to gloss over precisely how he spent the previous ten years. He eventually admitted to a past in Parkhurst, but claimed impressively he had been one of the leaders of the Parkhurst prison riots in 1969. He was a tremendous liar: although he did have a jail-breaking conviction. He also boasted that in his youth he and his friends had swindled a Belfast bank out of £30,000 from their night safe by a brilliant scheme.

'We put this scaffolding up in front of Barclay's bank,' he said. 'Then we put a sign over the night safe saying "Due to alterations, please place deposits in the letter box next door." We sat for three hours behind that letter box with a big bag. I was fucking terrified, but we got away with it!'

McCann was eldest of a Belfast family of 13 by his own account. He certainly had at least 7 brothers and sisters, one a hulking and taciturn soul by the name of Brendan and another, Peter, a former member of the Irish Air Force based in Dublin. He may have grown up in the Andersonstown district of Belfast as he says, but he did not give a faithful description of childhood under the English jackboot in an autobiography he later prepared in the hope of making a film of his life.

'At Christmas,' he said movingly, 'we were each given one banana. We never normally saw them.'

McCann certainly took to crime, but of a sordid kind. Scotland Yard's own Criminal Record office files show him jailed in May 1959 for 9 months, at London Quarter Sessions. He had broken into 14 shops. His career was as a London petty villain and south coast 'heavy'. Car stealing, forgery and threatening people were his stock-in-trade. He was picked up for innumerable driving offences, throughout the early 1960s, and for receiving stolen property. In 1962, he was arrested in Chiswick. In 1965 he was picked up for cheque frauds in France, in Puy-en-Velay. He worked with the notoriously criminal Weaver family in Brighton, whose patriarch, James Weaver, earned an honest few pounds in 1959 by describing to the *News of the World* how it felt to be reprieved from being hanged for kidnapping and murder (he said it made him feel numb).

This was the sleazy Brighton of Graham Greene's *Brighton Rock*, not Howard's chi-chi academic suburb by the sea. Some Weavers, Jim McCann and other thugs were employed as enforcers by young Nicholas Hoogstratten. He was fond of describing himself at the age of 21 as a property developer and 'Britain's youngest millionaire'. He generally omitted to mention the means by which he had acquired this status. They included stolen silver, slum landlordism and protection rackets. McCann described himself in this period as a 'debt collector'. Hoogstratten retired to jail for a four-year spell in 1968, where an impressed Father Gates, Roman Catholic chaplain at Wormwood Scrubs, told the appeal court: 'He thinks he is an emissary of Beelzebub.' McCann preceded him, retiring to Parkhurst in 1966 for a grand total of 60 cheque frauds throughout Europe.

McCann also admitted (or boasted) that he had links with the notorious London Richardson gang. There is some concrete evidence that he spent a period in Amsterdam selling stolen jewellery; it was a spot to which he was later to return. He was also seen in the early 1960s in New York, spending large sums of money at the opening of a smart night-club. The money was forged, of course: McCann later claimed to have unloaded 100,000 dollars-worth. This was, it was generally assumed by those around him, a great exaggeration. McCann's most tangible achievement in the 1960s seems to have been to purchase a warehouse full of tainted corned beef in London, and re-sell it in Amsterdam at a considerable profit to Nigeria. Since being paroled out of Parkhurst in 1969, he was wanted in England not only for the Wiltshire burglary, but for a couple of 'false pretences' in Cambridge and Manchester.

McCann was, in short, a con artist. He was, to those who liked rogues, a likeable rogue. His only real asset was his personality. He used it to generate a hypnotic atmosphere around him in which what he said became somehow regarded as true by otherwise reasonably sensible people. And, as a result, he could from time to time make the most extraordinary things happen. Marcuson was right in a way: 'This boy can do anything!'

McCann had his sights fixed on John Lennon, most famous and idealistic of the Beatles, whose mild, round, wire-framed tinted spectacles and long hair were imitated by millions, and whose Japanese girlfriend, Yoko Ono, was the last word in exoticism. Since the break-up of the Beatles as a group the previous year, Lennon was pursuing his more or less solitary obsessions – pacifism, revolution, universal love. He recorded 'Give Peace a Chance' in Toronto: he illustrated a record sleeve called 'Two Virgins' with pictures of him and Yoko stark naked. He appeared to be a harmless avant-garde musician with thoroughly stoned opinions. It was probably predictable that he would be assassinated in New York ten years later. For the moment, McCann had it in mind to stage a rip-off.

'Why don't you go and see Lennon?' he said to Marcuson. 'Get some cash . . . For the Irish revolution!'

'Yeah – amazing idea.'

'We could get Lennon to come over to Derry. Give one of those free concerts. For the Irish revolution.'

'Yes,' said Marcuson, excited. 'But I want to write more about the revolution first. Look, you please return to Belfast. I'll send over a team of real journalists – underground journalists. They'll tell the truth about Free Belfast.'

McCann had really little choice but to agree. He departed, back to his non-existent revolutionary comrades, sawn-off shotgun buried in the depths of his overcoat.

A few days later, the eager reporters arrived. There was Marcuson's own wife Jill; a Jewish Austrian called Felix de Mendelsohn, from the German sheet *Twen* who later went to work on *Suck* magazine, best described as a hippy entrepreneur; Joe Stevens, New York photographer who produced material for *Oz* and *IT* under the name of 'Captain Snaps'; and quite a crowd of others. McCann, nothing if not resourceful, had managed to make contact with a couple of local journalists already. They too, had fallen under his spell: and he had let them know that revolutionary activity was in the air. He was simply going to have to invent some. Within 48 hours of their arrival in Belfast, Jim McCann led the dazed hippy journalists to an 'action' against what he had decided was an appropriate bastion of 'Brit rule' – Queens University, Belfast. Petrol bombs had been made out of milk-bottles stuffed with rags. At midnight, after a break-in, they were hurled at the window of the staff common-room, missed and burst into unimpressive sheets of flame against the brick wall. At once the police arrived. All present ran away. Their car would not start. Most were arrested. Hotly pursued by the Royal Ulster Constabulary, McCann himself delved into the depths of his overcoat and produced the sawn-off shotgun. He had forgotten that the RUC are armed. Within seconds he was staring into half a dozen pistol barrels. McCann gulped, tossed the shotgun over the hedge, and surrendered.

He later described this episode in his 'life story' in a slightly more picturesque way.

There was a gun-battle for six hours. I had an Armalite and a .45. They blew down the wall with fucking percussion bombs. They were shooting through the window at me, the SAS! When the bomb went off, I was knocked completely unconscious. So I wakes up in this torture centre . . .

At the time, he did his best to recoup the embarrassing situation.

'I'm a political prisoner!' he cried, and bawled across at the others: 'You're political prisoners! Don't say anything!'

The whole party were hauled off to the Crumlin Road jail in Belfast. Excitement in England was at fever pitch. A group of enraged young students in London had already constituted themselves the 'Angry Brigade', and were letting off bombs at the homes of British politicians. They had connections with the Underground press and Scotland Yard frequently (and mistakenly) used to raid the premises of *IT* looking for them. In fact, their sympathisers were later to be found among the political activists and 'street hippies' who clustered round *Friends* the following year, after Marcuson left it. But police never realised this. Some of the youngsters of the Angry Brigade were eventually arrested and sentenced to long jail terms.

On 30 March, the following afternoon, Marcuson was strolling through London. He had just managed to organise the meeting with John Lennon and was feeling at peace with the world. He saw an *Evening News* screamer: 'Police smash Anarchist Bomb Gang'. Marcuson assumed the Angry Brigade had finally been caught. He bought a copy.

Police sources say 'We feel we have smashed an International ring of anarchists . . . Belfast . . . university bombing' . . . using the situation in Ulster for their own ends.

He read on, with a sinking heart, until he came to the list of those held. Oh, no . . . Felix de Mendelsohn, Joe Stevens, McCann, his own wife . . . And his last words before they left had been: 'Be careful. Don't get too involved.'

He would go to Belfast at dawn. This could be very heavy indeed. First he had the appointment with Lennon. He rode down in Lennon's white Mercedes to a private dining club in Mayfair where he held court. This attempt to get money out of Lennon was by no means ridiculous. The Beatles set up their 'Apple' organisation at the end of the 1960s to fund projects which appealed to them, although a Baker Street boutique and a record label had been the only concrete results so far. Lennon's B-side to the Beatles first 'Apple' disc, 'Hey Jude', was entitled 'Revolution' . . .

The atmosphere in Mayfair was uncongenial. Yoko Ono, by now his wife, who was to co-star on future records, was accompanying Lennon at the table. There were others dining around the room. They too, were presumably rich and famous people. Wasn't that man with the moustache the well-known English racing driver, Graham Hill? And didn't that woman over there look exactly like Ingrid Bergman? It *was* Ingrid Bergman. Yoko Ono plunged across the room:

'Please can I have your autograph, Miss Bergman? Here, write it on this napkin. Yes, of course you can have my autograph too. And John's. We'll write them on *your* napkin.'

In what seemed no time at all, the famous people in the dining club were busy autographing each others' napkins. Marcuson, having extracted some vague promises to consider finance, left rapidly. He was feeling somehow puzzled.

The next morning, he stumbled anxiously off the Belfast plane at Aldergrove Airport, past the blast screens and the heavily armed British soldiers. He found a local lawyer, Paddy McGrory, with expertise in Republican cases and organised liaison with the young civil libertarian London solicitor Bernard Simons. Simons had effectively handled a drug case for one of Marcuson's friends. This connection was to make Simons's career in one way, and be the bane of his life in another. Once known as a competent English defence lawyer in Belfast, he and his firm got a string of Irish cases when mainland bombings started in England later in the 1970s. And he was to defend Howard Marks himself with remarkable success over the next decade. But MI5, the Special Branch and the uniformed British police conceived a great dislike for him as a consequence – they were much later to be discovered, to their embarrassment, compiling dossiers on him, for the world as though they were the KGB and he was a Russian dissident. Simons was not the only one to get this treatment, of course.

Apart from inadvertently launching Simons into a career on the MI5 computer, Marcuson also managed to get all the gaggle of hippies, girlfriends and wives released without charges, leaving only the 'Belfast Four' in jail – McCann, Mendelsohn, Stevens and Peter McCarten of the *Belfast Newsletter*.

He went to visit the shameless author of all this misfortune. McCann in the visiting room at Crumlin Road jail was as manic as usual:

'Get me a fucking blade, Alan! I'm not staying in this place. Get me a blade!'

He was having a high time, and the other prisoners, including some genuine IRA men were, despite themselves, becoming rather impressed. Brought into court for bail hearings, McCann gave a clenched fist salute.

'You're an Orange Fascist!' he shouted to the RUC sergeant in the witness-box.

'I'd like to say something,' he demanded.

'Let's keep to the matter in hand,' said the magistrate.

'Now don't start interrupting me. I should like to protest the presence of a member of the occupying forces in this court room. This is not a people's court. There's no form of natural justice here. This is a political frame-up. A political conspiracy framed by Stormont and Westminster . . .'

On his next appearance, he ostentatiously sat with his back to the proceedings, reading the Black Panther revolutionary text by George Jackson: *Soledad Brother*.

'Look, er Jim,' said Marcuson. 'I know you support the Revolution, but the others are a bit worried. They think if there are these, er revolutionary gestures of yours at the trial they're all going to go down for 12 years each.'

'Alan, don't you worry, my good friend. None of youse should worry. I'll be fucking away from here before the case comes on!'

The astonishing thing was that, for once in his life, McCann was perfectly accurate. Somebody did bring in a hacksaw blade – sometimes he said it was one of his brothers, sometimes he said one of the guards had been bribed. The bars were sawn through, in best *Boys Own Paper* style and, two weeks before the trial of the International Anarchist Bomb Gang was due to open at the Belfast City Commission, he escaped. He shinned down a rope of – what else? – knotted sheets. It was generally considered by those who knew, that the escape had been organised for a genuine IRA man in his cell who changed his mind at the last minute in view of his short sentence. McCann had seized his opportunity.

The young Irish journalist, Peter McCarten, pleaded guilty and was jailed for a year. The others, just as McCann had predicted, were acquitted. They successfully blamed all the misadventures of that night on the deranged and absent arsonist, Jim McCann. Meanwhile, the editors of Oz had been finally acquitted of 'conspiracy to corrupt public morals', but convicted of publishing obscene articles. Judge Argyle – the same dispassionate soul who reacted to the 1967 'Legalise Marijuana' advert by jailing a Jamaican in Birmingham for five years on a cannabis charge – said how much he agreed with the guilty verdict. He ordered Neville to be locked up for 15 months.

'That's the same as I got,' said a fellow prisoner in the cells 'and I tried to murder my wife.'

Eventually the Court of Appeal let them all out again.

It was Oz which published the tape-recorded interview McCann gave a sympathetic journalist five days after his escape. They headlined it:

'Rage of Innocence.'

I'm in a prison cell, completely naked, degraded, a blanket over me. Over the next two days, I wasn't allowed to sleep. It was just a mock trial. I didn't even react to the pack of fucking lies. I just sat in the witness box reading a fucking book . . . I could cut those bars for about 15 minutes each day . . . Can't cut the last bolt . . . I tie my chain up again with bits of black thread. The two screws come into my cell every day. I tell them I'm fucking ill, give them a volley of abuse . . . two Scottish pig mercenaries on each turret . . . I leave a note: 'This escape is a demonstration of revolutionary freedom!'

Marcuson drew to the climax of his story. Howard and Plinston were gripped. A triumphant phone call came from McCann across the Irish Sea: 'The Kid's away! I told you.' The fugitive had crossed the border to Dublin, by pretending to be a bridegroom. He claimed he had solemnly driven through in a Daimler, with a bride in white by his side, white ribbons in the car bonnet, dressed in a black suit and a lustful smirk. He was now in hiding in the depths of the Republic of Ireland. Marcuson and his wife set out for a scoop meeting with the fugitive patriot and hero. They took a taxi out to Heathrow, and the 75-minute direct Aer Lingus plane to Shannon Airport, on the Limerick coast. They followed his instructions in a series of phone calls, and it was soon apparent why they had been summoned. McCann was discovered lying unromant-ically in a YMCA hostel at the very southernmost tip of Eire, on Valencia Island, a short ferry ride off the southern edge of Dingle Bay, among the kind of picturesque scenery enshrined in the soft-focus movie *Ryan's Daughter*. He was flat broke. It was just as well Marcuson, who had by now abandoned the extravagant *Friends* scene, had brought cash. He also brought, in view of the likely rigours of the expedition, a good deal of dope.

McCann watched for the first time, intrigued, as Marcuson warmed his little block of brown hash, crumbled some softened fragments on to the tobacco, rolled it up into a cigarette, and fitted a little piece of rolled up cardboard into the mouthpiece end.

'Hippy shit,' he said disgustedly.

'Try some,' Marcuson said.

'Well why not?' said McCann, always eager to learn a new game.

It had no visible effect on him, but he seemed to like it. Or to like the idea. From then on, at least in the company of the hippies, McCann was cool. He carefully avoided mentioning the subject of drugs in the company of members of the IRA, who, being Irish catholics, were puritanical over matters other than murder.

It was clear the little troupe could not stay indefinitely at the Young Men's Christian Association. They moved to a small guest house on the mainland. This was a mistake. Upstairs in one of the neat rooms they had rented, McCann cried: 'Roll a fucking joint, Alan.'

'Not here. They'll smell it.'

'Ah come on: that stink won't worry an Irishman.'

'OK, OK.'

Bang. Bang.

'What are youse doing in that room? What's that smell?'

'Don't worry lady. It's just some unusual French cigarettes we're smoking.'

'I'm going to call the Gardai. You're drug-takers.'

'All right, all right, we're leaving. Now.'

They went on the road for a while, driving around the little towns of the west of Ireland, Marcuson in love with their damp charms, McCann working out schemes for renting cars but not paying for them.

'I'm a writer,' he told hoteliers. 'My friend here's a journalist.'

As an Irish patriot on the run, he saw himself as a character out of *Bonny and Clyde*.

'We're getting low on money, Jim.'

'We can rob the fucking banks, Alan. Every time we come to one of these towns, we can stick up the banks. That's the way to raise funds among us Republicans.'

'It's not quite my style, really, Jim. Why don't I drive to Cork Airport and go back to London. I'm sure I can hustle some more bread somewhere.'

And so it had gone on thoughout the autumn. Eventually they had ended up back on the Kerry coast, staying in the house rented from a veteran Republican, Michael Murphy, to whom some cock-and-bull story of McCann's deeds had been spun.

McCann proceeded to take the village over, punctuated with trips to visit his relations in Dublin. He was a one-man hive of IRA activity. In the local bar he would confide heavily:

'I'm just down from the North.'

He would warm to this theme as the drink flowed. In a while he would have them roaring out the words of the old 1922 Civil War songs:

> Take that flag from the mast, Irish traitor!
> It's the flag we Republicans claim.
> It shall never belong to Free Staters
> For they've brought on it nothing but shame!

The climax was a dramatic visit from a quiet figure who slipped into the house and closeted himself alone with McCann for a conversation lasting several hours, and then departed. McCann, uncharacteristically did not mention his name, but Marcuson recognised him from newspaper photographs. It was Sean McStiofain, then none other than 'chief of staff' of the IRA. Years later, McStiofain was to admit to this meeting.

'McCann had certain propositions to put,' he said flintily. 'I was not impressed with him.'

On his return from his first hustling trip to London, Marcuson found McCann presiding in a newly rented cottage at Ballinskelligs over what appeared to be a full-scale Provisional IRA bomb-factory. There were iron filings all over the floor.

'What's happening?'

'I'm highly regarded, Alan, highly regarded. That escape of mine did me some good with the boys. They're out there now, in the mountains, testing their weapons.'

McCann was full of ideas for furthering the cause, some of which his new-found friends were later to try out in modified forms.

'The real way to escape from Crumlin Road would be to dig a tunnel *in* from the outside, not the other way round.'

That was one of them.

'Or you could get a helicopter, and land it in the prison yard . . . you could get the helicopter, and use it to drop bombs on Stormont. You could make the bomb and sling it out over the side.'

He was the expert escapologist, the first Republican over the wall.

Marcuson raised what was in his mind.

'I know a much better way of raising money than robbing banks, Jim.'

'What?'

'Well, I've been coming and going rather a lot through the Irish airports, Cork and Shannon. Their whole approach to Customs and checks and searches is pretty relaxed.'

'So?'

'I happen to know some people . . . it could be a very profitable way of getting hash into England. Through the back door as it were. There's a big demand.'

'What, make money out of that fucking hippy-shit rubbish? You must be joking.'

Later, McCann graciously agreed that perhaps it wasn't such a bad idea. If bribery and corruption was required, he was certainly the man who could do it.

Marcuson did have the stirrings of a few qualms. McCann had dangerous friends and considerable tendencies towards megalomania. He was also worrying.

They sat smoking joints after one of these conversations.

'We'll be rich, Alan,' McCann said ruminatively.

'Yeah.'

'When we're rich, Alan, we'll lie on the beaches in the sun.'

'Yeah.'

'We'll lie like this on a beach in, in . . . Sardinia, with two young boys sucking our dicks.'

'Oh, yeah.'

Funny. Could have sworn he said 'boys'. *Boys?* Hmm.

This was the man who Marcuson described to Howard Marks and Graham Plinston. He was Jim McCann, the man who could do anything, the potential dope connection who could make their fortunes.

'Where can we find him, Alan?'

'It's a place called Ballinskelligs. County Kerry. I'm going back there. If you want to come over, just give me a ring. You call the Post Office and leave a message for me to call. There aren't too many other phones in that part of the world.'

'Shall we memorise the number?'

'You don't really need to memorise it. Ireland is a bit different to here. It's Ballinskelligs 1.'

# CHAPTER 3

# The Shannon Scam

Howard Marks debated for some days with Plinston after Marcuson departed. Should they ring Ballinskelligs 1?

'We do need somebody who can straighten an airport.'

'But it means cutting a lot more people in. We'd have to offer Marcuson a share and McCann himself. You, me, Durrani in Pakistan, the Film man, McCann, Marcuson. We'd have to offer Marcuson 20 per cent.'

'Let's do it.'

'I've forgotten the phone number.'

'Very funny, Howie.'

British Airways direct flight 838 touched down at Cork Airport shortly after noon. Howard Marks and Plinston made an odd-looking pair of businessmen at the Hertz car rental counter – British drivers' licenses, a fistful of credit cards, faded denims, un-tipped Capstan full-strength cigarettes, and about £1,000 in cash stuffed in Plinston's back jeans pocket.

They swung on to the road north to Cork, and turned left on the city's outskirts, heading west towards the Atlantic. It was raining.

'Irish mist,' said Howard, knowledgeably.

Through the little town of Macroom, and on through the Derrynasaggart Mountains, going slower as they penetrated into County Kerry, it occurred to Howard that Ireland was a primitive country, ill-suited to such sophisticated operators as themselves. Kerry was, of course, the most remote part of Eire. The Irish make Irish jokes about Kerrymen. Ancient loyalties linger on, and ancient hatreds. In those hills, they still remembered the families who fought for Michael Collins in the civil war of 1922, and those who carried a Thompson gun for De Valera's IRA diehards. They still remembered the ancient wrongs done by the British. There was not much else to think about.

It was the slowest 100 miles Howard had ever covered. They turned south-west down the estuary of the Kenmare River.

South of the hills of MacGillycuddy's Reeks, they climbed precipitously around the coast of the Ring of Kerry. National Route 70, trunk road as it was, had tractors straddling the tarmac, more than one donkey-cart, and frequent crowds of cows crossing, lowing, surging, pounding mournfully round the bumpers. On the right, peat-bog stood sliced into trenches with stacks of wet divots piled by the roadside. On the left, beyond the cliffs, peaks and crags of pointed rock rose in silhouette from a damp, silvery sea. The fields really were bright emerald green.

The road twisted finally round a mountainside and dropped down into the minute huddle of Waterville – colour-washed cottages, a shingle beach and the fake crenellation of the Butler Arms Hotel.

'Where are we, Graham?'

'Ballinskelligs Bay.'

'This doesn't look so bad.'

'We aren't there yet.'

He gestured across the bay. Miles away on the far hillside, two dozen cottages could just be made out through the drizzle, scattered gracelessly at the end of a track. There was a tiny beach on a corner of the shore. The only sign of life was a thread of peat-smoke from the occasional smallholding. It was a good half-hour's drive yet, over the rough rock and bog at the head of the bay and out again towards the Atlantic coast.

'This place,' Howard said, 'looks to me like a complete dump.'

They drove on, down the track to the beach, turning off before the maroon-washed Mains Hotel, the only two-storey building in sight. The Ranch House appeared: a fisherman's cottage overlooking the water. The familiar figure of Marcuson rushed out, at the sound of the engine.

'Where's Jim McCann?'

'He's up at the hotel, getting some drink. He'll be back soon. But you've got to listen to me. I've made a mistake. McCann is dangerous. He's a liar, a maniac, he's probably psychotic. You don't want to get involved with him. For the sake of both your families. He'll take over your lives! He's . . . demonic!'

56

'Alan, what on earth are you talking about?'

They calmed him down. The immediate cause of the trouble seemed to be McCann's sexually predatory antics. A beautiful German girl had arrived at the cottage, a nomadic acquaintance of Marcuson. She was with her German boyfriend. McCann conceived a passion for her. He manouevred the boyfriend into leaving for a visit to Belfast, and tried all his conversational ploys. Nothing worked.

'Do you know what he did? We're all sitting there one night, and he suddenly says: "Shall I tell you what we used to do in Belfast when we were kids? We used to draw little faces on our dicks. With Biros. We used to draw little faces on our dicks." And then, do you know what he does? "I'll show you," he says. He actually gets it out. And he takes a Biro, and he does it. He draws a little face on the end of the damn thing. With eyes and a nose. And he goes up to this girl with it in his hand. "There you are," he says in this little small voice, "that's what we used to do in Belfast." I've never seen anything so blatant in my life.'

'What happened?'

'She slept with him. The same night.'

'Oh. Is that it?'

'No it isn't. The next night he's at it with my own wife, trying to take her away from me. He's desperate for women. Or anything that moves. I told him to cut it out and do you know what he does? He's lying on the floor drumming his legs like a four-year-old and screaming "Youse all hate me! Youse all hate me!" That man's power games know absolutely no limit. I warn you, he'll tell you things that aren't true. But you'll believe them . . .'

At this moment, Jim McCann walks in. He looks at Marcuson's face.

'What are you fucking telling them about me, Alan? Let's go down the pub.'

They adjourn to the Mains Hotel. To Marcuson's chagrin, the two visitors appear to be falling under McCann's energetic spell. Drink is steadily taken. McCann dominates the proceedings with his usual deplorable panache.

'What are you doing here with your Guinness glasses,' he demands of the grizzled Ballinskelligs Republicans, 'when men are dying in Belfast?'

The singing soon starts:

In the Crumlin Road jail all the prisoners one day
Took out a football and they started to play
While all the warders were watching the ball
Nine of the lads went over the Wall
Over the Wall, Over the Wall
It's hard to believe, they went over the Wall
The security forces, they were shocked to the core
They bolted each window and they locked every door
But all their precautions were no good at all
Another three lads went over the Wall!

McCann had a proprietorial air during that one, and a moist eye
for 'The Boys of the Old Brigade':

'Twas long ago we faced the foe
The Ould Brigade and me
By my side they fought and died
That Ireland might be Free.

And the whole bar joined in the most recent IRA tear-jerker about
mass internment and the Brit 'concentration camps' of the North:

Through the little streets of Belfast
In the dark of Monday morn
British soldiers came marauding
Wrecking little homes with scorn.
Heedless of the crying children
Dragging fathers from their beds
Beating sons, while helpless mothers
Watched the blood pour from their heads
Oooh, with tanks and armoured cars and guns
They came to take away our sons
And every man will stand behind
THE MEN BEHIND THE WIRE!

Howard, fortified by a joint on the way to the bar, warmed to all
this.

'It's a picturesque place,' he confided to McCann.

'Ballinskelligs,' said McCann poetically, 'is like when God made
the world. On a soft day, the hills roll. It's got purple, it's got green,

it's got bog and it's wild and it's free. William Butler, he said – said it very, very well and so profoundly:

> For come to me, o human child to the waters in the wild
> Walk with us on Skalleg strand, the world's more full of wonder
> Than you can understand.

And he wrote that standing here in Ballinskelligs, which is basically the Holy Grail of Kerry, of Ireland, the whole Celtic paradise!'

He paused for breath.

'What's that building at the very end of the bay, Jim?'

'It's a lunatic asylum for nuns.'

Howard began to giggle uncontrollably, and McCann joined in. Nobody pointed out that the poet's real name was William Butler YEATS.

McCann was full of Belfast chutzpah: it was clear that anywhere he was he could take over in five minutes, drawing those around him into a whirlpool of his own devising. Howard loved watching the Belfast Revolutionary on stage; he could cope with McCann's unsettling ploys – but they were a challenge. They stretched him.

The group clustered round the bar table.

'Do you like sex?' McCann demanded, seizing the initiative as usual.

'Not objectively, no,' said Howard blandly, in his best and thickest Welsh lilt. There was a baffled silence.

'I mean, do you like screwing?' lamely said McCann. He had definitely lost what chess players call 'momentum' to this working-class kid. But Howard was also clearly prepared to admire him. Relations with Plinston were stickier. For one thing Marcuson was whispering into his ear:

'McCann'll take everything from you. He'll have the shirt off your back if you let him.'

'Are you a revolutionary like us, Graham?' said McCann.

'Certainly not,' said the town clerk of Letchworth's son: 'I'm a monarchist.'

McCann tried a different tack:

'I like that Fair Isle sweater you're wearing. It's certainly a nice piece of stuff.'

Plinston's vanity responded to this:

'Do you really? It is nice isn't it?'

'I've always wanted a sweater like that. It looks so good on you. Would you mind if I tried it on?'

'By all means,' said Plinston, graciously struggling out of it.

'See. See,' hissed Marcuson: 'The shirt off your back.'

Plinston glowered at him. McCann joined in with a contemptuous stare. They got down to business:

'Can you arrange to get hash in through an Irish airport?'

'No problem, my good friend, just no problem.'

'What will it take?'

'I'll need some cash to get it organised, of course. Give me a week and it's as good as done. I've got a lot of connections.'

'We thought you might want some money. We just have to trust you. If this comes off, it could be very big. There'll be thousands in it for you on a regular basis. We'll give you 20 per cent of everything.'

'I have to have cash now. People have to be . . . spoken to.'

'How much?'

'At least £500.'

'Graham can give it you now.'

He fumbled for the roll of £20 notes in his jeans pocket.

'We'll meet you again in a week's time. Not here, it's far too remote. In Dublin. Alan will make the arrangements.'

Once again, McCann rose to the situation. Even Marcuson, to whom McCann was now behaving in a distinctly threatening fashion, had to agree that his conduct was masterful. McCann settled on Shannon Airport for the operation: it was small and remote, tucked away by County Clare, 100 miles north up the Atlantic coast, just outside Limerick, in the lackadaisical west of Ireland.

Shannon was an interesting phenomenon. It was strategically placed because it was the final European landfall before planes had to make the transatlantic crossing. Not only did jets regularly ply between Shannon and North America on the routes to and from Ireland itself; it was also both a connection point and a refuelling stop for European and Asian airlines on long hauls across the Atlantic. While most European connections went from Dublin Airport through Amsterdam, the tarmac at Shannon could see New York-bound Alitalia planes refuelling from Milan, or Aeroflot touching down before the long haul to Havana, or the big Seaworld freighters come in. There was a lot of activity in the air.

Furthermore, Sean Lemass, Eire's trade minister in the 1950s, had done his best to exploit this position as an airways crossroads – one of Ireland's few economic assets other than peat. The first duty-free shops were opened at Shannon in 1952, for transit passengers to stock up with drink, perfumes and wristwatches: an idea soon to be copied worldwide. The area around Shannon was declared a freeport, in which bonded goods could be shipped in for manufacture. A huge trading estate grew up, much bigger than the modest airport terminal building itself. Every day at tea time, lines of cars and trucks would pour out of the gates to the trading estate, waved through the airport checkpoint, many to disappear into the new township that had also sprung up around them. The Aer Lingus cargo terminal sat surrounded by what was, by Irish standards, a sea of frenzied economic activity.

McCann invested only a very small fraction of his newly acquired £500. He had a box of business cards printed. They read 'Seamus O'Neill. *Fortune* Magazine. New York.' Then he rang up Shannon Airport:

'Airport manager's office. My name's O'Neill, I'm an editor for *Fortune* Magazine, the top American business weekly. Put me on to the airport manager.'

He made his pitch:

'We at *Fortune* are doing a comparative survey of the world's airports, in depth. Advice to our readers – very influential businessmen – wouldn't want to omit Shannon: in fact, I've persuaded my colleagues to include it. Didn't want the ould country to lose out. Could be worth a lot of business. So I've just flown in. If you can arrange a conducted tour of the airport, how it all works, especially the freight side. Yes, as soon as possible – I've just flown in to Dublin and I've only got three days here before going on to Schiphol at Amsterdam. Thursday? Yes, hang on – I think I can manage that . . .'

Three days later, he was back at Ballinskelligs, beaming. He tossed down document after document on the table in front of a bemused Marcuson.

'International Air Transport Regulations.'

Thump.

'More of the same.'

Thump.

'More IATA rules.'

'Here's some maps. Every inch of Shannon.'

'And here's all the Customs forms they use. I nicked top copies off all the piles as we were going round. This is the main one. It's an

"Out of Charge" docket – this clears cargo to be released out of the freeport area on to Irish soil. You just need a Customs man to issue the form and sign it.'

Marcuson stared, thunderstruck, at the booty.

'Now, let me see my notes. When the cargo comes in, this is the mark they chalk on the crates, to signify they've been examined and cleared. When they chalk them, they move the crates across the floor of the cargo terminal – let me see the map – from here to just this side here. The main import from Asia – you won't believe this – is cheap religious tracts. They're printed in India. Oh yes, and they have two or three dead bodies coming in from the Middle East for burial here. The point is, they go through in hermetically sealed containers.'

'Amazing. What about doing our scam?'

'No problem. I had a little talk to this Customs man. In return for a little financial assistance he'll accept forged "Out of Charge" dockets.'

'Fantastic. How did you do it?'

'Well, he's under a slight misapprehension. I played the Green Card, you know. The Boys in the North, David O'Connell and all those Provo arms he tried to buy in Amsterdam last year before their ship got busted . . .'

'What exactly do you mean, Jim?'

'He thinks he's doing it for the ould country, for the north.'

'What does he think this stuff is going to be?'

'Well, guns, I suppose. Anyway, I can't stay. I've got a plane to catch.'

'Where are you going?'

'They do a flight very good direct through to Paris. It's only 3½ hours.'

'I don't understand.'

'Well, there's most of that £500 left, isn't there? I thought I might buy a few clothes. See youse all in Dublin after the weekend. Bye.'

Howard, Plinston and Marcuson gathered in the Pavilion Bar at the Dublin Intercontinental, in a gloomy frame of mind. Marcuson, especially, was convinced McCann was an unscrupulous menace. Howard rather liked him:

'Let's be practical,' he said. 'All we have to do is make sure McCann never has any more of our money in his hands. We can pay him on commission for the stuff he gets through.'

'How do you know he can get anything through? Maybe it's all just a con.'

McCann arrived, ebullient, with a new lightweight suit and a Pierre Cardin tie. He sensed the position, hinted heavily that Marcuson had lost his nerve, and wooed Howard and Plinston.

'All right. If you don't believe I can do it, let's have a test. Go back to London and fill up a crate with something – phone books. Airfreight it from Heathrow to Shannon, address it to some non-existent firm. I'll get it out of the airport for you.'

Marcuson said: 'I don't want anything to do with it. I don't want anything to do with you right now.'

The others tried to smooth this over.

'Where shall we address it to?'

'Why don't you label it to "Ashling Distribution Services". It's a good name, it's gaelic for "vision" – "Ashling", see – it's "hash" and "Aer Lingus".'

'Yeah, Ashling. That's quite funny.'

It was a joke of which McCann was to become inordinately fond over the next decade. And he turned up in Dublin two weeks later, for their next rendezvous, with the sample of the London telephone directory under his arm, straight out of Shannon Airport, just as he said.

It did appear that McCann could do the main thing – get it down from out of the air – but that still left problems. The next thing was to work out how to get a consignment through from Ireland to the English dealers. Howard and Plinston decided to use the basic driving method. Rent a car, stuff its panels, and simply drive to England, returning it to the hire company with some story about it having been temporarily stolen, in order to explain any peculiar smells or damaged bodywork.

Howard was thorough. He hired one car, drove west down the M4, across the Severn Bridge on the familiar route to Swansea, and on to the British and Irish Steam Packet company car ferry for the overnight passage to Cork. There were a string of ports up Ireland's west coast which carried cars to England – Cork, Rosslare, Dún Laoghaire, Dublin, Larne – and a string of English ports to receive them – Swansea, Fishguard, Holyhead, Liverpool, Stranraer. The traffic was enormous, and the British Special Branch were not to set up their Irish 'port units' for full-scale surveillance until the IRA began to organise systematic bombings on the mainland of Britain in the mid-

1970s. The Irish authorities were on the alert for guns and explosives coming in, but there seemed no special effort to detect contraband going out. Howard drove north round the coast to Dublin and booked a test-run back on the ferry from there to Liverpool. Things were looking good.

Jim McCann was waiting for him in Dublin, full of zest.

'When are we going to start?'

'This is what we'll try, Jim. We'll set up base on the west coast as near Shannon Airport as possible. We'll need to rent a house or a cottage, using a false name. It'll be needed for weeks: best for a three- or six-month lease, or whatever you can get. It has to be really remote, and have space for cars to be stashed.'

'When does the stuff come in?'

'It's going to be difficult to tell exactly. Graham's going out to Pakistan to organise it, and we want to do about 200–300 lb, just to start with – a single car load.'

'I've talked to my man. There are heavy problems. I've got all the problems my end, you know – it's me that's doing all the sweating. For a start, I'll have to know the Air Waybill number of the consignment, so my man can forge up the paperwork and I can claim it out of Shannon.'

'You'll be told – I'll call you with it, as soon as the stuff's in the air.'

'And the other thing is serious. It's going to come in on a particular day, right? Well, he works a shift system, my boy, some days he's there and some days he's not. It's got to come in on the right day.'

'We'll work it out. I'll give you my phone numbers in Oxford and Brighton. When the stuff's ready to go in Karachi, we'll speak. You tell me what days your man is on that week, I'll synchronise it with the airline schedules and cable Karachi to have the stuff put on the right connecting flight. According to my ABC they'll probably move it direct from Karachi on PIA to Frankfurt, and then transfer it to Aer Lingus for the Shannon run. When it's arrived, you call up the airport – what firm are you going to be?'

'Ashling Distribution Services, what else?'

'Right – well, go round there and get it. A small van will be OK. You bring it round to our base, wherever it is by then. I'll be waiting. You unload and clear off, and I handle all the arrangements from then on. I'll get the stuff over to England in a car.'

'We haven't fixed the cash. How much am I going to make? How do I get my share? I need it in advance.'

'Come on Jim. Be serious. When you deliver the stuff, I'll give you every penny you've earned. In cash. On the spot. We'll give you £10 a lb.'

'That's fucking nothing! I'm risking my neck going into that airport for nothing at all.'

'Well, it isn't nothing. It'll be two or three grand in your pocket and that's just for this test run. If it goes OK there'll be 10, 20 times that much, and not just once either. We could all be at the start of something tremendous.'

'£10 a lb, plus my expenses then.'

'OK Jim.'

The plot began to move into motion and the conspirators scattered purposefully. Plinston produced £5,000 in cash.

'Here you are, Howard, straight from my "accountant" in Geneva.' He then boarded a plane to arrange the purchase of hash from his connections in Karachi. Durrani's men would get it on the plane there and into the air.

McCann found a cottage. It was certainly remote, even desolate, high on the Clare hills overlooking the isolated northern shore of the Shannon estuary, but it was within an hour's drive of the airport. It was on what had once been Colonel William Henn's Paradise estate, a testament to the historic feudal grip of the Anglo-Irish squirearchy. Paradise House had burned down in the 1960s, but the unoccupied cottage a quarter of a mile along the wooded brow survived and was for rent. Howard gave it its most unlikely tenant to date – his unemployed chum from the Valleys, Little Pete.

'Go out there,' he said. 'There's no phone, but there's a little village called Ballynacally down at the bottom of the hill, and there's a lovely view out of the window. Just look after things, don't go away, and wait for me. It might be a week or two until I arrive – it's a bit uncertain.'

'Sure, Howard. Sounds fun.'

'There'll be £500 in it for you.'

Howard now set about preparing himself for the big-time, by constructing a 'front'. Long-haired Notting Hill ex-students with no visible means of support were bad bets for avoiding police interest. He decided to become a respectable small businessman, much as Plinston was with Hamdullah, the carpet firm. Not only would a couple of company 'fronts' provide a plausible explanation of Howard's swelling income and his travels. They would also, if carefully chosen, provide a means of 'laundering' it. Howard, too, would become a midget Al Capone.

He turned to the Oxford group of his friends – the magic circle who were to become, wittingly or unwittingly, the backbone of the Marks dope multi-national for the next 12 years. One such innocent was Redmond O'Hanlon, who had been an undergraduate at Merton and who, distressed by his mother's discovery and disapproval of his juvenile first novel at 17, had embarked on a mammoth academic work, which looked never to be finally completed, on the influence of natural history on literature, with special reference to the impact of Darwinism on the novels of Joseph Conard. This passion for birds and beasts gave him in the end a certain academic authority: he was eventually to work part-time for the *Times Literary Supplement* and to travel to Borneo with the poet James Fenton in a fruitless quest for the disappearing black rhino. O'Hanlon married Belinda, a student friend of Howard's first wife at St Anne's, a cool pretty woman with masses of pre-Raphaelite blonde hair, whose parents farmed 200 acres of hops and dairy pasture in Kent, and who had a penchant for dressmaking. She and Anna Woodhead, a Spanish girl briefly married to Anthony Woodhead (his brother was a psychology student at Oxford and another of Howard's friends) ran a little sewing partnership, advertising round the Oxford colleges for affluent women undergraduates who wanted special hand-made numbers to wear at May Balls.

This would do for Howard's plans. He offered the two women a deal. He would finance a move out of their modest workroom in Parkend Street to a full-scale boutique in the centre of Oxford. They would set up a proper company which he would direct. Rosie would vaguely help in the business, and they would both signal their commitment by living over the shop.

'Your job, Belinda,' he told her, 'will be to make the clothes, not to fuss about money. You'll get regular wages as well as your shareholding. I'll do up the premises, supply filing cabinets and office equipment, and just draw out £25 a week as a partner.'

How could she refuse? Henry Hodge, by now a solicitor, was commissioned to set up the company 'Annabelinda Ltd'. Howard and Belinda had 40 shares each. Rosie and Anna Woodhead had 10. Howard used his £3000 in the Port Talbot bank account as collateral security for a £3000 bank loan. With the money, he bought a lease on a corner shop-front with two storeys above it, at 6 Gloucester Street, just off George Street, an excellent city-centre location, where Annabelinda trades to this day. An arty sign saying simply 'Annabelinda' was hung over the door and the boutique was fitted out with the kind of decor likely to appeal to the young debutantes of Oxfordshire and Gloucestershire.

The interior decoration was carried out through a second company Henry Hodge was commissioned to launch: 'Robin Murray (Oxford) Ltd, 6 Gloucester Street, Oxford. Tel. 42428, Director D. H. Marks.' This operated from Annabelinda's basement. Howard had remembered another tip from Plinston – building, decoration and architectural improvement was an excellent method of soaking up bent money. He bought expensive fittings which 'Robin Murray' would install, invoicing 'Annabelinda' modest sums.

He put in sewing machines – 4 or 5 at a time – which never went through the company's books. He generated tremendous 'profits' from the sale of non-existent dresses, and drew out the laundered money for him and Rosie to spend. He bought a brand new BMW cash down for £2,500. 'Robin Murray' decorated a bathroom for customers for £100 and wrote it down in the books as a £1000 job. Howard printed up imposing business cards: 'Annabelinda Limited. Directors D. H. Marks, B. O'Hanlon', and organised the purchase tax to the satisfaction of accountants Thornton Baker. Neither the accountants, nor the O'Hanlons, nor Anna Woodhead, nor Henry Hodge, nor Howard's interior decorator friend Robin Murray, would have had the least idea what was afoot, nor ever did until Howard's eventual hasty departure from the shop.

Belinda sewed calmly away. She acquired a copy of *Burke's Peerage* to look up the family background of those of the county set who were buying dresses for the debby weddings. She renewed her annual subscription to *Italian Vogue*. She pinned up posters of her favourite Renaissance paintings, and samples of medieval coloured lettering round the wall. She complained that Rosie drifted about like a little rich girl, doing no work and spending money as to the manner born (which indeed Rosie was). She worked towards opening a branch inside Liberty's, the famous London fabric store. Belinda, characteristically, would hand-stitch tiny blue embroidered flowers on to a cream silk dress selling at today's prices at something close to £600.

Redmond composed baroque advertisements for rich Oxford tourists:

## ANNABELINDA
### Dress Designers
are pleased to be able to guarantee their eccentric and distinguished clientele a little languidly longer of liaisons dangeureuses in their forest chateaux, lakeside pavilions, perfumed gardens, beached brigantines, state barges, canopied couches, lost gazebos (and other seraglios of the summer subconscious) with a new collection of their originals in handwoven silks, hand-embroidered, pleated and quilted silks, silk crêpe de Chine, silk chiffon, quilted satins, Liberty printed silks, voiles and lawns at
Number Six, Gloucester Street.

Howard delightedly told his illegal friends a different tale:
'I'm making lots of money from dope, and sticking it into Annabelinda.'

Now, when the scheme had been going so well, it stalled.

The worst of these smuggling projects, Howard began to realise, was the delays. There was dead silence from Plinston, supposedly buying dope in Karachi. There was no way of reassuring Little Pete, sitting in the depths of County Clare without a phone. And there was silence from McCann.

It was lucky for Howard that he did not discover until much later how close the scheme had been to unravelling, as the days passed. He had given his Brighton address to McCann. What he did not know was that McCann, busy playing the Green Card with the Provisionals, had passed it on to Dutch Doherty, wanted on suspicion of killing two British soldiers, a formidable IRA streetfighter who was eventually to escape, like McCann had, from Crumlin Road jail. Before Doherty's arrest, McCann was eager to pass on the news that he had influential English contacts: Doherty obligingly fetched out his address book. Police failed to catch up with Doherty as he moved from house to house, until the end of October 1971, in the Ardoyne district of Belfast. Then they laid hands on his address book as well.

And there in it, was the name 'Howard Marks' and the Brighton address. Police passed it to the Special Branch in London. They paid a routine visit to the house in Lewes Crescent, each floor a different flat.

'Are you Mr Howard Marks?'

'No.'

'Where is he?'

'I don't know who he is, never mind where he is!'

'Doesn't Mr Marks live here?'

'No. Maybe he used to, but it means nothing to me.'

'His name was found in the address book of a man called Dutch Doherty you see, someone in the IRA. It's rather important we make these inquiries.'

'Sorry, I've never heard of him.'

Which was true. The London police did not follow up what was obviously a stale name and address. Had they arrived a few weeks earlier, before Howard and Rosie shifted operations back to Oxford, plans for the great Shannon scam would have come to a rapid and nasty halt.

Unaware that policemen were knocking on his former door, Howard waited, day after day, soothing himself by rolling frequent joints on the middle floor of Annabelinda, and turning up his record-player playing David Bowie's 'Changes' to full volume. Just over the rooftops, the students and townspeople drifted down the rainy Cornmarket. A new generation of undergraduates were living round the corner in the Balliol quadrangles, just beyond the Martyrs Memorial, in Howard's old rooms and up the staircase where he, Joshua Macmillan, Henry Hodge and all the others had first met. The new undergraduates were probably smoking lots of dope, too. At this rate, they were going to run out of anything to buy quite soon. Where was Plinston? What had gone wrong?

Two weeks passed. The phone rang. It was Plinston.

'All right. It's done. I'm on my way home.'

'What's gone wrong? What's been the hold-up?'

'Haven't you read about the crisis in Pakistan? With the new Prime Minister Bhutto? There's been a war and change of regime here. Rather a lot has been going on. It's been in all the papers.'

The next day, McCann rang in, and hoarsely gave the number of a Dublin call-box. Howard sprinted out into George Street, past the Apollo Theatre, to his car. He rang McCann back three hours later, from a London call-box.

'All right. The consignment of um, bananas is ready for shipping. Yes, I know there's been a delay. There's been a big war with India over there. It held everything up. It's been in all the papers, you know.

Now find out the days in the next 7 to 10 days when your friend will be open for business. Let me know as soon as you can . . . Any news from Paradise? No. OK. Bye.'

Plinston's plane droned through the skies back from Asia to Heathrow. McCann called in from Dublin with the shift times. In 14 hous, his man would go back on duty for three consecutive days.

Howard went shopping. 'Can you rent me a medium sized car? I'll need it for at least a week, perhaps a few days more. A two-door will be all right – have you got a Capri?' Then he went to the Ford main dealers in Oxford. 'I want some door poppers, yeah, that's right, those spring clips. Better give me a couple of dozen.'

On the way back to George Street, he called in at the hardware store, and bought a large Phillips screwdriver. Then he picked up the Capri. It was a rather showy shade of green. Howard looked with satisfaction at the pair of large, deep doors. He paid with his Hertz card, listed to the young director of Annabelinda Ltd. He'd already rung a couple of estate agents in Dublin –

'I run a dress shop in Oxford and I'm thinking of opening a branch in Dublin. Could you send me some literature on any suitable premises you might have available in the city?'

He loaded up his briefcase with their listings, fabric catalogues, Annabelinda notepaper and business cards.

The next day he strolled round to an Oxford travel agents, and booked a return passage on the overnight B & I boat with a single cabin on the upper deck both ways.

Then he swung the green Capri onto the M40, for the hour's drive down the motorway to Notting Hill. He paid a social call on Charlie Radcliffe, his new girlfriend, and Alan Marcuson.

'There should be a lot of stuff coming in soon, Charlie. We'll let you sell it for us, even though you've been too involved with your lovelife to help with the scam.'

'Am I going to get my percentage, Howard? I did set the whole thing up for you.'

'Yes, Alan, we understand how you feel. Don't worry.'

From the Warwick Castle, it was only a short drive down behind Paddington and along the ethnic bustle of Westbourne Grove, to Notting Hill Gate tube station. He pulled up outside 'Heads', his favourite haircutters:

'Can I have a wash and cut? And this time, will you cut it really short and neat? Well, fairly short anyway.'

Back in the Capri, it was south over Chelsea Bridge, picking through the clutter of Croydon and on to the Brighton Road. There were old friends to see in Brighton – dopers, dealers, 'Go'-players. Howard definitely liked this life. It was sociable. And while he was in Brighton, well away from Annabelinda, there was one particular thing to do.

He swung round the sugar-icing turrets of the absurd Regency conspicuous consumption of the Brighton pavilion, well before reaching the Palace Pier. Howard parked the car outside the main Post Office and went in. He selected an international cable form from the dispenser on the counter, and printed a telegraphic address in Karachi at the top. He had twelve more words to write:

'PLEASE SEND SPORTING GOODS TO ASHLING DISTRIBUTION SERVICES SHANNON AIRPORT.'

He hesitated and then added:

'BRENDON MacCARTHY

It was the first false name he was ever to use. A kind of line had been crossed.

The next morning, Howard drove back to Oxford, and waited. In the afternoon, the phone rang. It was Plinston back in London.

'That phone number you wanted,' he said tonelessly, 'is the local company, and it's 57248903.'

Howard wrote the eight digits down carefully. Then he took his ABC Airways Guide down from the shelf, and ran his finger down the list of three-digit prefixes universally used to designate carriers, until he came to Pakistan International Airlines. He wrote '214–' in front of the number on the piece of paper.

At 6 p.m. as arranged, McCann rang in, with a coinbox number in Limerick, close to the airport. Howard told him:

'The family are coming over to visit soon. I thought I'd let you know your uncle's phone number, so you can get hold of him. It's 214-57248903. If he's not home yet, he'll be in very soon.'

Then Howard took off. South to pick up the M4, along past Bristol, slowing down carefully as the wind from the estuary kicked at the traffic on the Severn Bridge, into Wales, down to the dock at Swansea and up the stern ramp of the big B & I ferry. He bought himself a large duty-free Jameson whiskey, went up to the dark and windy after-deck, smoked a joint, and tossed the stub into the Irish Sea.

The next morning, he queued in the line of cars going through Customs at Cork as the dawn sky lightened, and drove steadily north-west towards Limerick. Patiently trailing behind the tractors and truckloads of peat, he reached the little town by lunchtime. As he crossed the grey stone bridge across the river, wall posters began to appear advertising the duty-free shops at Shannon Airport. He drove past two Gardai, beefy men in blue shirts with peaked caps like bus-conductors. They were gossiping aimlessly outside a store with a shakily hand-painted sign. Howard tried not to stare at them.

Signs of airport life were beginning to increase. Here, a sign would advertise 'Transit Warehouse', or a huge truck chassis would be parked incongruously in a tiny front garden. Large hotels began to appear by the roadside, constructed in a low sub-Moorish style Howard did not yet recognise to be characteristically Irish-American. A huge ruined medieval keep appeared on his right. There was a signboard 'Bunratty Castle – medieval Banquets and Winery'. Motor Inns and restored baronial mansions appeared at every turn as the road briefly flowered into a four-lane highway for the left turn towards the sea and the airport. Howard accelerated the Capri past the turn-off and continued up the road towards the north side of the estuary. Within a few miles, the flurry of transatlantic activity disappeared. The road was silent. Howard crossed into County Clare and turned down the narrow lane with deep hedges that meandered 20 inconclusive miles along the promontory. He caught occasional glances of the silver water on the left. On the right, a ruined medieval tower stood like a stone cactus, its remaining knobs and buttresses green with ivy. He passed a wayside shrine dedicated to Our Lady of Lourdes.

This was Ballynacally. It slumbered in the afternoon rain. There was the Griffin Bar with its big Guinness sign. There was a second pub. There was a third. There was a little silent garage. Howard drove on through without stopping and on up the lane.

A mile later, he braked, and swung left through the remains of a long-decayed lodge-gate, and on to a stony track which disappeared into the woods. As the trees closed, dripping, over the Capri roof, the track veered to the right and plunged upwards. The car ground on in bottom gear, its wheels spinning. As it breasted the hill, a high stone wall and behind it the deserted ruins of a substantial farmhouse came into view. Howard stopped, backed, manouevred the car through a right angle on the narrow cart-track, and set off again, climbing on a second track along the brow of the hill. He ground over a crest, and a tiny cottage with low whitewashed walls suddenly appeared. Behind it, the whole expanse of the Shannon estuary spread out in a dim sheet of water, with the far shore of Limerick and the flat land jutting out into the estuary. A runway and some terminal buildings could just be seen there at Shannon itself.

A distraught Welsh figure poked its head out of the door and beckoned frantically.

'Did you see them? Did you see them?'

'Who?'

'The Pakistanis! They were here! I don't know what's going on.'

'My God. What Pakistanis? The solitude's destroyed your mind!'

'They come to the door. I haven't seen a soul for two weeks except the rats, right! Then there's this terrific bang at the door. I'm terrified. I open it. There's a Pakistani standing there, and another one behind him with a suitcase. Here, in the middle of nowhere. And the first one says, very solemnly, "Good Evening". Well, that threw me for a start, as it was lunchtime. And then he says "You Sir, I can see, have a lucky face." I was just staring at them. And he suddenly grabs this suitcase, whips it wide open and says "Do you want to buy a tie?"'

'He says what?'

'Ties. Do I want to buy one, the suitcase is full of ties. And he starts getting them all out of the case . . .'

'This is what we middle-class people, Little Pete, would call a travelling salesman. Let's try and relax. Let's have a blow.'

As Little Pete rolls a joint, Howard stares out to the runways of Shannon Airport in the distance.

Night falls. There is no sign at all of McCann. The silence is profound. Little Pete has spent his time laboriously stopping up the holes in the floorboard with wire wool. Every night, they are disturbed, proving the presence of rats. Suddenly tonight, they hear a faint, continuous scratching.

'It's rats,' Little Pete says. 'Shh. Listen again. They're in that cupboard. I'll get them.'

He tiptoes up to the cupboard with a raised hammer and flings it open. Inside, a butterfly, which has somehow got in, is flapping its tiny wings against a sheet of paper.

'It's a bit quiet here,' Howard says.

The next day, there is still no sign of McCann. Howard tries not to think about what could have gone wrong. As the light begins to fade they hear a scream of pained gears in the distance. Both peer out. A battered and old Volkswagen van is struggling up the hill. It crunches to a halt, blocking the entire track. McCann is at the wheel. As both men head for the cottage gate, McCann struggles with the loading door of the Volkswagen, flings it open and hauls out two small wooden crates, bound with metal straps.

'Look at that,' McCann says. 'The Kid's done it again!'

Howard pulled down the steep track the following morning, leaving Little Pete tending a crackling blaze outside the cottage of paraffin-soaked wrappers and pieces of crate. It had taken 2½ hours to unscrew the door panel fittings of the Capri on the inside, pull the fake leather trimmings out from their metal 'poppers', stow the slabs of Black Pak in the hollow doors right up to the window base, and pay off McCann.

'They're 50 kilo crates, Jim. That means it's 200 lb. At £10 a lb you're in line for two grand.'

'And my expenses. I've had to spend more than that just to straighten the airport.'

'You can't be serious.'

'Well, what about my accommodation in Limerick? And it cost me a few quid to get that Volkswagen from certain friends of mine. Tell you what, call it another £2,000 expenses, and I'll carry the rest.'

'Uh huh. Here you are. Don't spend it all at once.'

Howard drove on to the ferry at Cork, and smoked a large joint which helped him to sleep. The next morning he cruised into the Customs channel at Swansea docks, wearing a tie, with his briefcase full of 'Annabelinda' literature on the seat beside him.

'Purpose of your visit to Ireland, Sir?'

'Over on business.'

They waved him through. It seemed odd to Howard not to do what he normally did and call on his parents' home in Kenfig Hill. But he could not drop in on them. The truth was, he was feeling a little tense. It was only when he crossed the Severn Bridge, and paid the toll at the English end, that he began to relax.

In fact, he felt marvellous. As the Capri rolled along the motorway, Howard lit up another joint. He began to sing to himself Little Richard's 'True Fine Mama'.

74

'I'm very happy doing this,' he thought. 'I think the thrill is even better than the cash. And I can't see anything wrong with any of it.'

He felt so high that he drove through Oxfordshire to Milton Manor. Redmond and Belinda O'Hanlon rented a wing of the country house, and he had a standing invitation to visit. Howard drove up the drive. Later that evening, when Redmond and Belinda went to the pub, Howard said he was tired and would stay behind. He fished out his Phillips screwdriver.

It took nearly an hour to 'de-stash' the Capri's door panels and load the slabs of hashish into three large suitcases. He put them in the boot for Charlie Radcliffe to collect and sell in London. He would run on into Notting Hill in the morning . . .

It did not take much more than a week for Radcliffe to wholesale the stuff out. Plinston and Howard were letting him have it at £110 a lb: by the time all the payments were in, they were looking at a large cardboard box containing £22,000.

Now, they had to pay their suppliers. Durrani came over for a chat.

'How do you want the money, Mike?'

'At £35 a lb it's £7,000. You can give it me here and now in sterling in London. I've got some cigarette buyers over here who need paying.'

'Didn't know you were such a big smoker.'

'There's a boatload of Benson & Hedges we run into Pakistan. We do it from Dubai every Thursday, you know.'

McCann had already squeezed £4,000 out of the partners. No more than £1,000 had probably gone on other genuine transport and accommodation costs. At the end of the day, Howard Marks had made £5,000 clear profit, tax free. In just over a year, he had made more than £20,000 from smuggling. But there was a consideration much more important than that. The Shannon system had been shown to work.

Life on the middle floor of Annabelinda was becoming really rather pleasurable. Rosie was pregnant.

'It's good, isn't it?' Howard said. 'All this bent money and the prospect of really big loads. You can get to be so rich doing this.'

'When are you going to call it a day?'

'You mean like all these people who say "I'm going to make ten grand and then retire?" '

'Yes, and get a smallholding or something. Keep chickens.'

'What a pathetic attitude! That's un-professional. What's the point of stopping when you reach a figure written on a bit of paper? Anyway, it's interesting – the travel. Look at all the new things you find out about – freeports, life in Ireland, the situation in Pakistan. Do you realise when I switch on the TV news, I'm genuinely concerned about what's happening? I'm exporting from one war-torn country to another. World events really matter when you're doing this.'

'Well, I've got one child to look after already, and I'll soon have two. I know hash is a great cause, but I hope you're not going to be whizzing about the world for ever.'

'Let's get some people to come over. You look a bit jaded, Rosie.'

Later Plinston came round and talked business in a low voice.

'How much are we going to try next time?'

'Let's bring in a whole ton!'

'I don't think anybody's ever smuggled in a ton of hashish in one go – not in Britain anyway.'

'Exactly Graham. Let's do it!'

McCann took his usual aggressive line.

'I'm not doing it for chicken-feed this time. I've got the most dangerous job,' he announced at the Dublin planning conference. 'I want £30 a lb and my expenses. You can't do without me.'

McCann grudgingly accepted £20 a lb. After he left, the new project was crystallised.

'I don't altogether trust Jim. I don't fancy the idea of you leaving all that hash in his dubious care while you make half a dozen car trips to England.'

'No, what we need is a team of drivers. They can come over, all using different routes. I'll stash them all up and get the hash away quickly.'

'Where are we going to get the team from?'

'Aha.'

A few weeks later Howard met Plinston again, with something of an impish smile.

'I know a lot of poorly paid graduates, you know,' he said. 'They're very, very straight people, not a dealer among them. Doctors, architects. I'm offering them £10 a lb. And I can tell you that the list of refusals from these highly respectable people is very, very short.'

He had even approached the daughter of the Master of Balliol, the rumbustious Fanny Stein, it later transpired.

Fanny, who lived in a large Bohemian house in the academic quarters of north Oxford, had been greatly amused by the recent reappearance

76

of Howard Marks. He took his new girl, Rosie, round to Leckford Road to meet her.

'Fanny Hill!' she said.

'Rosie Brindley!' said Fanny. 'I used to be your games captain at St Christopher's in Letchworth, didn't I? You didn't know I'd had a progressive education, Howard, did you?'

'I know you're flat broke, Fanny,' he said now, with maximum charm. 'Why don't you take the two kids to Ireland and tour around in a camper for a bit? I'll pay. In fact I'll give you £2,000 to drive there and back.'

Fanny did not take him up on this highly ambiguous offer.

With the team of amateur drivers assembled, it was next necessary to find more property to rent. The track to the cottage was too small and primitive to handle large-scale 'stashing' operations involving a number of cars. It is also a motto of the hash-smuggling trade:

'Never stash up in the same place twice.'

They found a much bigger house to rent to the north of Ballynacally, with a driveway. The only problem was that a single farm was visible over the fields, not half a mile away.

'Never mind,' Howard said. 'It's got to be done. We can keep on Paradise Cottage and Jim can live there. It'll stop him having to rent that room in Limerick to sleep in, which according to him is costing such a fortune.'

Plinston snickered.

Jim was becoming increasingly trying. He had developed a violent grudge against the unpretentious Marcuson for his criticisms of McCann. He would ring him up in the middle of the night and abuse him gutturally. Then Marcuson's phone would ring with anonymous IRA 'death threats'. And finally, every time Marcuson looked out his window in London, he saw a burly figure leaning outside in a raincoat, ostentatiously reading the *Irish Times*. Suddenly, McCann forgave him, and decided to conduct a vendetta instead against John Lennon for singing 'Power to the People' but failing to hand over money for the 'Derry free concert'. A powerfully built figure arrived in London, introduced himself as one of McCann's relatives, and confided he had been sent over on McCann's instructions.

'What for?'

'I've got to burn John Lennon's house down.'

Shortly afterwards, a small fire did indeed start at Lennon's Surrey mansion. Fortunately, it went out again.

Howard went over to Ireland once again to brief McCann.

He checked in at the Shannon Shamrock Inn. It was a big, anonymous Motor Hotel he had spotted on the road north of Limerick, up past Shannon Airport. It sat right next to the picturesque restored keep of Bunratty Castle and its 'folk park' of Disneyland-style reconstructed Irish hovels. Outsiders and US tourists by the coachload obviously thronged such an institution. It would do very well. Howard registered as 'Brendon MacCarthy'. He noted with satisfaction that by the crowded front reception area was a payphone with a glass booth that gave privacy. These things were good to know.

McCann materialised in the lounge with its cork-lined walls, chandeliers and red leather benches, where Americans were drinking Jack Daniels rye whisky from the big dispenser behind the bar. He had with him a huge, bear-like man wearing the trousers from one blue suit and a jacket in a paler shade – clearly from another.

'Meet my good friend Gus,' McCann said, and watched delightedly as Gus crushed Howard's hand in his own, with a scowl. As they made their way to a table, McCann whispered:'

'Careful what you say. That man is a Provo assassin. He rubs out people who step out of line.'

Gus certainly looked the part. It was only much later that it occurred to Howard he was probably only another of McCann's relations.

They talked business.

'. . . all these cars coming here empty, yes, and going back stashed up?'

'Well, yes.'

'How would it be if they picked up a few things?'

'What exactly do you mean?'

'Well, there's no reason why we can't smuggle both ways, is there? You're screwing me as it is, only giving me £20 a lb.'

'Smuggle what, Jim?'

'Well, how about gelignite?'

'Good grief, no!'

'Well I'm surprised at you, Howard. I thought you were into interacting with the people. British imperialism is trying to shit over the Irish, and the only lifestyle is revolution. Isn't that what you fucking believe, too?'

'Yes, but I don't want anything to do with killing people.'

'Oh well, what about blue movies, then? There's a big demand for them over here.'

'All right, Jim, I suppose so.'

A friend of Ratcliffe's was found who could get blue movies.

'What sort do you want? Spanking? Leather? Boys? Naughty Nuns?'

'Just a few movies of people fucking each other, that's all. Maybe they'd like some naughty nuns, being Irish.'

The cars were loaded up with Naughty Nuns and sent across with Howard's friends. Howard himself flew over to Cork and was there with McCann to meet them at Ballynacally. The social atmosphere was a little difficult. As the middle-class Englishmen crowded into the house and handed over their movies, McCann gibbered with bestial gratitude and made vigorous masturbating gestures. Howard pulled him aside:

'Please Jim, cool it a bit. You might upset these people. They're all very straight you know. They're just doing this to pay for their home improvements, or to finance separations from their wives.'

'Let's get them to bring in Durexes next time eh? There's a big black market for them in this Catholic country. I'm going to get a company registered called "Durex Novelty Balloons".'

'What for?'

'So when they finally legalise contraception, they'll have to buy out my trademark.'

'This country is just like Chicago in the 1920s.'

'Well it would be – it's got nearly as many Irishmen in it.'

McCann worked the airport scam once again. He materialised with 20 crates of hashish stacked into the Volkswagen, despatched from Karachi.

No one noticed the nearby farmer's tractor coming up the lane until they saw him staring curiously at the wide-open doors and the removed seats of the car being worked on in the drive. The flock of amateur smugglers ran inside the house.

'He's seen us! What shall we do?'

'Don't panic,' Howard said. He tore on foot round to the farm, knocked on the door, smiled winningly and said:

'I'm sorry to trouble you, but would you have any gearbox oil?'

Whatever suspicions the farmer had must have been mollified by this apparent evidence of home auto-mechanics. No police cars arrived.

All the cars left for England on four separate ferry routes, with the hash in the doors and under the back seats. One skidded on the icy roads and crashed into a wall outside Fishguard in Wales. The police came. They glanced in the boot. There was nothing there. It limped home to be de-stashed into suitcases in a quiet Oxfordshire coppice. The pace of unloading was hectic: Rosie Brindley lent her Volvo fastback to one of their friends who was not in on the secret, several weeks later. He appeared at Annabelinda that evening.

'I was driving along, Howard, when this fell out of the door.'

He held up a two-kilo block of hashish, worth about £500 wholesale.

'I thought it might be yours.'

'Thank you very much. In the circumstances would you like to be on the firm?'

'Yes, please.'

The team did another ton of hashish. And another. Howard was working 24 hours a day, despatching, co-ordinating, hiring two-door Volkswagens and Volvos from half a dozen companies, driving to Heathrow and jumping on planes, keeping accounts, interviewing long-haired dealers who turned up out of the blue demanding to be offered a drive on Howard Marks's famous Irish run.

He began to hate the sight of every green and cream Irish coinbox, with 'Telefon' inscribed in Gaelic lettering. The Irish telephone system never worked and he never seemed to stop sprinting from one coinbox to another.

McCann would not ever simply deliver his van-load and then clear off. He hung around, carousing, complaining, practising psychological warfare.

Soon, he stormed in, indignantly waving an Air Waybill. Durrani had sent a small but valuable consignment through of very strong Afghani hash. It was not machine pressed, but hand squeezed into small discs, through from the airport at Kandahar. It would sell for up to 50 per cent more than Black Pak.

'Look at this!' said McCann. The Waybill said 'Antique Carpets'.

'Well?'

'It didn't sound like antique carpets. It's packed in linseed oil tins and when I picked the crates up, they rattled! It's just asking to get me arrested. It's a set-up! Look at this. It proves it!'

He pointed at the space on the Air Waybill for 'Shipper's Name'. It said 'JIMA KHAN'.

'What's wrong with that?'

'Well it's me, isn't it, my name? Jima Khan. Jim McCann!'

'Cool down. Let's have a blow.'

'No, I'll tell you what. Let's have a night out. Let's go to one of those medieval banquets at Bunratty Castle.'

It was a doomed project. McCann started drunk and got drunker. The 'serving wenches' handed out mead to tourists; sang 'The Jug of Punch', 'The Last Rose of Summer' and 'My Lagan Love'; served up medieval T-bone steaks; and tried to look as if they enjoyed having their bustles slapped by middle-aged men from Iowa in golfing trousers.

One of the features of the evening was that one of the crowd should be dragged off from his bench by medieval guards, and incarcerated in the medieval dungeon. McCann – who else? – volunteered to be locked in the dungeon, and shouted abuse at the medieval banqueters. He went slightly too far: on his release, words continued to be exchanged with a heavily built American businessman. As Howard looked on appalled, they began to square up to each other. The American hit McCann quite hard in the face. As he lurched back to his feet, hysterical with drink and humiliation, the two combatants were separated, and the banquet broke up in medieval disorder. The guests spilled out into the medieval car park, McCann fuming. Suddenly he ran over to the Volkswagen, leapt in, gunned the motor and roared away to the end of the car park and back again. As his headlights picked out the truculent American picking his way across the gravel, Howard saw to his horror that McCann was revving up, and leaning out of the window roaring obscenities. He was also waving what was unmistakeably a pistol. Howard hustled the American out of McCann's path, muttered an apology about his drunken friend and clambered into the car.

'What are you doing, you Irish ass-hole?'

'He was putting me down, the Protestant Fascist!'

'This is really uncool.'

McCann would ring up Howard and Plinston at midnight, or 3 in the morning, especially as the war between the Provisional IRA and the British worsened. He was full of hoarse, apocalyptic gossip.

'Be careful tonight,' he would hiss, 'the official IRA, the Stickies, are coming over to England tonight to blow up the Houses of Parliament.'

Dope deliveries round London were getting trying as the IRA started to blow up barracks and offices in London, and the police responded by random road-blocks.

One drive, a friend of Plinston's arranged to meet his wife at the Ballynacally pick-up on one run. He failed to report in. Howard fretted, made guarded calls to London, came back and said:

'There's a rumour that he hasn't even left London yet.'

'Right,' said McCann. He grabbed the driver's terrified wife and bundled her out the door.

'Where are you going?'

'She doesn't move from my custody until we hear from him!'

'For Christ's sake, Jim, there's no need to kidnap anybody. That's completely unnecessary. Now just bring her back.'

There was no doubt McCann was becoming wearing.

On the other hand, phenomenal sums were flooding in. Howard was clearing £50,000 a ton. Between the autumn of 1971 and the summer of 1973, he was to handle a total of at least 10 tons of hashish, most of it through Ireland. No policeman ever discovered the secret of the Irish connection – and when the Marks-Plinston-McCann partnership eventually came to the notice of the British Secret Service, they managed radically to misunderstand its true nature.

All this money made more laundering imperative. Howard had some new business cards printed up and took over the unused top floor of the Gloucester Street building. The address was that of Annabelinda; the phone number that of 'Robin Murray (Oxford) Ltd'. But the cards said 'Dennis H. Marks – International Stamp Dealer'. He sent out approval booklets to schoolboys.

'What are you doing, Howard?' Rosie asked.

'I'm buying unsorted stamps by the kilo,' he said. 'The idea is that you might find a very valuable one among them which you can sell for a large sum.'

In fact, he would also buy single valuable stamps for £1,000 a time cash at philatelists in the Strand, and then write them up in the 'Dennis H. Marks' books as lucky dip treasure trove. Pollard, the dealer, bought 10 tons of candles in Amsterdam hoping (wrongly) to cash in on the winter power-workers' strike. Howard took over the remains of his stock as proof of his accounting entries showing that he, too, had made vast profits from the candle sales. He put £30,000 cash into a safe deposit box in Brighton. There were cardboard boxes full of money strewed all over his top floor above Annabelinda. He gave lots of money away to his friends. They came to him with cherished projects, frequently dreamed up in a marijuana haze, which only needed £5,000 seed money to get off the ground. The projects invariably collapsed.

Dennis Irving, for example, Howard's silver-suited Oxford friend, turned up one day:

'We've got this great idea for a really anarchic record company, Howard. There's a group of us, we've got a guy who writes songs, and we've done this amazing number. It's called "Fuck You".'

'How does it go, Dennis?'

'Uh, like this:

> All I want to do-oo-oo is:
> Arse and cunt,
> Back and front
> FUCK you!'

'Oh yes, very nice. How much bread will it take?'

· 'A few thousand. We can form a company. I thought we'd call it "Lucifer Records". Then we get the single privately pressed, and we can sell it through mail order, put ads in *Private Eye* and that kind of thing.'

'Let's do it.'

They actually sold 1,500 copies of this pre-punk innovation. They then made a second single called 'Prick', whose motif was the line 'You're a P.R.I.C.K.!' Nobody bought it at all. Nor did anybody buy their long-play album called 'Big Gun'. Lucifer Records collapsed – its lyricist went on to write material for the Bay City Rollers, and Dennis Irving developed a new craze for designing musical synthesisers. He also told Howard about the new sport of hang-gliding.

'Dennis. I've got a present for you. Ernie Coombes has sent it across in a crate from California. It is your actual hang-glider.'

Howard actually liked to be generous, and in this he had a set of attitudes not entirely shared either by his wide circle of middle-class friends, or by dope-dealers like Plinston, to all appearances just as much a bourgeois hoarder as any other product of Pixmore Way, Letchworth. Howard liked to flash cash about – he had moved beyond the working-class Puritanism that used to flinch when Rosie put several hundred pounds in her handbag and come back from Bond Street with an armful of dresses.

'You should do it too,' she had said. 'It's not just a question of flared jeans when flares are in, and frayed jeans when they're all frayed. Let's go out and get you some designer gear.'

That was how Howard ended up with his green Yves St Laurent suit, for which he became rather well known. He also bought – and wore – a suit made out of purple satin.

He took his friends out, six at a time, for dinner at Englishes fish restaurant in Brighton and picked up the £100 bill. It included a £50 bottle of wine.

'Why not?' he said, amused: 'Aren't you supposed to spend the same on the wine as you spend on the food?'

What he liked to do was make a lot of money and spend it immediately.

'That sort of behaviour,' said one of his friends, who had just watched Howard buy the rounds in the pub five consecutive times, 'immediately characterises you as a Welsh proletarian. Middle-class people don't let everybody know how much money they've got.'

'Well, I despise the middle class, don't I? Why should you be coy about money? Everybody wants it; and I've got it.'

He would give his friends cash when they were poor –

'I'm not going to call it a loan: it embarrasses me having to ask for money back.'

He would also give them presents, or try to – he even offered the solicitor Henry Hodge a Norton Commando motorbike. Some of his friends thought one of Howard's cleverest skills was to manipulate people by acts of generosity. Others thought it showed a nicer nature than using the more conventional approach of trying to control others by intimidation and meanness. Howard, presumably, merely followed his instincts.

These dope-smuggling deals, with a circle of up to 30 to 40 people working essentially on credit, and handling goods which were not their own, depended remarkably on mutual trust. The deals worked, despite lack of recourse to the law courts, partly because most of the individuals involved did not regard themselves as criminals in any sense. They would have been genuinely shocked at the idea of stealing from their friends. The Sixties had not been about *stealing*. They had been about peace and love. Furthermore, so many of the dopesters were Oxford colleagues. It was the perfect milieu for a mutual Mafia to flourish. In this they were rather like the Cambridge Communists of the 1930s – concentric circles radiating outwards, of illegal activists; occasional accomplices; loyally silent friends; and a whole galaxy of people who would prefer to think the best of you because you were assumed to share the basic attitudes of the group. They were all, with the possible exception now and again of the turbulent McCann, *nice people*.

Unfortunately it was the atmosphere of the Sixties which also brought into general use the term 'rip-off'.

The Dutch Rip-Off was a bad business. Howard took a long break from smuggling, through the spring and summer of 1972. Rosie was heavily pregnant and they had a holiday in Cyprus.

'But I don't really like foreign travel, Rosie. It's a long way from Kenfig Hill.'

'What about all those drives across Europe?'

'Well, that's exactly why I wouldn't do them on my own. And going to Ireland's different. They all speak English there, even if they don't speak Welsh.'

'We'll be all right. I'll help you cope with the foreigners. It would be a good way of getting rid of some of this money, spending it abroad.'

They booked into a big hotel in Kyrenia and drove around the island with £2,000 burning a hole in Howard's pocket. They had the largest suite in the hotel: that was a start.

'Do you realise Cyprus is in the Sterling Area. We wouldn't have any difficulty buying some property here. Let's look around for a Dream Home.'

It soon became clear they could easily unload about £30,000 on a luxurious mansion in Cyprus with a swimming pool and an olive grove. It was probably as well they didn't, as the Turks invaded the island shortly afterwards.

'We've had a fortnight, has your £2,000 gone yet?'

'No, there's rather a lot left. What are we going to do?'

'We could fly back first class on the plane.'

'I didn't know they had first class on planes.'

Howard still had a lot to learn about the art of being rich.

The village of Yarnton is a rather slick hamlet, just off the main road north of Oxford to Woodstock. Surrounded by expensive farmland, White Cottage, up a slightly crowded cul-de-sac, soaked up a useful £10,000.

Howard set up a joint bank account with Rosie. He put a few pounds in it, and asked Richard Lewis, Rosie's husband, to put in a big cheque on Rosie's behalf. Thus 'straightened', the money was paid out for the cottage. Howard gave Lewis the £10,000 back in cash, explaining vaguely that the arrangement was a perfectly legal one: 'It's for tax reasons.'

In August, Howard and Rosie's daughter was born, with Howard, much stirred, present at the birth in the Radcliffe Hospital. Crowds of new people were soon flowing through the house at Yarnton, baby or no baby, and Howard began to disappear to London again 'on business'.

'Howard, this is Larry. Larry heard you were looking for new deals to get away from your famous Irish run. Larry's in carpets too. He's got a friend who's a sailor, an excellent man. Sailor Jo knows a great way of flying hash from Beirut to Geneva. Trouble is, he hasn't got any hash in Beirut.'

'It just happens I do know of a graduate of Sussex University, who knows a Lebanese banker. I could approach him – after all, they're all at it out there.'

A few weeks pass.

'Graham, I want you to come with me to Hyde Park. Yes, I know it's cold, but this Lebanese gentleman has come over specially with a sample of what he can get, and he wants to meet us in the park. If it's all right, we're going to give Larry the money, and send him off to Beirut to buy 50 kilos for his sailor friend.'

'Why only 50 kilos?'

'I think it's a straightforward "kamikaze" run into Geneva airport: the sailor has to carry it with him. I can hire a driver to run it in from Geneva – it's someone who was at Oxford with me.'

'You astonish me. Do you realise that we make about one million phone calls, pay off your driver, pay off Larry, pay of Sailor Jo, pay off the Lebanese – and at the end of all that we've barely cleared two grand each. I don't know why you dragged me back from my quiet little winter in Tangiers just to set up that.'

'It cuts Jim McCann out.'

'Yes, but it cuts a lot of other people in. I do, however, have a better thought. We'll do this one and if it goes, we'll do something a bit different for the second run. You remember Gary Lickert?'

'That American boy from your Frankfurt run who came over here to buy a cheap Volvo in Europe? Marty's garage friends welded him up with some Black Pak?'

'Uh huh. Well, there was a reason for him buying our Shannon stuff and sending it home from Rotterdam like that, inside his Personal Import.'

'Yeah: we had so much we couldn't get rid of it to anyone else.'

'Not just that. Hash is selling for a thousand dollars a lb over there. Three times the London price. All that Latin grass is no good for smoking in pipes.'

'So what do we do – call up Ernie Coombes to send some workers over here for it?'

'Nope. We call up Ernie to send some workers over to *Geneva* for it. He'll give us a great price and in fact we don't even have to move an inch. We just have to make a lot of coinbox phone calls. Of course, it's still only 50 kilos a time . . .'

'Graham.'

'Uh huh.'

'Let's do all that and then do another ton into Shannon. McCann or no McCann. Let's do a real monster again.'

At their summit meeting round a restaurant table in Dublin where McCann was safe from Brit justice, he was aggressively raising his voice:

'And I'm telling you that it's far too dangerous to use British drivers. Since Bloody Sunday in the North and the SAS secret agents at work all over the South, a Brit is going to get stopped by someone. I'm quite prepared to provide members of my family to drive the stuff over to you.'

'You must be joking, Jim.'

'Well, then, I'm not doing it for £20 a lb. It's got to be £30 – you boys swindled me last time. I know there was more than a ton really went through . . .'

'Jim, Graham's trying to say something.'

'Thank you. Perhaps there is a way through this difficulty. I spent much of last summer on the island of Ibiza where, you may or may not know, Jim, many important dealers are to be found. In fact, the place is swarming with hippies. I renewed acquaintance with an interesting Dutchman there called Nick. I am sure he could provide a team of Dutch drivers. They wouldn't be Brits, would they, Howard?'

'They'll all get lost, though. We'd really have to get somewhere new to stash up on this coast, close to Dublin. And we'd need a single spot for them all to de-stash in England. Could be done –'

Howard bought a six-month lease in the name of Annabelinda on a large modern house and garden. It was on a small street leading to the beach in the fishing village of Greystones – barely 15 miles out of Dublin on the coast road leading south to Bray.

It was an insignificant pretty port with sailing-boats, and a small white-painted anchor placed decoratively in the centre of the grass traffic island where the beach road met the sea-front. The villas were called 'Winslow' or 'Hillbury' or 'St Bridgets' or 'Holmedale'. They had a suburban air, although they were interspersed with allotments in which could be seen the occasional goat. Little girls with clips in their hair bicycled past betting offices, gateposts surmounted by plaster dogs, and fishermen mending lobster pots by the boats drawn up on the beach. Further south, the drives were longer, the trees shadier, and the hedges even better-tended, around the Greystones golf club. Through the white gates sauntered the family chihuahuas and chows, beneath the big red burglar alarms that hung on many of the mock Tudor gables. It was a neat, quiet little town.

Clearly nothing much went on there in the winter, and it would be easy to find from the nearby Dún Laoghaire ferry port. He told the owners of the house he was thinking of opening a dress shop in Dublin.

'Branches!' Belinda O'Hanlon said scornfully when he mentioned this to his co-director. 'If you want branches you should start selling jeans. I don't want you damaging the Annabelinda name by marketing tat.'

'No, Bebee. I certainly won't do that.'

He organised a second system at the English end. All the Dutch drivers would make their way south to Hampshire, to the welding and spraying shop Marty Langford's Welsh friends ran near Romsey, just outside Winchester. There the gangling, introverted Marty promised to stack hash into half a dozen cabin trunks. Howard would drive sedately down to Winchester, where he had rented another drab terrace house – in Crouchers Croft. From this discreet spot he could dole out the dope to his wholesalers, filling up a suitcase at a time from the anonymous monster warehouse out at Romsey. Dave Pollard, Charlie Radcliffe, the young Keble graduate with the upper-class manner, James Goldsack, and Charles Weatherley, formerly of Christchurch College, could reverse into the garage, slam the boot shut and be away into the Winchester traffic in minutes.

Dutch Nick flew out to Holland for the drivers' briefing.

'There'll be three other Dutch drivers – Pieter says he picked up stuff from you in Europe once before.'

'Yeah, I remember Dutch Pieter. Surly sod, thinks he knows it all. Always sort of looking sideways.'

The complex series of coded phone calls started to run, for once as precise and mechanical as a Bach Sonata. Plinston to Howard. The hash is delivered here in Karachi. Howard to Dublin. When is your Customs man on shift? McCann to Oxford. Here is his schedule. Howard to Karachi. Load it on this flight. Durrani to Plinston. This is the Air Waybill number. Plinston to Oxford. This is the Air

Waybill number. Howard to Dublin. This is the Air Waybill number. Here is the hash.

Howard returned to the White Cottage at Yarnton, pleased with the Monster deal. Rosie suggested, slightly acidly, that he might like to feed his daughter. As he held the baby in the crook of his arm and she sucked frantically, the phone started to ring again.

'It's Marty. One of the trunks has disappeared.'

Howard tore out of the house and into the BMW. He drove frantically south to Winchester. The 400 lb trunks were worth about £40,000 each to him and Graham. It was more than half their profits. Who? Who? The only people who knew the trunks were stored in the garage were the Dutch drivers. Shit! It must be one of them. It was almost certainly Pieter.

There followed some painful scenes.

'It can't possibly be any of my men,' said Dutch Nick. Hasty inquiries revealed that Pieter was still staying at a farmhouse in Hay-on-Wye, which belonged to a mutual friend.

'Come on down with me,' said Howard. 'We'll confront him.'

This was foreign to his nature. It was also useless. Dutch Pieter, carousing with girls, said nastily, 'I don't want to hear about your problems. I know nothing about them.'

'Go back home,' Howard told Nick: 'We'll soon see if he starts selling the stuff.'

Jim rang, of course.

'Where's my money? I'm not waiting for ever.'

'OK, Jim, some little thing's just come up.'

After a week, Dutch Nick called from Holland.

'He's selling. It's him.'

'He's one of your men. You'll have to reimburse us.'

'I am sorry. It would be quite out of the question for me to accept financial responsibility under these circumstances. But I am at your disposal for any help you need to recover the money yourself from this man.'

'Terrific.'

Jim rang and rang, demanding his money. Finally, Howard explained what had happened.

'Well, you'll have to fucking pay me in full. I'm not carrying the loss. You stupid Welsh cunt.'

'Thank you very much. Why don't you insult me, while you're about it?'

'You stupid Welsh cunt, you'll have to pay me and you know it. But I might help you with this Dutch bastard.'

Three days later, McCann called again.

'All right, you Welsh cunt. You don't need to pay me now. I've got my money.'

'What do you mean, Jim?'

'I went to Amsterdam. It's a city I know well, don't you forget. Dutch Nick told me your man Pieter was living on a houseboat. So I went round there, and broke in. I waited for him to come home. Then I persuaded him to give the money back.'

'Oh Jesus, what violence have you committed?'

'Not a mark on him. I just mentioned what terrible forms of injury might be wreaked upon his person. It's all a mind-fuck, Howard. You should never be reduced to actually having to carry out the threats. Anyway, he started whining about how Dutch Nick had been underpaying them, and how two of them broke the padlock on the garage, and then he gave me all the money. He got it out of his safe-deposit box. It's all in guilders, mind.'

McCann chuckled evilly.

'And he's made me a present of his houseboat as well.'

'Oh Jesus, this is all so harrowing and uncool. I shall never chase after somebody who rips off again. I'll just write it down as an error of judgement.'

'Ah, always collect, Howard. People take you for a cunt otherwise.'

'It's probably not a businessman's attitude. But I can't stand all this screaming and threatening. It's just too worrying.'

He was right to worry: more than a year later, the first whisper about the Shannon scam was to reach police in Holland. A vengeful Dutch Pieter was busted on a dealing charge, and offered up his knowledge. The extent of it was not very great: that Plinston had been running hash apparently from Dublin to Winchester, with the help of a man with a Welsh accent. But Amsterdam police fitted the jigsaw piece into their bulging intelligence dossier.

For the affair of the Dutch Rip-Off had another, even less predictable consequence. Jim McCann was reminded by his flying visit of his past successes and his many old contacts in Amsterdam. If it was that easy to intimidate Dutchmen, he reasoned, perhaps he was working out of the wrong place . . . From now on, slowly, but with gathering momentum, events began to spin out of control.

# CHAPTER 4

# Mac the Spy

For a start, Mac McMillan asked Howard to become an M16 spy. It was a fatal confusion on McMillan's part between different kinds of magic circle. He thought that because Howard was a Balliol man he could be drawn into the secret world of strong-chinned merchant bankers and super-patriots. These are the people – the 'agents' – who provide the bulk of MI6's chaps around the world. Gainfully employed and innocently patriotic, they carry messages, 'launder' money, allow their organisations to be used as 'fronts'; provide discreet contact points; pass on titbits of information and generally act as stooges and fall guys. Their attitude to the assorted black nationalists, Arabs and communists whom they help to betray is expected to be as robust as the third verse of the National Anthem:

> Confound their politicks
> Frustrate their knavish tricks
> God Save the Queen!

What was an organisation like that doing trying to employ an anarchist from the Welsh Valleys? It was, in the end, a question about which more and more people were to wonder.

But it was not the way Mac McMillan saw the position in the winter of 1972. It was then a little over four years since one of his Balliol tutors had carefully sounded him out. Beneath the mutton-chops and the corduroy jacket, it was plain there beat a stout English heart.

'You speak fluent German of course. Had you thought of the

Foreign Office? There are ways in which you can do Foreign Office work without necessarily having to pass the exam for the Diplomatic Service. You make what we call a "joint application". It's always satisfying in a way to be able to serve your country, don't you think? . . .'

In time, a formal letter arrived from the 'Co-ordination Staff, FCO'.

It has been suggested to me that you might be interested to have a discussion with us about appointments in government service in the field of foreign affairs, which occasionally arise in addition to those covered by the Diplomatic Service Grade 7 and 8 Competition.

The letter went on:

Should we ask you to attend for interview in London, your second-class return rail-fare from your home or college will be refunded to you minus £1. It will assist us to process your application if you complete the enclosed questionnaire and return it to the above address in the envelope provided.

The address given was 3 Carlton Gardens, London SW1.

McMillan waded through the questionnaire, which was long. He told them about his father's occupation and career history as a banker; the place of birth and occupation of all four of his grandparents; and that he was a regular reader of *The Times* and the *Daily Telegraph*. He told them that he was to marry a British subject, Carolyn Barltrop, and that Dr and Mrs Barltrop lived in Highmoor House, in the Oxfordshire village of Bampton.

They asked him to come to the Georgian house, positioned between the Mall and the hoary London gentlemen's clubs in St James's, which MI6 use as a frontier-post. A middle-aged man took three hours over the interview, which went well:

'The work is with the Secret Intelligence Service. We call it SIS in the office, although you probably know of it as MI6. What I'm about to tell you comes under the provision of the Official Secrets Act. So would you read carefully and then sign this please?'

He handed him a form. It was a declaration that he had read and understood the provisions of the 1911 Official Secrets Act; and accepted that they prohibited him from divulging information without permission from the authorities, whether it came into his hands as any document, sketch, plan, note or 'information' of whatever kind. This piece of paper did not have much legal force, but McMillan did not know that. Anyway, he did not mind signing it. He was about to be initiated.

The man explained:

'The SIS works on commission, as it were, from other government departments – chiefly the Foreign Office. Our job is to go and collect the information required. The work is very secret, of course – and I'm afraid this will cause considerable inconveniences. You will have to tell outsiders that you work for the Foreign Office, as some kind of low-ranking diplomat. If pressed, you may say you work for "the Permanent Under Secretary's department."

'There's no need to specify further. You will be listed in the Diplomatic Service List, which is available to libraries and the general public, as a Foreign Office employee. Eventually, when you go abroad, you will be working under the embassy cover and will be listed as a junior diplomat. It's what some people might call a "front".'

He smiled thinly:

'Your entry will never, I'm afraid, for reasons of security, rise above that of First Secretary.'

'What exactly will I have to do?'

'Well, if you are suitable – and we only recruit about half a dozen of you chaps a year from the universities, linguists mostly, and a few direct from the Army – then you'll spend two years in London. You'll move around HQ a little bit, see how it all fits together, go through old files in Registry, be taught the ropes. Once we've got you house-trained, we put you through an induction course – how to do dead-letter drops, make contact with agents, codes, secret writing – we send you down to Fort Monkton in Gosport for a spot of physical smartening up – you like rugby, that sort of thing, don't you – it's all rather stimulating.'

He waved his hand vaguely.

'Then off you pop, into the field. We'll attach you to one of the major stations abroad for a tour of a couple of years, working under the local station officer. In your case, I should think it would be somewhere you could use your languages. By the time you're 25, if you're any good, you'll be running your own operations somewhere. Naturally, you'll be under direction from London.'

'Am I under the control of the embassy, like other diplomats?'

'No, no, you're not a diplomat at all. It'll make your FO colleagues a bit shirty sometimes. The purpose of your activities is known only to the Ambassador.'

'Yes, but what exactly do I have to *do*?'

'Well, you cast around. You cast around for information and for contacts, the more contacts the better. The idea is to recruit people on to the strength as agents and informants. It's buying people in a way. You don't have scruples about handling people in such a fashion, do you?'

'No.'

'Well, it's the only thing we can do. It's using people, you see, but we don't entrap and blackmail agents into working for us in SIS. We can offer asylum, of course, to chaps in Communist countries, if they want to defect. Other than that, it's just money, I'm afraid. We leave the rest to the KGB, the rough stuff. Tell me, you've read about these chaps who hi-jack airplanes, take hostages, that kind of thing. What do you think the authorities ought to do about such situations?'

'Well, it's up to the authorities to bring it to an end, I imagine. They have to do whatever needs to be done.'

'Even if that means killing the chaps who've taken the hostages?'

'If it's actually necessary, yes, of course.'

There was a brief silence.

'May I ask a question?'

'Indeed.'

'What are the pay and conditions?'

'Not glamorous, I'm afraid. We rely on a sense of patriotism quite a lot in this work. The days when everyone was assumed to have a private income are past, thank goodness, but you'll probably be not as well off as your colleagues in the Diplomatic. When you're abroad, there are comparable allowances, – naturally, overseas allowances, education allowances for British boarding schools, loans for a house, a car. Not too many questions asked about expenses. Otherwise, well – you can retire at 55. In fact, you have to. Field officers get a bit burned out, and with 300 chaps on the strength, there can't be promotion for everybody. It's rewarding work, though. In a way.'

McMillan joined up. He worked at the 12-storey glass office block with the opaque ground floor windows, the TV cameras, and the missing name plate on the revolving doors, next to Lambeth North tube station, south of the Thames. It was called Century House. The days were long past when MI6 had operated out of the creaking lifts and Dickensian corridors of No. 55 Broadway, St James's, famous home of its war-time exploits.

Mac and Carolyn married in Oxford itself, in September 1969. It was natural enough to invite Howard, the amusing Welsh hell-raiser, to his wedding, and his wife Ilse. They had kept in touch on Mac's frequent visits to Oxford. More than once Mac had driven out to the cottage at Garsington and engaged in beery evenings with Howard and Bill Parkinson.

Howard went along – champagne and speeches in the good old undergraduate ambience of the Stocker Room at Brasenose College – and was charming to Mac's chemistry graduate bride. Howard presented them with a set of spice pots and half a dozen drinking glasses. He also explained that he had moved, lock, stock and barrel, to Sussex University, to plough on with his attempts at a doctorate.

Mac and Carolyn found themselves a tiny one-bedroomed basement flat in Battersea – 205a South Lambeth Road. It was conveniently south of the river, indeed, almost within walking distance of Century House, where Mac was spending his two years learning the spy business. There was no point in getting a permanent place, in view of his imminent foreign posting. Nor could Carolyn take up any permanent work for the same reason.

Mac consulted Howard about the Carolyn problem towards the end of November that year. He wrote:

We've settled down – rather unsalubrious area, but we get by. Carolyn has just started a clerical job in a bank, characterised merely by its monumental tedium. I was wondering whether the tutoring line you were once engaged upon in London might prove a viable proposition for her. Is there a demand for tuition from qualified female chemists? I should hope so. Anyway, perhaps you would give a bit of advice about this: I can't for the life of me remember that outfit you were with or how you got your foot in the door.

He asked politely about Howard's work:

Hope you have settled down in the provinces and that Brighton/ Hove hasn't proved to be an insufferable place. Do most of the undergraduates really fornicate all day long, only surfacing for the occasional protest march?

95

And he extended a friendly, if clumsy, invitation:

> If you come to London, you should look us up. There's not enough room to bed down but this should not deter you from coming. We, on our part, will certainly take the opportunity of visiting you some time, should this prove convenient.

The one thing Mac was diligently careful not to do was say a word about his work.

By now, he had learned quite a lot about MI6. He had discovered something of the politics of this most secretive institution. For example, the identity of his boss. This would hardly have rated as a discovery of note in any country less furtive than Britain. The head of the richer sister organisation, the American Central Intelligence Agency, for example, was publicly announced, like other senior political appointments. The director of GCHQ, the much larger and more important, code-breaking secret organisation was openly listed. But the British secret service loved its aura of mystery. Sir Martin Furnival-Jones, the head of MI5, the counter-espionage police in Curzon Street, was fond at the time of telling politicians:

'Other countries . . . do not adopt quite so restrictive an attitude to these matters. I doubt whether they benefit.'

They told Mac:

'We're being pushed around by Harold Wilson and the Labour government. Sir Dick White was in charge here for years. He came over from M15 in 1956 after the terrible balls-ups.'

'Which ones?'

'You name them – there were so many. Half the chaps were trying to assassinate Nasser over the Suez business, and the other half were being discovered by Russians swimming around in frogman gear under their cruisers in Portsmouth Harbour. Not to mention Kim Philby, of course. Anyway, Harold Macmillan put Sir Dick in over here. Then all the balls-ups started happening over in MI5 – they have to tell the Queen an important member of the Royal Household is a Russian spy (that was all hushed up of course) – then the Ivanov defector ploy turns into the Profumo business, and they end up rigging up TV cameras in their own deputy director's office, because half of them think he's working for the Kremlin. Serves them all right, the dozy bunch of policemen.'

'So Sir Dick's not in charge any more?'

'Oh yes, sorry. No, he retired last year. Just in time too. These two Americans, Ross and Wise, wrote a book about the CIA and printed that he had an office at 21 Queen Anne's Gate. Do you know what they said? "Sir Dick Goldsmith White, the head of MI6, one of the most powerful, but least known men in England".'

'What's wrong with that?'

'Nobody had ever printed his name, that's what. It was a secret. Nobody had published that fact anywhere in Britain, although anyone who was anyone was quite naturally aware of it. It had been kept dark for a good 10 years.'

'How'd they do that?'

'There's a very neat little thing called the Defence, Press and Broadcasting Committee. It's got these senior press chappies sitting on it, very much the right sort of blokes, been in the war, that sort of thing. We go along and tell them not to print things. Then they send out these little bulletins called "D-notices" to the papers and the BBC and so on.'

'I never knew that.'

'Well, we tell them not to tell anyone what the D-notices actually say, either. Can't have the government admitting it runs a lot of spies in foreign parts. The FO would get very tense.'

'So nobody knows the name of the new man?'

'Thank goodness, no. That's what I was telling you. Old Sir Dick retires, bless him, and everything's all set for his Number 2 to take over. Maurice Oldfield – dumpy, round-faced little fellow, never married, comes from Bakewell in Derbyshire, sort of local accent. Chess player, thick glasses – but sharp as a pin. Lives in a little flat in Marsham Street, just over Lockets restaurant. He won his spurs back in the 1950s in the big counter-insurgency campaign against the Malayan guerrillas: the old days of Empire, they were.'

'So he's the new boss?'

'Well, no. That's what I was telling you. Wilson gets in again – all those namby-pamby pinkos don't like spies, do they? Especially after the Helen Keenan business. It was a bit upsetting to Wilson, in all fairness. There's the Rhodesians and the South Africans busy getting Cabinet Office papers off one of his own typists in London, and meanwhile, MI6 in Salisbury can't do a thing to help make sanctions stick. The Foreign Office jump in, scenting their moment – "Oh we quite agree, always said these boys should come under tighter control."

Etcetera. The upshot is, they produce one of their own. John Rennie. Brook's Club, amateur painter, fearfully rich, total cold fish. His only qualification is that he used to run IRD after the FO finally got their hands on it.'

'What's that?'

'Oh, it's another one of our secret things. They list it as the "Information Research Department", but that's just a cover. It's a big propaganda project. Ernie Bevin set it up after the war to try and counteract the Russians. They wade through all the Russian provincial journals, things like that, and then set to in the back room and compose little newspaper articles based on them. "Look at all these items about drunkenness. See how it shows what miserable alcoholics they all are in the Workers' Paradise" – stuff like that. Did a lot in Malaya. Plus, trying to foul the Russians up generally – denouncing their front organisations, explaining how they're trying to take over some miserable country no one's ever heard of, pinning the Red Label on assorted guerrillas. When they've composed all this stuff, they dish it out to their chaps in the embassies. And they employ certain ways and means of getting it into the local papers. They used to control a few news agencies, and they spread some under-the-counter cash about, They've got a big new place over on the other side of the river – Riverwalk House, on Millbank.'

'So he's not popular.'

'No, Sir. Oldfield still does the donkey-work, of course, and Rennie sits in his office like a clam. I don't think he likes any of us much either. Of course, you'd probably get on well with him.'

'Why?'

'He's another Balliol man.'

It was now time for McMillan's induction into work as a blooded field officer. It was the most bizarre experience imaginable. He never told any outsider precisely what happened, but one of his contemporaries, a nicely spoken young Oxford history graduate with gold-rimmed spectacles, did not keep his own secret so well.

The MI6 training officer said to him:

'You now have one final task. We wish you to demonstrate your newly acquired skills by carrying out a mission. You will collect a package from another agent, and bring it back here.

'This is the routine you must follow. Tomorrow, you are to take an afternoon train to Northampton. It's not very far away. At 7.30 p.m., you are to go to the bar of the Angel Hotel – it's in the city centre. Your contact will meet you there. He will have a rolled up copy of *The Times* under his arm, and he will exchange passwords as you have just been taught. You will collect the package he gives you, and he will then leave. You are to remain at the bar – have a leisurely drink or two – for at least an hour, and then return to London by a late evening train. You will then come to the office and make the hand-over. If anything goes amiss, you are to remember what you have been taught. It is more important to protect the integrity of your department than to complete any particular mission.'

The young spy left on the electric train the next day, heading north from Euston through the flat countryside. He was wearing a new trench-coat. A short trudge up the hill from the station brought him to the Angel Hotel. It was a typical hotel to find in the middle of an un-interesting county town – a small cream-painted lobby with a payphone and a bell to push for hotel service, alongside a sizeable bar which was clearly well-filled with beer-drinkers and local youngsters at the weekends. It was quiet now.

He bought a half pint and tried to look inconspicuous. Four minutes past the designated hour, a middle-aged man walked in with a rolled up copy of *The Times* under his arm, and came up to the bar. They exchanged passwords. When the man left, he left behind a small package.

The man from MI6 placed it unobtrusively in his pocket. What a relief. The whole business, odd as it was, was successfully concluded. He was working his way through his second self-congratulatory Scotch when an extremely appealing young woman leaned across as they both stood at the bar.

'Would you have a light?' she asked, and cupped her hands round the flame. They fell to talking. No, he wasn't from Northampton. He was just up from London on business. No, he was going back tonight as a matter of fact. It seemed the most natural thing in the world to be talking to pretty women who were obviously interested in you, having just accomplished a secret mission for MI6. The words 'James Bond' floated briefly into his mind.

'I'm sorry,' he said regretfully, 'but I'm going to have to go for my train.'

'I'll give you a lift if you like – I've got my car outside and it'll save you the walk down the hill.'

How kind she was . . . how interesting. Pity in a way he had to report back to London tonight. It was a ridiculous way to organise the mission: it was only a dry run after all . . .

As she swung the green Mini away from the kerb and down the hill, he wondered if there was a later train. He was opening his mouth to delicately raise the question of a further final drink together, when the girl driving braked heavily. A solidly built figure in a blue uniform peered through the driver's window.

'Just pull over to the kerb, would you, Miss? Routine check.'

There were two policemen, both with sergeant's stripes, standing by a patrol car.

'Would you get out, Sir, please?'

'What's all this?'

'Drugs squad, Sir, just making a check.'

They peered into the back seats of the car, and in the glove compartment.

'Open the boot, please, Miss.'

She swung it open. One of the sergeants called the other over to the rear of the car.

'Look at this.'

'Oho.'

It was a small, greenish-brown slab, wrapped in polythene:

'I have reason to believe you two are in possession of a large quantity of cannabis, which is a prohibited drug. I must caution you that you need not say anything, but anything you do say will be taken down and may be used in evidence . . .'

Cannabis? CANNABIS? He'd never even smoked dope while he was at Oxford, and now he was discovered driving in somebody else's car stuffed with it. How embarrassing.

'This is nothing to do with me, officer. Actually, this lady was just giving me a lift to the railway station. I've never even met her before.'

'Yes, Sir, of course. People frequently drive round in cars with ladies they've never even met before. You'll be able to make a statement down at the police station.'

'You mean you're going to arrest me?'

'Well, it wouldn't be very chivalrous just to arrest your lady friend and not you, would it? Come along, now.'

They were bundled into the squad car, the woman in the front and him in the back, for the drive of a few hundred yards to the Campbell Square police station. Through the doors, into the charge room. He was listening to the sergeants describe their arrest to the duty sergeant.

There was another woman sergeant in the room, and two or three other uniformed constables. One was nudging another and whispering in apparent surprise.

'Good order in the charge room, please,' said the duty sergeant loudly. He asked:

'Name?'

'What?'

'Name, mate, what's your name?'

He wrote it down in the charge book.

'Address?'

He gave his London flat address.

'Occupation?'

There was a strained silence. Finally he said:

'Postgraduate student. At Oxford. Er, art history.'

This information was silently written down. He saw that the young woman, her particulars similarly processed, was being ushered away.

'Look, I want to contact a lawyer.'

'You can do that tomorrow morning, Sir, after you come up before the beak.'

'What do you mean? Are you keeping me here?'

The sergeant explained, patiently:

'You're not going anywhere tonight except down in the cells. This is a very serious charge.'

A young constable took him to the cells and locked him in.

The embryo James Bond looked round miserably. The cell door opened again. The young uniformed constable returned.

'I've brought you a mug of cocoa.'

'That's very decent of you.'

The constable hovered.

'Do you want the mug back now?'

'No, no, no bother, you can hand it out in the morning.'

He disappeared. The cell door closed.

Early next morning, a different constable brought him a mug of tea and two slices of bread and jam. Then he was taken out of the cell, up through the police station, and further up a flight of tiled stairs. The clock said 9 a.m. He was in a magistrates' court, apparently in the same building as the police station. The constable gestured him to a bench. In front of him was a clerk, scribbling intently. The door from the cell-stairs opened and a second dejected looking young man was brought up to be sat down on the bench beside him.

After a few minutes, the constable prodded them to their feet. A middle-aged figure entered from a side door and arranged himself on a raised bench, above the clerk. The clerk called his name. The spy, who had just sat down, stood up again.

One of the sergeants who had arrested him, said:

'Your Worship. The charge is a serious one, that he and another female were found driving through Northampton in possession of a large quantity of prohibited drugs. We would request a remand in custody for 7 days, for further enquiries.'

'Yes,' said the magistrate: 'Do you want to say anything?'

'I would like to contact a lawyer,' he said in a dazed voice.

'Yes, well that will most probably be arranged by the authorities in Bedford prison. You will be remanded for 7 days.'

Two men in grey suits stepped towards him.

'This way,' they said, and gestured him through a side door. They were out in the street. One held open a car door for him, and they climbed in.

'What's going on?' he said.

'You've done very well,' one of the two men said, as they swung the car towards the motorway sign for London. 'You've passed the test.'

'What test?'

'It was all a test. To see how you'd behave under pressure. You've passed because you didn't say anything about your work, even when you were in the cell for the night.'

'I don't quite follow.'

'That young constable who brought your cocoa. He was under instructions not to talk to you, but to make a careful note of all you said. If you had mentioned to him, or anybody else for that matter, that you worked for us, then you would have failed the test.'

'Aren't we going to Bedford prison?'

'No, we're going home, back to the office – you can have the rest of the day off.'

'It was all a set-up?'

'You have grasped it at last. That young lady who was so charming to you last night is in fact, Woman Police Constable Sue Edwards. She will receive approximately £2 expenses for her petrol and a letter of thanks on behalf of a "nameless organisation". The page in the charge book about you has already been torn out. There was a bit of commotion when you came in, because one or two of the PCs in the station recognised WPC Edwards – she is a pretty girl, isn't she? – they used to work at her station.'

'But I thought that was a real courtroom this morning.'

'Oh, it was. But the chap who remanded you wasn't the magistrate – he's the local clerk of the court, fellow called Brooke Taylor. And the fellow in front of him was a local solicitor, sworn in for the purpose.'

'Well, what about the other bloke in the cells, the one next in line to me?'

'All part of the act. He's the solicitor's articled clerk. Most responsible young man. The real magistrates' court starts in a few minutes at 9.30 a.m.'

'Good grief. Do you do this to everybody?'

'Yes. Of course, it's different things. We do them in rotation. We've got a sympathetic chief constable here – I think it was three or four years ago we last did this particular technique in Northampton: nice police lady called Doreen Murray. She's an inspector in Wellingborough now, the CID chap was telling me this morning. They rather like doing the work – it's a bit like playing Mata Hari, isn't it?'

The young spy blushed.

'We vary it. Sometimes we have your colleagues stopped at roadblocks. Then the police find fuses or explosive components in their cars. That's quite testing too.'

'Don't any of the trainees get a bit annoyed when they find out what's been done to them?'

'They do a bit, mmm. It was embarrassing once, with one police force. Won't tell you which. The arresting officers were a bit zealous – rough, you know – overdid it a spot. Our chap was really quite upset in the end – being beaten up for nothing, as it were.'

'But there must be dozens and dozens of people involved in all these charades.'

'Wonderful thing, the Official Secrets Act, old boy, wonderful thing.'

Mac McMillan, having passed his similar mock persecution with flying colours, was at last sent abroad. They set him to work in the Vienna station, listed as third secretary, and attempting to conduct espionage against East Germany. In 1972, his first tour over, he came back. Mac and Carolyn bought a modest house in Dulwich, and discovered that two dramatic events had occurred at home. One was that yet another Balliol man had come to power – the stubborn Tory bachelor, Edward Heath, was Prime Minister. This was to have unsavoury consequences for MI6. At the same time, Sir John Rennie underwent a bizarre eclipse. His name became known to the general public. It came about in a strange fashion.

The wealthy offspring of an older generation of Balliol men simply could not cope with the drug culture. While Howard Marks drank beer and smoked dope at university, young Charlie Rennie was getting 'smacked out' on heroin. Like the teenage Joshua Macmillan, he drifted about the world cash-rich, but unbalanced. His mother, Anne-Marie Godat, died when he was 16. His Foreign Office father re-married two years later, and despatched Charles Rennie to Princeton University. There he smoked dope like most of the Ivy League hipsters, and dropped acid too. He also took a lot of heroin. The US police found him in possession of marijuana, and discreetly deported him back to England.

There, the worst possible misfortune occurred to him – as he had anticipated, on his 21st birthday, he came into an inheritance from his grandmother of £63,000. The Rennies had a family firm in South Africa. His father sat grimly in his office at MI6 – he had a good deal to be grim about – as Charlie Rennie worked steadily through the money, buying heroin. The trouble with a full-scale heroin habit is that larger and larger doses are needed to get an effect, and eventually, merely to be able to continue to function at all. Heroin addiction is no fun and it does not, like alcohol, take ten years to work up to it. It takes a few weeks.

Clearly, as far as Charles Rennie was concerned, patriotism was not enough. He married a girl from Plaistow, in the East End of London, who had left school at 15, and who he took on as his secretary when he decided to set up in the music business. They did a lot of heroin together. He spent £250 a week. They registered at a clinic – then the standard, and humane, British method of dealing with heroin addicts, by letting them have maintenance doses on prescription. The way Rennie told the story:

'I just went through the money like water. I was taking 10 grains a day and only getting one grain from the clinic. I just couldn't survive on that. I took more than that in one fix.'

By 1972, he had spent all his inherited money, sold his car, his gold watch and his TV. He had been 'busted' three times for possession. He was a wreck.

It was a well-understood rule of British upper-class life that, when you have sunk into the gutter as far as you can go, there is only one more really verminous thing you can do. Charlie Rennie did it. He sold his story to the Sunday papers. In June 1972, he went to the *People*, after his latest suspended sentence. He was flat broke.

It was a good story. He described how he was getting 15 ampoules of physeptone – a heroin substitute – every day from the clinic, and selling them for £1 a shot to his unfortunate acquaintances. With the money he bought a quarter-ounce of Chinese heroin every three days.

'Nothing else matters to me but heroin. I'm so badly hooked that every vein in my arm has collapsed. I can no longer hit a vein. So I have to skin-pop – inject into the flesh of my arm. There's a great risk of blood poisoning because Chinese heroin is so impure.'

But there was only one thing made the tale, as he well knew. He pointed out to Clive Entwhistle, the *People*'s man:

'My father is Sir John Rennie. He's the head of MI6.'

The *People* got round the problem of the D-notices easily enough.

'The son of Britain's top spy, head of the secret intelligence service known as MI6, has become a drug pusher in the West End of London,' Entwhistle wrote, all over the front page.

'For reasons of national security, neither father nor son can be identified. But I have traced the young man's astonishing and sickening career.'

After that, it was only a matter of time. Shortly after Christmas, Charlie's wife Christine made the mistake of trying to sell physeptone to a plain clothes policeman in Piccadilly. The couple's flat in Ealing was 'spun' and the drugs squad found a pile of stolen travellers' cheques, some opium and a stock of about £15,000 worth of heroin. The newspapers had a good time.

' "M" TO QUIT,' yelled the *Express*. 'Son faces drugs case.'

They added just to tease:

'The Director, whose name is always kept secret at the Government's request, is 59 this month.'

Charlie's privileged anonymity lasted slightly less than two weeks after his arrest. A German magazine *Stern*, which did not care about D-notices, printed the whole thing.

Rennie bowed out, and Oldfield was in. The British papers plastered portraits of Rennie's gloomy and patrician features about their pages. The D-notice committee agreed that now his name had appeared in the German press, the Congolese, the Syrians and the Kremlin had probably already done their worst, and the D-notice no longer applied. Clutching the remnants of this nonsense around him, the D-notice secretary, Rear Admiral Farnhill, said:

'Nobody is going to confirm or deny that this man is what he is said to be.'

Poor Charlie Rennie got a very stern berating from the judge at the Old Bailey:

'You had the exceptional opportunities of being at a great English school and an equally famous American university. In addition, you inherited a very substantial fortune on the very threshold of your manhood. These attributes of a highly privileged kind you have abused with an unbelievable, reckless indiscipline. Compassion, understanding and tolerance have been shown to you, to no avail. You have been intent on your own self-destruction by the most hideous means known to society. By your own hand and free will, you have made yourself an odd lot on the human scrapheap, useless, faceless, inadequate and incapable.'

In case this did not make Charlie Rennie feel bad enough, Judge Gwyn Morris then sentenced him to jail for 4¾ years, and sent his 24-year-old wife to Holloway for the same length of time.

He said it would be good for them, and perhaps he was right. Five years later they were still together, reasonably healthy, and still at it. This time they were picked up shoplifting dresses from Liberty's – the famous store in Regent Street. It was not said in court whether any of the dresses were made by Annabelinda.

Oldfield presided over an extraordinary change in MI6's work. Heath and his Tory cabinet were trying to stem the tide of domestic anarchy apparently sweeping over the British Isles. MI6 were ordered into Northern Ireland, along with all the other under-cover departments of the old Imperial machine. Oldfield did not like it, and said so. He was over-ruled by Heath.

People were dying – soldiers, policemen and innocent civilians – as the ambitious gunmen of the 'Provisionals' squared up to the truculent 'Loyalists' led by the Rev. Ian Paisley.

'The beastly Bel-fascist,' as Jim McCann was fond of putting it around the bars of County Kerry, 'has dragged from the social bog the mildewed skeleton of Ireland's historical neuroses. And now we all mediate the mad dance to the tribal music of gun-fire, petrol bombs, and the whines of the mongol idiots in the northern Irish government.'

The old Protestant self-governing regime at Stormont was abolished, and so were the ' "B" Specials' – the National Guard of the settler establishment. Heath's men set about dealing with the unrest among the natives by the classic Imperial methods which had worked so well in Malaya against the Communist guerrillas – a co-ordinated intelligence drive, a big propaganda campaign, mass round-ups of suspects, attacks on the guerrillas' arms-supplies and cross-border sanctuaries – and then, if all else failed, negotiations from strength.

None of these grand political designs worked very well. This was partly because the basic colonialist method of extracting intelligence, as refined by the army in Malaya, Kenya, Cyprus and Aden, consisted of subjecting prisoners to various forms of near-torture, until they went to pieces. This caused a row when done so close to home in Ireland. The basic colonialist method of dealing with violent rioters – by shooting them – did not work well in Ireland either. The killing of 13 civilians in Derry by British paratroopers caused just as big a row.

Could MI6 carry out their classic post-war 'political action' brief in a nearby country like Ireland, without causing a row too? It would have been surprising if Balliol men of the old school were so far out of line with each other. MI6 did their bit, and also caused a lot of big rows.

The first MI6 officer to be sent over to Ireland was Craig Smellie, Scots veteran of the Sudan and Iraq. He installed himself on the first-floor of Army HQ at Lisburn where the Army intelligence men worked behind a steel grille. He affected a tam-o'-shanter with a pom-pom, carried a gnarled stick and called his office the 'political secretariat'. Unsuccessfully, he tried to recruit agents in the Republic of Ireland.

Oldfield attempted to put the operation on a more business-like footing. A new structure was invented. Northern Ireland was given an 'Ambassador'. He was called the 'UK Representative in Northern Ireland'. The incumbent was Howard Smith, a Foreign Office man who knew about Russians. (He was to move on to the Cabinet Office intelligence machine, become Ambassador to Moscow, and finally to be given charge of MI5 in London.) His resident 'deputy' was Frank Fenwick Steele, an old Middle East hand. James Allan, with a background in South Africa and Cyprus, became chief of station and kept negotiation lines open to the IRA.

Throughout 1972, Oldfield was trying to buy MI6 agents in the south. The Republic of Ireland was swarming with IRA fugitives:

skulking, propagandising, training, arms-buying. This was their major sanctuary. Jim McCann was vaguely aware of what was afoot when he complained it was too dangerous for the team to use British drivers any more. Of course, Maurice Oldfield and MI6 were not to know that the Republic of Ireland was also swarming with Balliol-educated British hash-smugglers. They could not be expected to know everything.

No one knew at the beginning of the year, either, that the damp towns of County Kerry held even more than gunmen and dope smugglers. In the little town of Cahircaveen, a few miles north of Ballinskelligs, lurked yet another fugitive from British justice. This was one of the world's more incompetent robbers, a snatcher of medium-sized pay-rolls in Birmingham. He was pretending to run a little front clothing import company called 'Whizz Kids'; and pondering gloomily how he could soothe the apparently implacable hostility of the West Midlands police.

His real name was Kenneth Littlejohn, ignominiously discharged from the Paratroops 12 years earlier, after being discovered stealing a cash box.

Littlejohn drifted around Ireland. A lot of time was spent boozing and boasting in bars. He also talked to his younger brother Keith. Skinny and sharp where his brother was fleshy and square, Keith was good at striking up relationships with welfare workers. It was as well, under the circumstances, for he too was a robber by profession, and not a very good one. Many members of the Littlejohn family were regarded unenthusiastically by the law.

Towards the end of 1971, just as Howard Marks and Plinston were driving to their dope-smuggling rendezvous at Ballinskelligs with the fugitive James McCann, Kenneth and Keith were having an earnest little talk in another part of the Republic of Ireland.

Keith then rang up Lady Pamela Onslow, a member of the Tory establishment, and a personal friend of Lord Carrington, defence minister and *éminence grise* of the entire Heath administration. She was an unlikely chum for Keith to have, but they had met in a young offenders prison (known as Borstal after the site of the first), in 1967. Keith was in there for robbery. Lady Pamela was in there to visit the inmates. She had continued to befriend the young man in a patrician fashion.

'My brother, a former soldier, has important information about IRA activity in Ireland.'

Lady Pamela was sufficiently thrilled to tell Peter Carrington all about it. He was sufficiently unwise as to send his junior army minister, Geoffrey Johnson Smith, along to Lady Pamela's house in Notting Hill (the up-market end of Notting Hill, near Holland Park, a short stone's throw from Howard Mark's Notting Hill. If Lady Pamela had been the kind of person to buy dope, she would not have had to walk for more than five minutes.) At the house, the Minister met Kenneth Littlejohn in person, and listened to a tremendous story – as good as one of Jim McCann's.

'I decided to go into export,' Littlejohn said. 'That led me to the Irish government department responsible for Aran knitwear factories and cottage industries. During a pub crawl with some of the officials in Galway, the talk inevitably got round to Ulster and the troubles. I always got pleasure out of telling the militants they lacked basic military knowledge, training and imagination. This character didn't like what I was saying. We're having coffee back at his flat and he pulls a rifle on me. It's a Kalashnikov, Russian-designed, Czech built.'

He went on to speak of mysterious submarines landing arms on lonely beaches in Connemara. He dwelt on a Dublin car dealer of his acquaintance who had offered to take him at his boastful word and set up a £10,000 contract for Littlejohn to use his military skills and blow up ships in Belfast Lough. He intimated that his IRA sources were hatching a plot to assassinate John Taylor, the hard-line Stormont Minister for Home Affairs.

Johnson-Smith agreed to bring it up with 'the appropriate authorities'.

It is a mark of the desperation with which M16 was conducting its Irish operations that they should ever have met Littlejohn at all. But they did. He had a series of meetings with an officer calling himself 'Douglas Smythe'. He agreed to furnish information about IRA in the South, whose organisations he would 'infiltrate'.

He then took up with a gang of Irishmen, through his family connections, and proceeded to egg them on to rob banks under his direction. Keith helped him. Kenneth told people afterwards that they were a group of 'Official IRA' private soldiers led by Paul Tinnelly and based at the seaside town of Clogherhead, whom he had persuaded to become renegades in order to discredit the IRA. This was another good story.

The Littlejohns and their gang robbed the Allied Irish Bank in Grafton Street, Dublin, early in the morning of 12 October 1972. They kidnapped the manager, at gunpoint, and left with £67,000, most of it in used notes. Kenneth Littlejohn left his fingerprints everywhere. He was subsequently individually identified by no fewer than 14 of the bank's employees. His car, at Dublin Airport, had an electricity bill tucked inside with his address on it.

The Littlejohns returned triumphantly to England, hoping to buy a restaurant in Torquay. The Gardai were not, however, completely stupid. Within a week, they put together enough evidence to request Scotland Yard to arrest the Littlejohns. As the year ended, the Little- johns were sitting moodily in Brixton Prison, working out how best they could exert some leverage in their predicament. It would not, would it, look very good were it to emerge that the British Secret Service had been employing notorious criminals for secret work in the independent Republic of Ireland?

As if this were not bad enough, there was another reason why the men at Century House were looking forward to a miserable Christmas. The obvious way to find out what the IRA actually were up to in the Republic was to look at the files of the Gardai in Dublin. The Irish Special Branch were just as unenthusiastic about the resurrected IRA as any of the British – they were violent men, one of whose declared objectives was to overthrow first the British rule in Ulster, and then the comfortable bourgeois regime in Dublin. But relations with Dublin did not work like the easy relations with – say – South Africa. Dublin was prickly about its independence and inclined to extreme lack of co-operation with the 'Brits'.

For six months a British agent called John Wyman, sent out to Dublin with the cover that he was employed as a private investigator by Bateman Investigations of Long Hanborough, near Oxford, had managed to get hold of a steady flow of IRA files out of Gardai Headquarters. He was getting them from a sergeant called Patrick Crinnion, who had access to C3, the Special Branch section dealing with terrorism and subversion. A second British intelligence office, Andrew Johnstone, was helping him.

Unfortunately, on 19 December, Crinnion's superiors decided to pick him up on route to the Burlington Hotel, in Dublin, with 10 file sheets hidden under the carpet of his car. They picked up Wyman too, and locked them both up, announcing – in public – they were to be charged under the Irish Official Secrets Act. It was all bound to come out.

This, then, was the state of affairs at the office when Mac McMillan returned to England, anxious to 'cast around' for contacts and information. Shortly before Christmas he was in Oxford again – it was where his wife's parents lived. He ran into Bill Parkinson, the Beat poetry enthusiast whom he had last met round at Howard and Ilse's, in the Garsington cottage.

'Bill, how are you? It's more than two years since I saw you, isn't it? How's Howard? Still doing his PhD in Brighton?'

'Oh, he's back in Oxford. He dropped all that. He's really busy now. He's in business. He's a director of this boutique called "Annabelinda" in Gloucester Street. It's quite big, but he's so busy with his various enterprises that I actually manage it for him – look after the orders and things. He's away a lot. Travelling.'

'How fascinating. It sounds as if he's doing well for himself. Would you be so good as to give him my regards and tell him I shall certainly look him up in the future. He's to be found there, is he?'

'Oh yes, sometimes anyway. It's Number 6, on the corner, halfway down. You can't miss it.'

Bill Parkinson was right. Howard was terribly busy, racking his brains to think of a smuggling system which would cut out Jim McCann.

Poking around Plinston's carpet shop one day in his absence, Howard had pursed his lips on finding a letter in McCann's characteristic aggressive black capitals.

. . . SO IF WE CUT MARKS OUT OF THE NEXT DEAL THINGS WILL GO AHEAD IN A MORE BUSINESSLIKE MANNER. THEN THAT MAKES IT EASIER TO COVER MY EXPENSES, AND MORE FOR YOU GRAHAM . . .

'Very nice,' Howard said to himself. 'Right.'

'I know how you feel about Jim at the moment,' Plinston said. 'I've got something new that's surfaced. He's a Lebanese called Somir. He has some idea that he can get stuff through Montreal. There's a French gangster there who's got the airport Customs straightened. Let's give him a suitcase of Durrani's Black Pak, and see how he gets on.'

Somir got on very badly indeed. He left for Montreal, via Paris, and was picked up in Paris on the way through. He had a suitcase full of dope and a little piece of paper with the number of Plinston's Swiss bank account written on it, for eventual transmission of the cash. The French pursued this lead energetically.

111

'They've frozen my Swiss bank account, Howard.'

'That's bad.'

'They say it's a form of action they are obliged to take because "the French Authorities state" I am a suspected dealer of drugs, "and they have agreed not to provide banking facilities for the proceeds of such crimes." '

'This sounds serious.'

'I'm not too worried. They say they wish me to demonstrate that the money is not what the French say it is, and then they'll unfreeze it.'

Plinston departed on a major series of airplane flights – first to Canada, to see what the French had gleaned about Somir's system, then to Switzerland, accompanied by his 'accountant', Patrick Lane, and home again to Hamdullah and the Warwick Castle.

'No sweat, Howard. We've explained to the Swiss that I am in fact a sort of money-dealer, and that's why Somir had my number. They're happy with something formal on their files, so the French can't say they didn't co-operate.'

'But you actually did six months in Germany for hash-smuggling. Surely they know that?'

'They're lovely people, the Swiss. They like money. Also, this Frenchman in Montreal is now our connections, Somir being in jail. He'll take air freight, provided it's not of Pakistani origin. That's too risky.'

They ran a little through from Heathrow that way, from the Shannon stockpile. But what was the point of smuggling a little box at a time?

Howard and Plinston were starting to act as independent distributors in the provinces, as well as supplying to the big London wholesalers. They were employing numbers of people to do deliveries, and would-be employees constantly knocked at the door. Some Lebanese hash would come in – could they please handle it? A dilettante smuggler would arrive triumphantly with a suitcase, knowing Howard's firm would offer him a price.

'One suitcase. It's borin',' Howard said to Robin from Oxford, a man he liked.

'Cheer up,' said Robin: 'You should amuse yourself like I do. Take up karate for example. That's not boring.'

'I don't like fighting.'

'Well, what about gambling? Do you know, the first grand I made from running dope, I put it all in premium bonds and won another two grand, just like that.'

'Premium bonds!' said Howard, disgustedly.

What Howard did do was give Anthony Woodhead, Anna of Annabelinda's ex-husband, a commission as researcher.

'Will you please go away and find out everything there is to know about international freight, how docks work and so on. I want to understand the system.'

Woodhead, a strange, silent, guitar player with a ruthless manner, took £100 from Howard, and disappeared into the libraries for a week. He came back with a file of material on international airfreight. Howard gave him another £100 to continue. He disappeared. This time for good.

'Where's your Anthony gone?' Howard said.

'He said something about Japan.'

'Oh.'

Howard and Plinston now thought of another brilliant idea. Hydroponics. One of their friends produced an information sheet from the US Department of Agriculture, offering handy hints on the proportions of chemical nutrients which would facilitate the hydroponic production of hemp for rope.

'It's perfectly simple: we take all these proportions which it says produces good hemp for rope, and ignore them. Then we take all these proportions which it says make bad rope, and do it. Good rope, bad dope. Bad for rope, lots of dope.'

'You'll try anything, won't you, Howard? You're such an enthusiast.'

'Think about it. Home-grown! We don't have to smuggle any more. Hydroponics. Under cover: perfectly safe. It's not like growing it in fields. Don't worry about helicopters or anything. If it worked, we could rent some of those big covered-in railway arches. We could run gigantic market gardens.'

'All right, you win. What do we have to do?'

The two of them shifted some of Howard's three tons of stored candles out of the way, and constructed a large hydroponic table in the basement of Annabelinda. Hydroponics is the art of cultivating plants by artificial means, using a controlled light supply fixed just above the growing plants, and rising with them as they grow to keep a constant intensity. A tray with a shallow tilt holds the seedlings, and is dripped with a monitored water supply, while the temperature and humidity are maintained at a constant level. It is all very scientific and by no means simple. They bought a book on horticultural lighting and set to work.

First you have to get some marijuana seeds. They must not be too old, too green which suggests immaturity, or too black which suggests fungus. Ideally, they should come from the same batch to grow at a uniform rate, be plump and mottled brown-grey, and have been stored in an airtight container in the vegetable compartment of the fridge, in the dark. Howard and Plinston did not know much about this but they did their best.

Then they had to get vermiculite, top it up with soil, and make up a fertilizer solution. The seeds had to be soaked in a 5 per cent bleach solution (to prevent fungus growing), carefully planted and watered, and installed in an elaborate wooden frame, with pulleys and a bank of fluorescent tubes surrounded by big hanging reflectors of white cardboard. This was to increase the light efficiency and distribute it evenly across their little dope garden. They had to buy two different kinds of fluorescent tube, eight foot long – Cool White for the red spectrum and Natural White for the blue. Their eight-foot-square garden needed 16 fluorescent lights, suspended on an unwieldy set of gantries, and burning more than 1000 watts. The idea was to leave the lights on for about 16 hours a day, with the utmost regularity, support the little plants with sticks as they poked above the ground, and hoist the banks of lights up little by little every day, at an awkward slant as the plants grew at different rates, making sure they did not have to strive too high to reach the light, and so become spindly. They had to be thinned, pinched, pruned and tended, as well as watered, checked for phosphorus deficiency and nitrogen deficiency. Then they had to wait for six months, cut down the light cycle to 12 hours a day, wait another six weeks for the females to flower and form clusters, and finally harvest the crop. If they were lucky, this would produce about four pounds of grass.

'And that's not counting in the cost of all this electricity, is it?'

'No, Howard.'

'It's quite dangerous too, the big electric bills and having it all sitting here in Annabelinda.'

'Yes, Howard.'

'It's all a bit borin', actually.'

'Uh-huh.'

They were not really gardeners by temperament, either of them.

Yet another of Plinston's independent connections, his would-be straightener of bent Nigerian millions, was arrested in Frankfurt, running 500 lb of hashish in a truck. This would no doubt lead to another entry under 'Plinston, G.' in the ominously swelling file at Bundes Kriminal Amte headquarters in Bonn. Heat everywhere, and no big loads. Neither of them could seem to break out on their own. Inevitably, greed got the better of the pair of them.

'Graham?'

'Uh-huh.'

'Let's do another monster with McCann.'

It was not quite so easy this time. Jim McCann had risen in a little more than a year from cadging drinks in the public houses of County Kerry to becoming the possessor of almost £200,000 in used notes, some of them in guilders. He was Cannabis King of the Western World, and bent on becoming an international playboy. Everything had to move faster and faster. His approach to life was not merely crazy – although it *was* fundamentally crazy. As he told Marcuson in the spring of 1971:

'You can end up spiritually bankrupt in many ways. It's better to burn it all up in fantastic intensities than to live 50 fucking years of slavery and boredom. Living death.'

He was regurgitating something he had read somewhere. When McCann saw old Cagney movies, he was Cagney for weeks afterwards. When he read the *Republican News*, he was Martin Meehan the Street Fighting Man. And when he read Sartre, he became Sartre. It was part of the madness that Howard half-liked about him, for Howard too was an energetic fantasist. James Dean. Marlon Brando. Elvis Presley, the Welsh Robin Hood.

McCann finally answered the call at his relations in Belfast – it was the McCann family answer service at work.

'If you want a meeting it'll have to be in Amsterdam, I've developed a good many business interests over there lately. Meet me at the American Hotel. I'll be the fellow wearing the good suit.'

He appeared, by the sound of his voice, to be chewing a large cigar.

Howard kitted himself out with stamp-albums and correspondence about opening new Annabelinda branches – in case anybody should ask. Then he booked into the American Hotel on Leidse Plein, and caught a plane. McCann was looking very flashy. He had a dove-grey silk suit, gleaming hand-made shoes, a designer tie; and a Cartier briefcase with a little gold combination wheel.

'The last time you marketed my stuff I'm bringing in, it was a shambles.' He said rudely, 'Calls were late, the organisation stank and you let that Dutch creep get away with a trunkful of our hash. If it hadn't have been for me pullin' the situation together . . .'

'Marketed, Jim? Marketed? It's our hash.'

McCann swept on:

'That's exactly what I'm saying. From now on, I want to meet the head man in Pakistan, reassure myself. For all I know you're making a total fuck-up at that end, too. Now you get me to meet the Films man, or no deal.'

'How do you know about the Films man?'

'Never you mind how I know – I want to meet your big-shot Karachi Airport man or it's no deal.'

'I'll talk to Graham – we'll go back to my drivers this time, if you don't mind.'

'That's not an easy thing. I'm in business over here very big now – I'm going to get through lots of guns for the Provies. I've got a container system all organised. Now, if we do another ton and you use your own drivers, what guarantee have I got you won't sell some of the stuff on the spot over in Ireland? Then word would get back to the Provies I was bringing drugs into Ireland.'

'Jim, we never have sold the stuff in Ireland. The whole idea is to ship it through to England. That's the purpose of the exercise.'

'Well, it's absolutely necessary for my security. None of the stuff to be sold in Ireland, right?'

'Sure.'

'And I want £30 a lb.'

'We've been through all that before. What about £20 plus legitimate expenses?'

'You're squeezing me again. I don't know why I tolerate it. £20 plus expenses, plus I want the bread delivered here in Amsterdam.'

'No problem.'

'If we're not using the Dutch, we don't need to keep on with Greystones. We can get somewhere fairly remote again.'

'I'll organise that. There'll be a phone problem if we move out into the country again. I'll keep on Greystones, and put a man in there to sit and answer the phone at the Irish end. One of my old schoolchums can be doing it. I've got another one who's at a loose end – used to be a croupier in a casino – I'll set him up at the London end as a 24-hour answer service for me and Graham. I want to spend as much time as

I can being visible at Annabelinda – farming out sewing assignments, delivering dresses around.'

'Delivering dresses, eh?'

McCann chuckled:

'Where's your bottle?'

'Just occasionally,' said Howard with what he hoped was dignity, 'I wonder if the police will ever notice anything.'

McCann guffawed.

'Let's go and get a few drinks.'

They cruised round the Amsterdam bars. McCann, the international businessman, drank gin and tonic at all times. He rattled on about the IRA.

'Them bombs at the Old Bailey – they were nothing. These boys are going to make London entirely uninhabitable.'

They moved on from one dark little canalside drinking house to another. McCann explained about his new front company, Tara Engineering, and his past successes 'diamond-smuggling' in Amsterdam. McCann offered to get Howard a false passport through his contacts. He was in town, he explained, as 'Jim O'Neill'.

'Do you want to get laid tonight?' he said nasally.

'Whyever not?' said Howard.

'I happen to know this very, very exclusive private brothel. Only the finest for the Kid. Wait here while I make a call.'

He returned from the payphone.

'OK, we're on our way.'

They got out of the taxi outside what was apparently a medium-sized private house miles away from the shop-window girls of the red-light district. McCann rang the bell. A peep-hole opened, and then the door. No one is in the downstairs parlour except some girls, serving out drinks to the two of them – the flushed Welshman, and the flushed Irishman.

'Look at the furniture,' McCann says. 'This is a class place.'

'The chicks aren't bad too.'

'What more could you want – young, really-nice-looking, all speak English – and four of them.'

'We got all four?'

'Sure do, partner.'

They retire to the rooms above. They roll joints and smoke them with the girls. Scenes of a Roman nature follow – soapy showers, massage oils, mirrors, vibrators, mouths, vaginas, penises, first one girl then another; and yet another. A perfectly normal orgy in almost every respect.

'Jim.'

'Jim.'

'Uh-huh.'

'That's not a girl.'

'No.'

'It's you.'

'Who's paying anyway?'

They both start to laugh at the same moment.

Back in London, Plinston and Howard had a brief and businesslike chat while Howard sorted through his list of workers.

'We'll let Robin drive. He's tough, lots of bottle. Not Steve – he's in Amsterdam too now, living on a barge he made out of the last run. Mike Clarke from Wales can come off helping manage the shop. We'll give him a try. Marty can handle the de-stashing again – let's spread it about the countryside and then store it through in Winchester again, at Crouchers Croft. But we'll keep well away from that garage in Romsey. Dutch Pieter knows where it is and he doesn't like us after Jim's spot of thuggery, I shouldn't imagine.'

'What's Jim playing at with this Films man business?'

'Clear enough, I think. He's just edging us out to put together his own connections. I bet all this talk about guns and the Provies is just a cover. He's going to smuggle his own stuff if he can get it. Maybe market it in Amsterdam, through Dutch Nick.'

'Let's con him. Let's introduce him to Mike Durrani instead. He won't know he's our smuggling man.'

'Yeah, we'll tell Jim he's the Films man. He won't know one wog from another as far as he's concerned.'

'Wonder why he keeps insisting we're not to sell in Ireland?'

'Search me.'

McCann appeared to fall for the subterfuge. They took Durrani over to Amsterdam for the encounter. McCann, gratified, produced a false Irish passport in return for the two photos Howard supplied. It was in the name 'Peter Hughes' and valid for another five years.

'What do you want for this, Jim?'

'A favour. Go back to England and see if you can look up my old girlfriend Anne McNulty. Persuade her to come over here. She's in Bristol somewhere.'

'I'll put Marty on the case.'

Howard, the international criminal, returned to Schiphol for the trip home, with his false passport stuffed in his flight bag. Howard, the international gourmet, loaded up with Dutch cheeses at the airport shop, and had the girl assistant help him get them in his bag.

She looked at him questioningly when she observed the passport at the bottom of the bag, especially as Howard appeared to be holding one already in his hand. He gulped.

'It's all right,' he said instinctively. 'It's mine.'

He flashed her his best self-deprecating smile and tried not to run for the boarding gate.

No sooner had Howard arrived back in Oxford than Mac McMillan the spy turned up at the shop, as he had promised he would. He looked much the same: fleshy and portentous, with the Jorrocks muttonchops. He nodded to Belinda, and followed Howard upstairs.

It was a momentous meeting.

# CHAPTER 5

# Reefer Madness

'Shall we have a joint, Mac?'

'No thank you.'

'Oh. Well, let me show you what I've been doing in your absence abroad. Downstairs is Annabelinda, which I run. Then here in the basement is my candle-store, from the days when I was going to cash in on the power-strike. Those fluorescent tubes? – Oh it's just a stack of old lighting, it's rubbish now. Then right up on the top floor here is my stamp business.'

'That's interesting. I'm still quite a keen collector. Can I browse through your albums?'

'What about you? How's the Foreign Office? Was Vienna exciting?'

'Oh, very low-level clerical stuff. Quite tedious. Glad to be back.'

'Look, it's great to see you, come out to the cottage, meet Rosie and eat.'

'This is yours, is it, the orange BMW? You're really doing rather well.'

'When we get home, remind me to show you my new video camera. You can take films and play them back on the spot with the videotape player and a TV set. They're pretty novel.'

'Must cost a bit.'

'Oh, about a Grand. . . .'

'Nice house, Howard. Where'd you get the enormous sofa from?'

'Harrods, actually.' And so on.

'I'm thinking of opening up a few branches, actually. Dublin, Amsterdam. . . .'

The two old friends had a good evening round at Yarnton – Howard sucking on a sly joint, McMillan drinking. It turned out McMillan liked the subversive music of Frank Zappa as well, which they played loudly on Howard's superb stereo. Mac did a very fair imitation of the low gravelly voice of Captain Beefheart singing 'Sun and Spark' on Zappa's LP *Clear Spot*. They retired to the Red Lion, a few hundred yards down the road, animatedly discussing politics.

'Well, what would you do about society if it was you in charge?'

'Smash it!'

'Good Lord. I'm really surprised to hear you say that. Think what it would mean to your parents if the Communists took over here.'

'Yeah, and they'd rape my sister, I suppose. I don't know what you achieve for society by doing some typically boring straight job writing up reports in an embassy all day about what's supposed to be occurring in Vienna.' McMillan, in his sports coat and grey flannels, changes the subject:

'This Annabelinda business, seems to have really hit the jackpot. How exactly did you come to set it up? Oh yes, mine's another pint.'

'I shouldn't be telling you this, Mac old friend, but I have a feeling some of the initial capital from a few of the people might have come from smuggling hash.'

'Blimey. Cheers. This, um Foreign Office work, you know: there isn't really the clear distinction between the embassy side of it and the secret service kind of thing. I work more towards that end of the spectrum, actually. Let me tell you, some of the work we do is very, very, interesting.'

'You mean it's the secret service, that's what you do?'

'It's that kind of thing.'

'Oh now that isn't borin'. That's really interestin'.'

Mac was just one of the individuals who surged through the house that winter, as Howard pursued his gregarious career. The next day, for example, a tall and swarthy Afghan tribesman arrived off the flight from Kabul – one of Howard's rock music friends, moving around Afghanistan for nameless purposes, sent him to Yarnton with a letter:

'Very nice man. Family have sent him to London for medical treatment. You'll love him. Be sure to give him a smoke. P.S. He doesn't speak any English. He is a Pathan.'

'What's a Pathan, Rosie?'

'God knows. That's your problem. I suppose you're just about to leave town again.' Howard did set off for London within a day or two. He was intrigued by what McMillan had said. Perhaps, he fancied, they'd both been rather indiscreet. Mac had given him his phone number: he went to pay a social call, and found Mac and his wife spending their evening in a featureless modern home in Putney.

'I was really interested in what you said, Mac. About the secret service. That sounds amazing work.'

'Mm, yes. Well, would you ever be interested in that kind of work, in – helping?'

'Always like to help people, Mac, Especially chicks.'

'What I mean is, if there was anything ever that you could do, not for me, for the office, would you do it?'

'Yeah. Absolutely.' It was just one more thing – like the hydroponics, like the Pathan tribesman, like the Afghan carpets Howard was thinking of importing to make a study of their freight procedures.

Then he caught the plane for a prolonged burst of Irish activity. Carlow is a typical central Irish market town. Its straggling high street has a ruined keep at one end, regarded indifferently by the crowds of juveniles from good Catholic families who throng up and down, and a bicycle shop at the other. In between are a disproportionately high number of betting offices, bars, undertakers and bakeries, reflecting the abiding local interest in horses, liquor, death in all its forms, and doughy food. A dozen miles north of Carlow, on the Dublin Road, is the entirely featureless village of Moone, its two pubs and a wayside shrine not strictly counting as features in that district. In a rented farmhouse just outside the village, Howard saw in yet one more ton of hash.

It was as nightmarish as any venture connected with McCann. In the dark of the rural evening, watching 'Gardai patrol' on the TV, Howard was stunned to hear an all-too-familiar hoarse bellow:

'Pull your fucking aerial up! I can't hear you!'

He dashed outside. There was McCann, in a car, waving what Howard recognised with sinking heart was another pistol. The Volkswagen was fifty yards back along the track, down on its springs with crates of contraband.

'Shut up Jim,' he hissed. 'You'll be heard for miles. What the hell's going on anyway?'

'It's these walkie-talkies. I got them in the Amsterdam duty-free shop so we could travel in convoy. And it's pretty fucking uncool of you to come here dressed like that, if it comes to it.'

'There's nothing wrong with green suits; you don't want to be prejudiced. What's the point of buying walkie-talkies, if you have to shout? Come inside.' The load was a crate short. McCann said, 'I keep

122

telling you to organise your suppliers better. We'd be better off if I handled them.'

They ran the consignments successfully back to London, and Howard discreetly asked Richard Lewis to drive Jim's share over to him in Amsterdam.

'It's all quite legal,' he said. 'The money's in dollars so it's not in breach of exchange control. You're not breaking the law – it's just some tax scheme. I simply don't want to do it myself. Run £50,000 over and I'll give you 5 per cent.'

Lewis motored across in his BMW and met McCann in the lobby of the American Hotel. McCann was at his thickset, charismatic worst:

'Just give me your car. I'll be back. Do you know this Patrick Lane? Howard tells me he's thrown his girl out "for professional reasons". What sort of reason is that? Is he a poof, do you think? Would that be it?' He returned the car eventually, minus the money inside it.

'That's a very nice machine.'

'Do you think so? Howard's got one just the same, and his friend Graham Plinston.'

'Have they now? Well, I'll get myself a BMW too.' He bought one, cash down, in Amsterdam the next day, and tore around the streets.

Howard and Plinston had not been strictly truthful with McCann when they said none of the Shannon hash was ever sold in Ireland. It all went back to London, but then an appreciable amount was wholesaled out to a dealer who in turn wholesaled in Dublin. Dublin, like Dundee, sold at a high rate because of its provincial remoteness. None of the buyers realised it had originated in Ireland, of course. It was London hash. This time something went wrong. The Dublin dealer kept complaining about his rate.

'You're charging me too much. All the down-the-line dealers in Dublin say it's on the market there already at less than my price.'

'Yeah, well that's what dealers always say, isn't it? They're just trying to beat you down. People are so mercenary these days.'

'No way. These big dealers on Sean McDermott Street, who are very tough characters, have a supply of Black Pak they're selling cheap.' So that was why McCann had been so insistent they were not to market in Ireland.

He brazened it out well, of course:

'Jim, you've nicked 30 cwt of dope and you're selling it to the guys on Sean McDermott Street.'

'Of course I did. I've got to cover my arse, haven't I? I'm not getting

123

what I should be getting. You're putting the squeeze on me and you know it.' Oh dear. This was definitely going to be the last time. Definitely this time. Jim could always come back punching, however completely he was in the wrong.

'Listen Howard, and the Provos have found out about me selling that dope in Dublin. They're putting a lot of pressure on me to ship them arms from Amsterdam. Can you let me have the services of some of your drivers? Not for your product. For, ahem, my product?'

'You must be joking.' Days later, two of Howard's drivers were indignantly on the line:

'Jim McCann's been calling us up, asking us to drive for him. Where did he get our phone numbers? Off you, we suppose.'

'Not me. He must have been through your clothes while you were sleeping at Moone.'

McCann invited over his old antagonist Alan Marcuson – so that Marcuson could see what a triumph McCann's life had turned out to be. He had bought the £7,000 lease for cash on an expensive flat in Loosdrecht, 30 miles outside Amsterdam, and rapidly exerted a hypnotic influence around the 'Pink Elephant' discotheque just beneath the premises. Marcuson told Howard the story when he got back:

'Jim takes me round for dinner and there's this young, swarthy character at the table. "For God's sake don't tell him you're Jewish," Jim hisses in my ear, "He's an Arab sheikh!". Half the night I believe this, as he sits there silent, until the phone rings and he goes and chats away in fluent Dutch. Turns out he's of Indonesian origin and he's "Black Peter". Peter Elia, the club barman.'

McCann was floating higher and higher on the image of himself as gun-runner. In March, the ship *Claudia* was intercepted en route from Libya to Ireland with a hold full of guns. McCann's imagination now knew no bounds. His conversation was sprinkled with talk of 'end-user certificates', 'RPG-7 rocket launchers' and 'the Omnipol arms factory'. He persuaded Elia to ring round and try and obtain guns. Elia claimed to know a man called 'Pistol Pete'. From somewhere he obtained some decomposing World War II grenades, and kept them in the Loosdrecht flat.

No one ever saw Jim McCann with a real consignment of weapons throughout this period – or indeed ever in his history. He had a sawn-off shotgun at one point in his life, and a couple of pistols at another. Nor did anyone ever work out precisely what McCann *thought* he was. But he was a dope-smuggler by occupation, then, before, and afterwards. He was almost certainly trying to play the Green Card again, and set up his own private dope-smuggling run into Ireland under cover of a dedication to the Republican cause. That was why he was trying to get to the Marks-Plinston team's supplier in Pakistan, and to recruit their drivers. That was why he was setting up a dummy container firm. If one of his unlikely contacts had actually produced some guns of course, McCann would certainly have tried to run them into the Republic and live off the ensuing credit with the IRA for as long as he could.

In fact, the only people not fooled by McCann's posturings were the Provisional IRA. His friends half-believed him. The Dutch police could scarcely do otherwise than believe him, confronted with an Irishman who so openly went about asking for guns, and so ostentatiously lit his cigars with 100 guilder notes in restaurants. They began to compile an intelligence file and photograph his movements. And, as they started to process 'International Terrorist' shared Euro-reports, British intelligence began to believe him too.

Howard did not know about this. Howard was still trying to solve the same old conundrum: was there a way of independently moving big loads and making big money, while dispensing with the services of the abominable McCann? Slowly, the outlines of a completely new major scheme began to take shape in his mind. It was a brainchild which was to fill out and grow throughout the spring of 1973, until it reached its prime in a truly spectacular disaster – the Great Mediterranean Fiasco.

Meanwhile, there were always gregarious little deals. Duncan Lowry would arrive once a week with a suitcase of 'Leb': obviously he had a middle Eastern diplomat squared somewhere. They sent off a small air freight box to Graham's new gangster friend in Montreal, and they supplied workers of Ernie Coombes, who came over the Atlantic to weld up the occasional car with hashish for the United States.

One weekend, a bubbly Californian redhead of 25 drove up the village cul-de-sac at Little Blenheim, and banged on the door of White Cottage.

'Hi,' she said. 'I'm Ernie's girl. I'm just over from the West Coast. One of Ernie's drivers brought some money out, and I'm along to London for the ride. We're going back in a couple of days with me as the passenger. I sit in the front: because I'm the Front'! She giggled. 'Graham said you'd let me stay for a country weekend in Oxfordshire.'

'Delighted,' said Howard. 'I'll get out my video and we'll make some home movies. Would you like some tea?' They pranced about, making movies, drinking afternoon tea, smoking joints and talking about life on the West Coast. If there was a Mecca for dope-heads it was California. Ernie's girl was definitely where it was at.

'Ernie's been organising these runs for years, you know,' she said. 'He's a really nice guy: his father's some kind of millionaire oilman in Houston, Texas, Everybody's a millionaire in Houston. They're hungry for hash, it's amazing out there. A couple of years ago, Ernie and I were living in this great house on stilts at Laguna Beach. It was at the top of the canyon, on San Remo Drive. There was a crowd of renegade Scientologists that had it before. They used to spend their time flying in Mexican marijuana over the border, by the half ton. The father of one of these guys rented a ranch out in the Arizona desert and it had a little airstrip. But Mexican grass is really cheap weed.'

'That's quite interesting. What was the distribution system?'

'You know, pretty basic. Some guys pick it up from a cache in the desert, run it up to LA and San Francisco, stick it in a warehouse, sell it around. There's nothing to it. California is awash with that stuff. They started flying it when Nixon launched "Operation Intercept" along the land border, and now they move more stuff that way than anyone ever did before. Thousands of tons. To anybody in California, dope means pot means shit Mexican. I've been all over, scouring around Europe on Ernie's searches for his "exotica". I went out to Frankfurt in '71 with a guy and we shipped back 70 lb of hash in the fenders of this Volkswagen Variant. God knows where it came from. Last spring he had this crazy scheme to send an overland expedition to Pakistan. He offers this guy who lives with my girlfriend 50,000 dollars to do it.

'It takes practically all year. He buys this Chevvy truck in February, and the guy drives it all the way across to New York. Then he ships it over to Germany. We all take the plane to Europe and sit around in the Frankfurt Intercontinental for a week getting it together. He takes off: he drives to Pakistan. And that is not a simple trip. We have it loaded up with a false floor in Rawalpindi. The guy's destroyed by now with driving. He has to put the truck on a boat. It finally turns up in Rotterdam, and we move it about a bit, put it on another boat to Canada. The guy flies around, gets it out of Customs, hauls it back across the top of the continent and over the border in Oregon. There it finally is, on the West Coast, 400 lb of black Pakistani hashish. It's

November. Winter when the guy leaves, winter when he comes back. Wow!'

'Still, 400 grand is an awful lot of dollars. I wish there was some smooth way we could move hash over to you. I've actually got a friend called Lebanese Sam who's sitting on 500 kilos of shit he got down somehow in Paris, and doesn't know what to do with!'

'What's that, 1,000 lb? Ernie does know this Englishman at home who's actually operating a potential air-freight system. Guy called Jim Morris in the music business. He's a roadie – well, a very sophisticated one – used to be Robert Stigwood's chauffeur. He's really in New York: he makes up sound systems and rents them around to groups. Listen, may be you two could work something out.' Americans work quickly. Within two weeks, Jim 'Flash' Morris arrived in London for talks. He too, was only in his mid-20s, an East Ender with scarves. high boots and a pocket calculator.

'I've made a lot of money from different aspects of the music business,' he said. 'I've supplied the sound systems to a lot of groups – we started working for King Crimson. In those days we were "Kelsey and Morris". Me and Bill Kelsey had our own travelling sound systems built in London, and we were known as the best. Kelsey's never been in the dope scene, though. I've written songs for the Bee Gees. And my wife used to sing with Tina Turner. Now I operate from New York – "Circus Talent" – we supply a lot of PA gear to groups over there.' He sucked on his joint.

Howard and Graham were impressed. Howard had always wanted to break into rock music.

'What's the scam?'

'It's beautiful. There's a thing called an ATA Carnet. We use them all the time for European groups doing American tours. We get a group that's going on tour. They hire a bloody great sound system from us – those huge speakers in wooden boxes, amplifiers, all the other odds and ends. It's our job to lug it around from spot to spot, with the documentation – all the gigs they're going to perform. Then we ship the gear back to London, and send them the bill. In other words, there are a number of very large, more or less hollow wooden boxes, shuttling around between Europe and the United States.'

'What's the Carnet?'

'That's the loophole. This sort of activity comes under the heading "Temporary import of Professional Equipment".' He tossed a brochure over the table at Plinston's Maida Vale flat. It was from the

London Chamber of Commerce, export documents service department in Cannon Street and headed:

'ATA Carnets, and International Customs facilitation scheme.
ATA Carnets are now commonly used by professional people – educationalists, engineers and entertainers fulfilling overseas engagements and taking equipment with them.'

They flipped through the dozen pages of detailed instructions and sample forms.

'So you deposit a large sum of bread with the London Chamber of Commerce, and on the strength of this, Customs at all the countries you visit just let you in?'

'Yeah. They know if the goods aren't re-exported as promised, they have a guarantee of cash to pay the import duties. So they just tear a copy off the top and wave it through.'

'I'm beginning to get it. They can meet the hash anywhere in Europe?'

'That's it! Out with the screwdriver, stuff the hash in the speaker cabinets, and bang them on a States-bound plane! We'd need to carpenter up some special cabinets of course. But I know guys in the music business who'd do it. There's a man who became a roadie for "Emmerson, Lake and Palmer" I know needs cash. And some others already working straight for me.'

'Clever, clever. Let me put you in touch with Lebanese Sam. You'll let Graham and me buy into the Paris shipment, of course.'

'Sure, sure: we'll give you something. If it works, there may be other sources you can tap for us in Europe.' It worked all right. It was so simple and trouble-free a system that Morris's new purpose-designed company Transatlantic Sounds stopped bothering to pack stones in the cabinets to keep the designated weight constant. Then they stopped troubling to use real rock groups at all. Why bother? You just designed your itinerary, bought your Carnet, and sent off a truck full of speakers to the freight forwarders.

Lebanese Sam seemed to have quite a few diplomats organised to move furniture by diplomatic bag. He popped up with some more hash in Vienna – 400 lb of Afghan this time, and then another 900 lb of Lebanese. Howard and Plinston bought into the consignments for cash, paid over to Lebanese Sam – and Ernie Coombes, in far-off California, sent over couriers with six-figure sums as the boxes of speakers winged their way across to Phoenix, Philadelphia or Portland, Oregon, to be collected. This was all a cash business. Howard and Plinston were little more than investors, taking a piece of the action. Jim Morris, as the chief smuggler, got another share, and Ernie Coombes, as the US buyer, financed some of his purchases by letting his wholesale dealers invest alongside him. A little group of sellers were shuffling cash with a little group of buyers a very long way away. But Howard was not collecting more than £20,000 a time. When the next of Sam's consignments materialised in Italy he set out to scramble back up the independent smuggling ladder.

'Doctor John, you must be a bit bored with your PhD. How would you like to continue your research in Italy for a bit? A free holiday. We need a seaside villa there for doing a bit of collecting and loading.'

'Flash, I've organised an Italian villa for the Rome collection already, with a worker in place. It's at Cupra Marittima, on the Adriatic coast . . . Well, I like to pull my weight in the firm.'

'Fred, are you still enjoying life at Sussex? It's nice to see you again. Do you remember that Lebanese banker who supplied us with a little suitcase of hash when the sailor flew it to Geneva? The one we met in Hyde Park? How would it be if he was to be given a very large amount of bread, say £40,000 in dollars – to make available something like three quarters of a ton. On the beach, as it were?'

'Larry, how's that excellent friend of yours, Sailor Jo? Do you think he'd like to buy a sea-going boat and sail it about a bit in the Med? Yes, I know he won't sail stuff through to England because he hasn't got the bottle to go through the Straits of Gibraltar. But he wouldn't mind sailing to Italy, would he, up the Adriatic coast? From the Lebanon. It's not far. He'd have the whole thing financed for him, up to about 60 grand.'

'Graham, I am getting a major scam together for three-quarters of a ton to follow up the Rome deal. We have to put up about £50,000 each. Cash in front. I know it's a lot of loot, but we'll have a boat at the end of it and we'll have cut out Lebanese Sam. These are my own suppliers, yes . . . Sailor Jo and a Lebanese banker. The sailor will land it in Italy and Ernie and Jim will come in 50 per cent to move it to the West Coast of California. They're tested already my two. Of course it's a lot of money, but so's the quarter of million we're going to make . . . OK Graham, we'll invest in a bit of insurance as well. We will do just one more monster as well through Shannon with McCann.'

It was at this point, a couple of months after their first encounter, that Mac McMillan of M16 suddenly poked his muttonchops round the door of Annabelinda.

'Still prospering I see, Howard? I've got a little proposition if you're still interested in helping the office. Are you?'

'Oh sure, I'm not busy.'

Howard's head was filled with visions of toiling figures. In far-off Asia, loaded mule trains were picking their way down Himalayan passes towards Karachi. In the Middle East, women laboured in the fragrant fields of the Beka's Valley, guarded by riflemen of the Palestine Liberation Organisation. Little ships fought their way north through the same heaving Mediterranean storms that once shipwrecked Ulysses. Enormous Boeing freighters droned westwards, high above the Alps. In the shadow of ghostly battles fought long ago over Ireland's wounded soil, men watched and waited. Huge trucks, with bearded drivers and tremendous exhaust pipes, rumbled arrow-straight across the cactus-strewn plains of the Far West. In Zurich, bankers with gold-rimmed glasses fingered the doors to their vaults. In Italy, in Amsterdam, in Shepherd's Bush and Oxford, in Intercontinental Hotels wherever civilised life was to be found, hands were poised over a dozen telephones.

'I'm not busy. Would you like a joint?' he said.

'No thank you. Now, there is something come up with which you might be able to assist. You'll perhaps be aware that a lot of the Soviet Bloc diplomats in London are here as spies. They work for the Russian secret service, the KGB. There is this woman at the Czech Embassy in Bayswater who my superiors suspect comes into this category. Now, part of our job at the office is to neutralise these people. We leave it to the boys in the Security Service to stop them getting up to no good in London, but we're thinking more of the long term. They move about, you see – get other postings. . . .'

'You don't want me to assassinate her do you?'

'Good Lord, No – you've been reading too much about that Little-john nonsense in the Sunday papers. My superiors make it extremely clear that assassination is no part of the brief of the modern British secret service.'

'I was only joking. Why don't we have a joint?'

'Certainly not.'

'Half the government do, I don't see why you can't. Look at Lord Lambton: what is he, the Air Minister? He smokes dope. And he goes to bed with two prostitutes at once in a brothel!'

'Do be serious, Howard.'

'It's true. One of them was black. I like him. He's really very laid back. Did you see he said all the fuss was only because of her being black? He doesn't give a shit really, does he? I suppose it comes from being a millionaire. Do you think if I was discovered in a brothel with a lot of girls, smoking a joint, I'd have to resign from the secret service?'

'Yes, well it's your notorious penchant for "chicks" which we thought might make you useful. Would you be prepared to befriend this woman?'

'You're not joking, are you?'

'Absolutely not.'

'All right Mac. Sorry about the witticisms. This is rather serious work, isn't it?'

'Absolutely. Can you meet us at lunchtime in London, the day after tomorrow. In Henekey's, on Holborn? If you have any problems, let me leave you my office number. It's extension 706, and the number is 928 5600.'

At the pub, it was made clear that Howard was now ripe for the next stage.

'I would like you to meet my superior. And there is another person cooperating in this project.' They gathered at the Angus Steak-House in Regent Street – it is the kind of restaurant to which American tourists go because it looks normal. Check tablecloths, plate-glass windows, low-paid waiters and straightforward pieces of meat to eat, but not chic in any way. No one who was anyone was ever likely to be seen there, except by mistake.

Mac was there with two men. One was young and Canadian. The other was middle-aged and English, with an expression of craggy propriety.

'Thanks very much for offering to help,' he said. 'Now this gentleman works for the Bank of Montreal here in London. He is intending to hold a small party at his home very shortly. Among those he will invite are three girls from the Czech embassy, young McMillan here, and yourself. Your brief is, simply enough, to try and pick the young lady in question up. We want you to strike up a relationship.'

'Well, I'll try – Sir.'

'Good. Well, we must leave you two and return to our duties. Goodbye and thank you again for your help.'

'Hey, Mac, this is right up my street isn't it?'

Mac smiled, fleshily: 'I thought this would appeal to you. I told you it was really interesting work, didn't I?'

'But look, Mac, if I succeed, I do pick her up – I mean where do I take her? I haven't got a place in London, have I?' Howard thought it best not to mention the seedy room Mike Clarke kept on at 43 Saltram Crescent as a safe contact point for phone calls.

'Yes, that's a problem. Haven't you perhaps got a friend with a flat you could borrow?'

'There's Graham, I suppose. Do you remember Graham Plinston at Oxford? He's just leaving for Tangiers and I know his family are already off in Ibiza for the summer. His place has a bit of style – Eastern carpets, big stereo, wine racks and all that.'

'I think I do recall him, yes. It might be a good plan. Look, why don't the three of us have dinner together this week? I'd quite like to get acquainted with your friend – or renew the acquaintanceship. But don't say we're especially close or anything, or let on about confidential business, eh?'

'Mum's the word, Mac.'

It was an odd little dinner. The three young Oxford men worked their way through some sophisticated curries at Shezan, an expensive West End Pakistani restaurant in Cheval Place. Plinston, reminded that Mac had been at Balliol with Howard, and under the impression that he was a Foreign Office diplomat whose contacts might come in useful, talked expansively about 'straight' business – his carpet shop, and his property company, 'Zeitgeist', the Spirit of the Age. He waxed eloquent about the speculative property boom generated by the fiscal policies of Heath's finance minister, Anthony Barber.

'Like they say, you can buy for one million, sell the day after for two, and see it sold again the next day for three.' He praised market forces:

'It's the small independent businessman who has always been the economic strength of this country. He is the purest and most successful form of capitalism, who can respond instantly to the demands of the market. If only the small businessman was left alone to supply those demands, he would benefit and the consumer would benefit. Instead, socialists try and legislate us out of existence.'

'True.' said McMillan. 'May I say how much I agree. But business needs a climate of political stability within which to thrive. That is why I consider we are fortunate in Britain to have so solidly-established a monarchy.'

'You're absolutely right,' said Plinston. 'My father, who was town clerk in Letchworth, used to say to me "The Royal Family is one of this country's most priceless assets." '

'Well I'm glad to meet at least one of Howard's friends who isn't tinged with anarchism. I feared he might only associate these days with dope-smoking revolutionaries.'

'Don't get me wrong. I think there should be free trade in cannabis as with everything else. Let the state bow out and leave it to the market.' Back at Plinston's well-appointed capitalist lair in Marylands Road, the two of them shared a joint, and Howard could contain himself no longer:

'Do you know what he is. He's a spy! He works for MI6. All this Foreign Office thing is a cover.'

'No kidding?'

'Nope. He keeps sounding me out, would I like to do things for him? "Help the office" he says.'

'Amazing. What a laugh. I never met a spy before. Do you think that this could ever be of any use?'

'Well he did seem rather impressed with you Graham, and all that bread you're making. His father's a big banker.'

'Good job he doesn't know just how I make it. He'd have a fit.'

'Hey, it's a good job Jim McCann doesn't know either we're dining with "British Intelligence". His feet would really leave the ground.' Howard giggled.

'Mac the Spy is definitely to be cultivated from now on, right? What a laugh. I suppose I'd better go home, Graham, I haven't been there much, what with deals and spies and chicks.'

Things were spinning faster. When he got home, Rosie Brindley was determined for a show-down.

'Howard, I can't cope with much more of this. I left my husband to share my life with you, but instead of you, all I ever see is your back disappearing out the door to find three different call-boxes in a row to make dealing calls. And that's when you're not heading for some airport or other. We can't plan anything together – it's always, you've had some delay, a call hasn't come through, a man hasn't arrived, suddenly you've got to leave town. It's a nightmare. God knows I like seeing people, I like the dealing life, I *believe* in it. But there are crowds of people through here everyday, looking for you, leaving messages, talking business. Ever since you got involved with this heavy American project, things have started getting right out of hand.'

'But I'm working hard and I'm going to make ever such a lot of bread.'

'Howard, money is irrelevant to me. I've always had some money. I know there'd always be a roof over our heads. What upsets me is that you never come home, and when you do, if you're not doing deals you just slump in front of the TV, just acting like some heavy straight businessman.'

'Well I'm sorry. When I come home after a hard day being an international dope-smuggler, my head's just buzzing. I need to relax.'

'That isn't funny. I think the truth is you're not really interested in me at the moment. I've decided to go to Ibiza for a while. Graham's girl is out there, and I'm going to rent a villa and get Richard to drive me and the kids over. We'll stay for a while. You can come over and join us, if you really want to.'

'Yeah, well I know your family's loaded with bread – and so is Richard Lewis.'

'That's not the point either. I suppose you were never cut out to think of yourself in the husband-and-father role.' So Rosie took herself and the orange BMW off to the little Balearic island of Ibiza – it was a spot as fashionable to the Sixties dope set as St Tropez was to movie stars, or Long Island to New York stockbrokers, or Tuscany to the British middle class. It was a brave move to leave Howard to his wheeling and scheming, for there were lots of girls in Oxford and London who liked being groupies to rich young dope-smugglers. Howard, pursuing his latest role, promptly set off for Oxford Gardens in North Kensington where he had been requested to present himself and demonstrate his skills as an MI6 gigolo.

'Hi Mac, I've sprayed myself with aftershave all over. Where's the chicks?'

'Oh I expect they'll be along. Let's get a drink. There seems to be some white wine on offer.'

'Look, what is this? I thought it would be some smooth diplomats' party. It's just a little semi-detached in W10, two glasses of Moroccan Chablis, a few boring guys in suits and no chicks.'

'They've probably been held up. I'll go and confer with mine host.' They went into a huddle. The Canadian started making phone calls. Still no Czech chicks.

'Howard look, I'm most awfully sorry. It does seem as if they've decided to give it a miss. What a cock-up. I am really, most awfully sorry.'

'It's probably just as well. I've been sitting here thinking: What if she doesn't fancy me? I mean, it's all right being given these projects, but what am I supposed to do, take it out and wave it at her?'

'There's no need to be coarse. I'm really disappointed for your sake, Howard. I don't want you to worry. We really will find something interesting for you.'

'Don't fret. I mean, I expect this sort of thing happens hundreds of times in your work.' Some things happened hundreds of times in Howard's work too – or so it was starting to seem. He tried to contact Plinston, supposedly re-charging his batteries in Tangier. Plinston had disappeared. His girl explained in the end, on the crackling phone from Ibiza.

'The Moroccans arrested him. They flung him in jail. It seems there was some sort of general alert put out – maybe the Swiss or the French were behind it – to watch his movements. But the Moroccans misunderstood apparently. They went round to his villa and hauled him away. It was terrible.'

'Well, what's happening? What's happening?'

'Oh it's all right. He spread some bread around, and they let him out again yesterday, with apologies. He's on his way over here to Ibiza now – he wants to get out of the way for a bit.'

'How are Rosie and the baby?'

'Terrible. They've both got some kind of influenza and they're really miserable.'

Howard headed for Heathrow, caught a plane to Barcelona and on to the villa at Santa Eulalia in Ibiza, and stayed for a few days. When Rosie had recovered her health and Plinston some of his composure, the two partners cantered back on to the tarmac. Plinston flew to London, and Howard eventually on across the Irish Sea to Dublin. Although neither of them knew it, the last act of the Shannon scam was about to begin. It was May: springtime in Dublin, in the village of Moone, and in the seaside house at Greystones on the Dublin coast where Howard would still occasionally stay to see such deals through.

En route through London, Howard heard from Yarnton that a letter had arrived. He made a point of writing:

Dear lovely Rosie, I've just read your letter. It's great to get a letter

135

from you and I just had to get in the car and drive down to read it. I miss you a lot. I'm back in London now in Mike's flat, sitting tied to the phone.

He wrote in code – 'Tony' and 'Stew' – to explain progress on the simultaneous Great Mediterranean Fiasco. The project to sail three-quarters of a ton of US-bound hash from the Lebanon to Italy was going extremely badly:

> It's been a really hectic week since I last wrote to you – everything going wrong – Tony was only able to get half of what he was meant to, and Stew's man hasn't arrived there yet, and hasn't in fact been seen by anybody for two weeks. Tony and Stew can't phone each other because the lines between their two countries has been broken. So all phoning is being done through me here, and it's very chaotic. I haven't heard from either since Monday. It's very difficult to escape the conclusion that this month's possiblities in that scene are extremely minimal. However, assuming that Stew's man hasn't disappeared forever – then next month can go ahead as planned, and things will be a lot easier. Tony now has a good relationship with his contacts.

Fred, out in Beirut, had successfully arranged the purchase of at least some of the boatload of hash they planned to sail across the Mediterranean:

> And everybody involved has now a better idea of the reality of this activity. It's still a drag that it hasn't happened yet, particularly with all this bread tied up in it.

Howard then turned to the state of the Shannon scam.

The Black Pak was Up, and to get it Down needed the discreet but rapid transmission of the PIA Air Waybill number from Mike Durrani in Karachi, via Howard in London, to Jim McCann who had returned from Amsterdam for the purpose to the vicinity of Shannon Airport:

> Jim rings up every half-hour, so as you can work out, the business with him is literally off the ground. But things have been pretty fucked up there too, nobody really knowing what the hell's going on. Yesterday there was a strike of international telephone operators,

along with everybody else. We couldn't get the vital information from K. All we knew was that it was on its way. This sort of vagueness really upset Jim. However things have cleared up a bit over the last hour, and if Allah is willing I should be going to see Jim this weekend. In the meantime, I have to stay stuck to this fucking phone.

*Anyway*, enough of this dealing rubbish.

I do hope you really are better now. Richard rang me on Monday and gave me the latest news on you. He said that you seemed to be 'getting in' to it all there. Is it sunny now – I love you, when you are brown. I hope the kids are better, and not too upset by Richard leaving. I keep looking at the photos of the three of you to remind me what you are like. I so much want your face close to me. It's lovely that you just want to talk rubbish to me. I'd love to listen to your rubbish right now. I love you so much, Rosie, and always will. I love you.

Howard was attempting some running repairs on his emotional life, but business immediately called:

I have to go now to Mike and Anne-Marie's place because we're expecting a call from Mike. David (the other one from Kenfig Hill) has just arrived to relieve me. Please think of me and write more to me. Love, Love, Love, Love, Howard XXXX.

Howard then boarded the plane on Friday morning. He had churned over the Irish channel so many times. But today, his route was odd. He took the British Airways morning flight direct to Cork. There he picked up a hire car at the airport, drove off in the direction of the harbour, and returned to the airport later that same afternoon. He caught the Aer Lingus plane on to Dublin at 4.20 p.m.

At the seaside house at Greystone, he wrote another letter. He was alone, with the dusk falling, and he was feeling a little nervous. Well he might. Plinston had agreed they should get their own back on Jim for the last ripped-off consignment sold behind their backs in Dublin. They would despatch some of this load, not in a fleet of cars to England, but direct to the US along the infallible ATA Carnet pipeline. And McCann would never know, partner or no partner. If they could pull off the trick and get a quarter of a ton on a plane and out of Ireland behind his back, the two partners would pick up around

£70,000 profit. And then they could make as much again selling the remainder over in England. But cheating Jim McCann was a novel, and possibly dangerous, exercise.

My dear, darling Rosemary,

Howard wrote, in his neat, widely-spaced hand:

You must have guessed by now that I'm sitting around waiting for the inevitable O'Neill to give me the first instalment of his birthday present. Everything *seems* to be all right, and if all goes well, I should be doing some rather strenuous physical exercise in the next hour or so.

I'm sure that I don't have to tell you that my head is in rather a confused state at the moment. I'm a bit frightened and a bit lonely. It would be so nice to pick up the phone and ring you. It would be bliss to hold your hand, and heaven to kiss you. I love you and miss you.

This business I'm involved in really takes its toll on me. I suppose it must be worth it, and presumably the ability to do it is by now part of me.

I think of you quite literally all the time. I hear your voice sometimes in my head, advising me, and keeping me cool.

Howard shared another coded joke with Rosie – all their dealing friends had code names for conversational use, and Ernie Coombes was always referred to as 'Dr Foster', especially in front of the children:

I think of Muffin (Rosie's daughter) a lot too, and her little sayings. Whenever I go to Annabelinda's 'Dr Foster' went to Gloucester Street with Howie' rings through my head. I can't think straight about Podge (their baby), I can only look at her photo and kiss it.

I must stop writing soon, because it makes me all sloppy and weepy. I've got to be a man of the world very soon – a tough, hard, cunt – which I'm not really, despite what you say.

I had my hair cut yesterday at Vidal Sassoon and I look a bit like an 18-year-old schoolboy. I've also got a stye (sty!) in my eye, which makes me look revolting. But I hope it'll go by the next time I see you, which had better be soon before I go completely to pieces.

I must finish now, and go to Jim's house. Trust me, lovely – I'm with you, love you, and need you. Howard.

He stuffed the letter in his pocket, pulled the villa door behind him, and pulled out of Greystones, driving south-west away from the coast and north of the Wicklow hills, along the 50 miles of agricultural back roads to the farmhouse at Moone. It was black and dark when he arrived – a good night for smuggling. McCann's Volkswagen hauled the crates of hashish 150 miles on the quiet roads of Limerick and County Tipperary. He delivered them: all twenty were present this time; he and Howard, staggering and grunting, hauled each crate out of the side door and stacked them in the farmhouse garage. McCann eventually went away, £50,000 richer when the hash was sold, as he thought, in England.

The next morning dawned damp, but soft. The team of university drivers were on their way, filtering in through the four car-ferry ports. Howard said nothing to two of the drivers as they stowed the slabs snugly into the door-panels. But when the cars left, they did not drive to the ferryport of Cork. Instead, they drove to a cottage 10 miles out of the city. It was an addition to his stable of Irish properties that was even less well-advertised than most of his rentals. There, Robin, Howard's tough operative from Oxford, was waiting. Quietly and rapidly, the door panels were all unscrewed and unpopped again. All the hash was taken out and stacked in the house. The two cars left, empty, for a chaste passage past the English Customs.

Later that night, a Luton box-truck, rented from Avis in Dublin, backed into the drive, its bodywork dusty from the 150-mile-run south. At the wheel was 'Captain Flash' – as Jim Morris liked, for purposes purely no doubt of disguise, to be known. It was he who Howard had met off the Swansea-Cork ferry early on the Friday morning, in his furtive diversion from the direct path between London and Dublin.

Morris and Robin loaded twenty of the big wooden speaker cabinets, from the 'Cripple Creek Case Company'. They left on board the other gear – the amplifiers in their thick metal boxes, the heavy-duty connectors, the mixing console, and the coils of cable. The speakers screwed open and inside were a series of specially designed grey fibreglass baffles with lids. They would hold almost 30 lb of dope a piece. It took more than three hours of manual labour to complete the task, and despite the polythene and sticking plaster around the slabs, a sickly smell of linseed oil and dope resin filled the air. The box-truck drove off northwards into the night. It would pull in at the cargo terminal of Dublin airport in the morning, and its contents be loaded on a transatlantic jet, waved through by Customs.

It was a coup. Howard's pipeline was running hashish something like 10,000 miles, from Pakistan to the West Coast of America entirely by air freight. It was going through five airports – Karachi, Frankfurt, Shannon, Dublin, New York – sometimes more. It was being handled by three different groups of physical smugglers – Durrani's team getting the consignments on to PIA planes; McCann's crypto-Republicans pulling them off Aer Lingus connections; and Jim Morris's music crowd whisking them through on Carnets into the continental US. The farm-gate price in distant Pakistan was around 10 dollars a lb. The seven principal traders – Ernie Coombes and Durrani as importer and exporter respectively, the Pakistani 'Films man', McCann and Morris as smugglers, and Howard and Plinston as overall brokers and fixers – each took a profit of at least £30,000–£60,000 on every shipment they could move: sometimes a lot more. If the masters at Garw Grammar School could have seen Howard's progress 12 years later, they would have been bound to have been thrilled. This boy, who could quote you dollars for lbs or sterling for kilos, or the other way round without even having to think, was the same one they had criticised for one thing only: his 'disappointing' lack of skill in Applied Mathematics.

In a frenzy of activity, Howard now got the first passenger plane he could from Dublin back to Heathrow. He rented another car, and drove to the little village of Trelleck near Tintern Abbey on the Welsh border. A new cottage had been rented here, in some attempt to preserve security by constant movement. There, acting as caretaker, was the faithful Marty Langford. He and Howard 'de-stashed' the three-quarters of a ton that had come over to England in suitcase and trunks, ready for the small fleet of wholesalers to carry away to London and the provinces.

'Let's send some more of the actual London stuff over to Ernie as well,' Howard said. 'It's a marvellous price, it gets it out of our hands that much faster, and he might take as much as 800 lb.'

There was another bout of telephoning. The whole enterprise was complicated by the archaic nature of the British telephone system. Only in London itself was it possible to direct dial calls to the United States – indeed, that was why the partners kept an answering service at Mike Clarke's London flat. Howard could not make international coinbox calls from Oxford at all.

140

But a fake itinerary was constructed. A truck of speakers was sent out to the cottage at Trelleck, and Marty toiled to help install the hash, which trundled off to the Cargocentre at Heathrow.

Howard got on the line to Ernie Coombes, the Laguna Beach dope connoisseur:

'This is Transatlantic Sounds. Tomorrow's concert equipment is arriving on TWA flight 703. We've sold 800 tickets at this end. The Air Waybill number is 006-5351-6212.'

'OK, no problem.'

New York, or Cincinnati, Las Vegas, Los Angeles, or Seattle. It didn't matter where. Ernie's men always picked them up.

'Those pop music people are so neat and laid back,' Howard said. 'It's such a nice way to work.'

'Yeah, it's quite easy isn't it – it's refreshing after trying to handle the crazed McCann.'

While the roads and skies of the British Isles were seething with these criss-cross consignments of dope, Mac the Spy turned up again at Annabelinda.

'How's business, Howard? Still prosperous?'

'Can't complain, Mac, I suppose.'

'I wonder, are you still interested in helping us? I know the latest incident was a bit of a let down.'

'Oh yes, sure, why not?'

'This is the thing. You're on the verge, if I remember rightly, of opening up branches of Annabelinda, in both Dublin and Amsterdam.'

'Yes, I told you that, didn't I?'

'These are both places in which the office is interested, for reasons you can imagine. The IRA, international terrorism, espionage – these things go on in cities like that. Well, if you were to open these branches as you intend, would you be prepared to let us make use of them for some of our people, as a cover?'

'You mean they'd work there, selling dresses?'

'Far from it, old chap. One of our people might describe himself, say, as a representative of the firm, have it printed on his cards and so on. And if anybody asked, you would of course, be prepared to say the chap was working for Annabelinda. He could be flying round Europe anywhere.'

'It's just a front?'

'The very word. And you never know, but the system might expand if it worked. We're always looking for deep cover. For example, maybe you could even open up business in the Communist satellites, say Romania: that would be useful to us. Naturally, if you did such a thing there would be discreet financial assistance to help you get started.'

'Uh-huh. I think I can say, Mac, that I would be definitely prepared to do such a thing.'

'Definitely prepared' was an understatement. Howard was definitely prepared to fall in with such a scheme, the way the Black Widow Spider was definitely prepared to eat its mate. It was a truly delicious idea. MI6 would help Howard to consolidate his own 'front', and even pay him to do so. Their 'front' would be his 'front' and it would always be in their interests to shore up its credibility. How wonderful.

It was romantic and patriotic, and it was tremendously good business. It is also possible that, lurking in a corner of Howard's mind was the word 'leverage'. Who can say?

Howard felt soothed and happy enough to snatch a couple of days for family life. Rosie appeared to have calmed down somewhat, and so had the pace of dealing. The Great Mediterranean Fiasco was in a helpless lull. He offered to return to Ibiza, spend a day or two with Rosie and then escort his family home again.

Summer in Ibiza in 1973 was a wild and peculiar time. On this tiny Spanish island, in the western Mediterranean, close to Majorca, the rich dope-dealers lived through the balmy season in the pastoral villas, much as the Emperor Tiberius tried to do on the Island of Capri. The town, with its narrow pungent streets and its fort, had little to commend it other than the big cafe in the centre where visitors lolled about all day. It was the second level of the summer population – one sharply different from that of the dealers – that consisted of the town hippies and the low-lifers. Ne'er-do-wells thronged the bars looking to get laid, looking to get someone else laid, or trying to touch some dazed dealer for the loan of £500. Petty thieving was endemic, and it was easy to lose your wallet to some hollow-eyed bead-twirler in cut-down jeans and a psychedelic sweatband. Nuttiness flourished: there was a witches colony on the island of Formentera, and enough tripped-out tarot-shufflers and i ching throwers to hold a freak's ball every night. The more grandiose of the dealers would let the hippies sleep in the courtyards of their villas, after the barbecue which so often was the social focus of the evening. Charcoal, fresh sardines and marijuana were the smells that mingled on the faint evening breeze. The dealers could be distinguished from the package tourists and yachtsmen around Ibiza: they were the ones eating the giant grilled prawns in the dearest restaurants, with the piles of brand new snorkelling gear in the back of the biggest Seats that could be had for rent on the island. Gradually that summer, many of the people round the European dope scene drifted down there for a while. Rosie Brindley and Plinston's girl had relaxed into it by the time Howard arrived.

Howard, of course, made Ibiza move faster. With such a conglomeration of cool persons, his essentially international trading interests came rapidly to the fore. While the cafe crowds were all trying to score hash off each other, Howard walked around with a briefcase. He couldn't help it.

In no time, he and a tall athletic-looking coke-snorter with long blond hair, the Dutchman Arend ter Horst, were talking business over a joint at the Dutchman's villa in St Juan.

Howard offered to buy surplus dope that ter Horst sometimes found himself with in Amsterdam. The Dutchman agreed to visit London and give Howard a few tips about opening a branch of Annabelinda in Holland.

Another line was out, another contact made, another proto-deal swirling like a gaseous cloud, ready to cool one day into a nuggety little planet. Howard caught the plane home, trying to act like a husband and father.

There was an ominous smell of burning in the air. Plinston said:

'You better come round to Marylands Road right now. It's a question of heat.' Plinston and Patrick Lane, his money manager – 'My accountant', as Plinston put it – were together in the house, looking tense.

'You remember James Goldsack?'

'Yeah, he's that dealer. Nice upper-class boy. A Keble man, isn't it? Married to a judge's daughter. He came round to Trelleck with a red Capri when I was doing the de-stashing, and took 100 lb off us.'

'Exactly. He's a good friend of Dave Pollard and me. Potentially very professional. Only he's been busted by the Customs just tonight.'

'Oh, Christ. With our dope, I suppose?'

'Yep. I have certain sources of information, and this appears to be the position. He's inside. We don't know whether he's said anything. They busted his house – he's got a place in Shepherds Bush – Barons Court Road, near Flash's flat. They found 20 or 30 lb of our Shannon consignment in the house, and that's what they're charging him with. They also found the key and the rental agreement with the registration number of a red Capri.'

'Oh, shit. If that's all they found, it means the rest of his stock is in the car. They'll grab it when they get to the car. . . .'

'They don't know where to find it – yet.'

'Well, where the hell is it?'

'Aha. As a matter of fact, his wife knows where it is and was thoughtful enough to mention its whereabouts to me. That's the good news.'

'But? . . .'

'Well, we don't have a key to it, of course. That's part of the bad news.'

'And? . . .'

'The other part of the bad news is where it is.'

'This is killing me, Graham. Where is it?'

'Parked outside Hammersmith police station.' Eventually Howard spoke. 'I really liked the way you did that, Graham, I almost enjoyed it. So what do we do: write off the ten grand and pray Goldsack doesn't talk? With that quantity they'll threaten him with an importation charge unless he gives them some names. He knows all of us and he knows Trelleck.'

'Well, we close down Trelleck right away. You'd better drive out there tonight, speak to Marty. Make sure every scrap of evidence is gone. But for God's sake don't let Marty clear off. The place is rented in his own name and that would be really uncool. Tell him to stay put, and look legit.'

'Yeah, fine. But there's one thing you've forgotten. We didn't want to keep a big warehouse in England, did we, after that Winchester rip-off. So we've been moving it slowly over.'

'I know that, but Marty can just burn all the evidence, all the bits of garbage and paper, can't he?'

'That's not what I mean. There's one more car to come across. And it's coming next week. Where the hell do we de-stash it?'

'You'll have to do it at Yarnton.'

'That's really risky. It's my own house, you know.'

'You did a car load like that once before, when we were de-stashing all over the place. What's the alternative? You want to do it in Hyde Park?'

'OK. Shit! Shit!'

Patrick Lane, who had been listening quietly, said:

'I'm not scared of Hammersmith police station. I'll go and get the hash back.'

'You're crazy. How?'

'Wait and see. I can't do it tonight. I'll go at 8 tomorrow morning. . . .'

Later the next day, he returned to Marylands Road. Howard had not been home the previous night, of course. They were both waiting nervously.

'It's round at Dave's, safe enough. No sweat,' Lane said. He rolled a fat joint.

'Tell us Patrick. Come on please, tell us! Jesus, we could all be facing 10 years for this!'

'I rang up the AA.'

'What?'

'I rang up the Automobile Association.'

'You're kidding.'

'I am a member. It was perfectly all right. I explained that, foolish fellow as I was, I had locked my ignition keys in the boot of my red Capri. Would they mind very much sending a patrolman with a bunch of keys to get it open for me.'

'And you hung around outside Hammersmith nick for an hour until the AA turned up? Amazing.'

'Well, I didn't try to look too closely associated with the vehicle in question. There was a slightly bad moment when the patrolman got the bootlid up. Inside were four bloody great suitcases and a rather unmistakeable set of scales.'

'I'd have run away on the spot.'

'No doubt. I gave the patrolman a fiver for his trouble, and managed to get two of the suitcases under each arm. I staggered down the road and caught a cab on Hammersmith Broadway. I'm afraid I had to leave the scales behind.' Goldsack lived up to Plinston's praise of his professionalism. A few days later he emerged on £5,000 bail. What etiquette in these circumstances demands, Goldsack did. He presented himself at Plinston's house in Maida Vale. He would produce, he promised, the signed statement he had made to HM Customs. Howard and Plinston would then both see that he had said nothing to implicate them, or to disclose the existence of the dope-store at Trelleck.

But the partners took no chances. Or at least, that was what they thought. Trelleck stayed shut down. Rosie was appalled to find Howard meeting men with cars outside her own house, and disappearing into the garage with them for hours.

'It's not going to be here much more than overnight,' Howard said. 'I'll give it all to one dealer and have him collect it quick.'

'This is just the kind of scene I couldn't stand before. What about all that?' She gestured at two black polythene dustbin bags, bulging with sticking plaster, paper and polythene, and reeking with the smell of dope.

'I took all the wrappers of the slabs before weighing them. I thought I ought to be careful about fingerprints – after Goldsack's bust I daren't let them go out with wrappers on, and I can't make a bonfire in the back garden here. There's too many neighbours.'

'Well, for God's sake, get rid of them quickly.'

'I'll put them in the car first thing tomorrow, and dump them in the country.'

Neither of them noticed their eldest child, a tidy 4-year-old, holding an envelope in her hand and looking for somewhere suitable to dispose of it.

That weekend, Howard's mother and father drove up from Kenfig Hill with Howard's elderly grandmother, to pay a state visit to their family. The neat young Oxford graduate and boutique-owner (it gave some pleasure to his parents to see that he had got over the long-hair phase of his life) brought tea out on to the lawn. It was a hot Sunday afternoon, and the children played on the well-kept grass – Rosie used to mow it.

Two uniformed policemen opened the gate and made their way in. One held in his hand a polythene-and-sticking-plaster wrapper from a 2 lb slab of machine-pressed Pakistani black hashish. In the other he held an envelope with a name and address written on it.

'Does Emily Lewis live here?' he asked Howard, ignoring the family group. Howard realised, in a sickening intuitive lurch, exactly what had happened, and exactly what was about to happen. 'And in front of my mother, too, and my grandmother,' he thought miserably. His arrest, trial and 10-year jail sentence flashed in rapid detail before his eyes.

'This is her mother,' he muttered hastily, pointing at Rosie. Rosie, cool, well-dressed, middle-class, attractive, did her best.

'Have you ever seen one of these before, Madam?' the policeman asked.

'Oh yes,' she said. 'The damp-course man. He's been here doing some work. It looks rather like his rubbish.'

The Thames Valley constable took her name down and the name

and address of the damp-course man. Then incredibly, they both went away.

'What was that about, dear?' asked his mother.

'Oh somebody dropped some litter,' he said abstractedly. 'They were making inquiries.'

He felt confused. He suspected he looked ashen. The afternoon wore on. His parents passed remarks: he did his best to answer them. Rosie disappeared into the bedroom, and stayed there quite a long time. Eventually, his family left with thanks and kisses, for the drive back to Wales. Barely had their car turned the corner of Little Blenheim, heading right for the main Oxford Road, than Howard started to throw clothes and shaving gear into a holdall.

'Where are you going?'

'I'm clearing off. I'll go and check into a hotel in London. They'll be back for me, I know.'

'What about me?'

'Tell them that I lent the garage to some friends of mine from Ibiza. Say they wanted to change their oil. It was them who left the rubbish behind.'

'Howard, I'm frightened. I don't want them coming back here and grilling me again.'

'Me neither. Bye.' Howard went to London and dialled Mac McMillan's number. Maybe something could be done. Maybe he could call this MI6 situation in somehow.

'Mac, can we have a meeting? I have something to tell you. Yes, look meet me at Saltram Crescent. I'm staying in London.'

Howard explained. More or less.

'I was doing a very small amount of dealing. Just dabbling really. But I took the wrapper off this block of hash, and this was what the police picked up in the country lane. I felt I should tell you because I felt you should know in case it affected my position.'

'Most responsible, Howard. I'm glad to see you're taking your assignment seriously. I'm really pleased you bothered to notify me of this.'

'Don't you think I'm in danger of being arrested?'

'Oh no, I shouldn't think so. Unless it was for litter, of course.'

'Look Mac, I am a bit worried about this wrapper business. Could you possibly find out whether the police have got any information on me? I know you've got easy ways of doing that.'

'Oh, I don't know if I could. If I do that, it'll certainly increase your debt to the office rather a lot.'

'I don't mind.'

'We'd certainly be calling on you to do something in return.'

'Fine, fine.'

'Look, no promises. I'll see what I can do. I'll come back and see you in two or three days.'

McMillan materialised, three days later.

'Now look Howard, you've got to make me a solemn promise. You'll never reveal what I'm about to tell you.'

'No. Promise that.'

'Not even if they tear your toenails out, must you reveal to a soul that I've told you this.'

'No. OK.'

'Well, the police definitely do not have a file on you. But you have been screened by MI6, to see whether you would make a suitable employee.' He paused impressively:

'I have to tell you there was some concern about your Uncle Danny, who lives in Pontypridd.'

'What for?'

'Well, he is known locally as "Danny the Red" isn't he? He always used to vote Communist.'

'You've got to be kidding. He's barely a relation. He's my father's first cousin. Anyway, he's not a heavy militant or anything. He's just an ordinary bloke. He works in this aviation factory. That's crazy. He doesn't make any secret of his opinions: crowds of blokes were in the Communist party down in the Welsh coalfield, right up to Hungary.'

'Oh well, they're not really worried. There was just a bit of concern expressed, that's all. What they're really concerned about is very different. They're concerned with the person you are meeting in the American Hotel in Amsterdam.'

There was a silence. 'They know about McCann!' Howard thought frantically to himself. 'All the time, they've known about McCann. They're watching him. Are they watching me? What do they know? Jesus, what do they know? Talk about out of the frying-pan. First Goldsack, then the wrappers. Now this. They know about McCann!'

What he said as casually as he could was:

'Do you mean Jim O'Neill, the Irishman?'

'Yes, that's the one. Just what exactly are you doing with him, Howard?'

'Oh, he has connections in Amsterdam. It's something to do with dope, actually.' Don't say anything about Ireland, he said to himself. Just don't even mention anything about it.

'Do you know he's an arms smuggler into Ireland?'

'Uh, well, I think he might do arms smuggling sometimes, as well.'

'Are you prepared to co-operate with all you know about this man?'

'Well, yes Mac, I suppose so.'

'I'll be back in touch very soon.'

Howard called Rosie. She was frantic with rage and anxiety.

'Look you don't even know how bad it is,' he said. 'It's much more involved than anybody realises. I've got a lot on my mind, so don't give me a hard time.'

'I thought we were going to be together again. You promised me you'd stop all this, and now it's worse than ever. I'm not going to hang around here all on my own, waiting for the police to come again and start grilling the children. I'm going back out to Ibiza with them, until all this cools down. And if you've got any sense. Howard – and if you want us to stay together – you'll disentangle yourself from whatever you're still plotting with Graham, and come on out there to find me pretty soon. Goodbye.'

Howard realised he was getting rather lonely. Rosie was gone. He could not very well tell his partner Plinston that he was slipping under an obligation to MI6. And it turned out that all the time, he was being watched. That was the most worrying thing of all. He settled down with a joint in the sleazy setting of Saltram Crescent. He couldn't sleep: he tried to work it out.

McCann has been under surveillance. FACT.

He scribbled down a list of notes on a scrap of paper.

In Amsterdam. FACT.

They know he is called 'Jim O'Neill'. FACT.

QUESTIONS. Do they know he is really called Jim McCann? Maybe. Maybe not.

Do they know we have been working together in Ireland? Apparently not.

Do they know we are smuggling hash? Apparently not. They think 'O'Neill' is an arms dealer.

He started on a fresh sheet of paper.

OPTION (1) Simply refuse to co-operate. Difficult to justify. Will merely arouse their suspicions. Might put me under 24-hour surveillance. Mac knows I'm involved in the drug scene, and knows about wrappers. They've simply got too much on me.

He stared glumly at this, and crossed it out. He started again.

OPTION (2) Agree to co-operate. Will incriminate self. Main thing I know about M is that he has been smuggling hash for me since 1971. Can't tell them that. Can't tell them about his boasted arms dealing either because (a) don't really know anything (b) don't want to get Jim into trouble. If they put Jim out of action, also puts us out of action.

He sucked the end of his pen for a while, then added:

You don't grass on friends. Is the worst thing.

He paused again, and resumed writing:

Everyone would find out. Stool-pigeon. Grass. Fink. Informer.

He savagely crossed out everything on the piece of paper, scoring the lines until the paper ripped. He rolled another joint and stared unhappily at the ceiling. How did they know about Jim and all this arms rubbish, anyway? He remembered the way Jim had proudly shown him on their last Amsterdam trip of a copy of *Playboy* magazine.

It had a long piece about Jim O'Neill, the lovable Provisional IRA 'intelligence officer' in Holland. It was obviously inspired by Jim himself, fanning the Republican legend. And presumably British Intelligence could read. An irrelevant picture drifted into his mind of a British MI6 man, in pin-striped three piece suit, locked in the office lavatory with the latest *Playboy* and suddenly sitting upright as he found the name O'Neill leaping out between the pages of soft-focus dirty photos. Howard pulled heavily on his joint. Maybe there was something harmless there to fob McMillan off with. The last trip but one to Ireland, McCann had said:

'Come with me, Howard. I want you to be a Dutchman.'

Then he drove him to the little private port of Greenore, 65 miles north up the coast from Dublin, virtually in an enclave nestling under the troubled South Armagh border with the British. Greenore was at the mouth of Carlingford Lough, where it ran inland for 10 miles at the foot of the Mourne Mountains, on the other side of the border. This was cowboy country, where unguarded tracks sidled across the border towards Crossmaglen and Newry. On the other side of the narrow Lough stood Rostrevor and Warrenpoint, where the Provisionals were to detonate a giant bomb from the Republic side, before the decade was out, and blow up 18 British soldiers.

McCann had dragged him in to see the Harbour authorities.

'This is Mr Bergen, from Amsterdam. As I explained to you in my call, he is thinking of importing cash registers from Holland through my container company. He would be most grateful if you could give us a quick tour of the available facilities, with special emphasis on the ways you have met the problems of Customs clearance and other handling formalities which can so often cause delay to the foreign businessman. You're very kind. After you.'

Howard had hissed at him: 'Jim, what are you doing?'

'I'm thinking of bringing a lot of dope direct from Amsterdam. Lot of contacts there now, you know.'

'What's the point? It's going to cost you £80 a lb there and you'll only get £100 a lb here. The price differential simply isn't worth the effort.'

'Ah well, perhaps you've got a point there, Howard. Let's say no more about it.'

Howard drew another sheet of paper towards him. He wrote on it:

OPTION (3) Appear to co-operate.

He underlined the word 'Appear', and then he took out his cigarette lighter, and carefully burned all three sheets of paper in the ashtray, crumpling up the bits of ash.

McMillan reappeared, fleshy, friendly once again.

'I'd like you to meet another of my superiors. Tomorrow.'

'Look, Mac, I can't very well talk to this guy without disclosing that I've had connections with cannabis dealers, that I might even have bought and sold cannabis myself in the past in small quantities. You can't expect me to do that.' McMillan did not hesitate.

'My superiors do not give a damn about that. It is not their responsibility. There will be no embarrassment to you. They will not question you about any illegal things you may have done in the past. And don't start telling me about it now. Let's leave it all until you meet my superiors. I'm acting under precise instructions about this matter. I'd like you to meet me at 12.30 tomorrow lunchtime. Do you know a pub called The Pillars of Hercules in Soho? It's in Greek Street.'

The next day, Mac was waiting at the bar. He took Howard through into the back of the pub.

'This is Donald.' 'Donald' had slicked black hair, thick black glasses and a scowl. For all Howard knew, when he went home at night, he had blonde hair, perfect vision, and a broad grin. Howard started off hesitantly enough:

'I have this dress business, and, well, one of the partners, not a partner exactly, just someone who works in the business – I think he might be involved in cannabis smuggling, although I couldn't say for certain. . . .'

'Yes we know you people have certain kinds of business into which we do not need to further inquire at this point. Please go on.'

'He was rather busy this partner, this man who works with me, and he asked me to help him out. As he was so occupied, he said, would I go to Amsterdam and meet this man called O'Neill, and give him a message. So I went out there, and I did this, I met him at the American Hotel. We became quite friendly in fact, and have seen each other since, from time to time. On a social basis. O'Neill was offering a facility . . . a smuggling facility for my friend. He was saying they could use a system that O'Neill had organised, a system for running weapons into Ireland. The idea was that they should use some kind of shipping arrangement, from Rotterdam. It was going into a port in Southern Ireland, called Greenore. That's it really, that's what I know.'

'What does he look like, this O'Neill?'

'Oh, 5 ft 10, rather pointed nose, quite thickset, got a strong Belfast accent.'

'What has he told you about his past?'

'He did once tell me he'd done time in prison. I had the impression that was in England, but I'm not really sure, or what it was for. I don't know how long he served in prison or anything.'

'I see. When, then, was the last time you saw him? Do you know where he is now?'

Howard knew very well where McCann was. He was on his holidays. He had taken Anne McNulty and a suitcase of cash to Kenya.

'I have certain interests in Africa,' he had said enigmatically, but it was to be presumed he was touring the safari parks in best rich White Hunter style. Then, later in July, he had decided to drop in on Ibiza, subject of so much languid talk among his colleagues.

'Might see you there, Howard,' he said. 'Where all the action is.'

Howard calculated frantically when he had last flown over to Amsterdam to hand over that cash from the second Moone run. He did not want to get it wrong, when it was obvious they had been under surveillance for some time.

'About three weeks ago. In Amsterdam – I don't know whether he's still there.'

'And when are you envisaging that you might see him next?'

'Well, hard to say. He has my various phone numbers and I'm expecting to hear from him at some point in the near future.'

'Good. Give McMillan here a call when he does surface again. It would be nice if we could organise something. We would very much like to lay hands on Mr O'Neill, and that means doing so either in England itself or in Ireland. It will be a great help to have some idea of his movements. Thank you for this meeting. And goodbye to you.'

As 'Donald' left, still black-haired and scowling, Howard exhaled as quietly as he could. But Mac was euphoric.

'That's very pleasing, Howard. You appear to have passed all your tests in flying colours. Things are going to get really interesting now . . .' He bought them both more pints of best bitter. 'Anything else we can do do help you, Howard? Valuable fellow, you are, popular if you can give us assistance.' Howard passed in a minute from nervousness to a gambler's euphoria. He had carried it off. These boys were like the Customs men and the police. Spot of fast talking, and they were watching your dust.

'Yeah, you know Graham, Graham Plinston, who we had dinner with. Can you find out for him what you found out for me – whether the police have a file on him?'

'I can look into that question for you, certainly. Anything else?'

'Well, yeah, this is sort of a personal thing, nothing to do with your office, but I make quite a lot of bread in my dress shop and things. I'd like somewhere to deposit it, it's some that's generated abroad, you know, never comes into this country. Your family are bankers and experts at this kind of money business – can you find out for me how I go about getting a Swiss bank account?'

'Well, funnily enough and as it happens, I'm just on the point of having a meeting with a banking friend of my father's: about MI6 business in fact. I'll see whether I can arrange to introduce you to him. I'm sure he'd know how to help. This police file business – happy to help with as many other of your friends as you like, you know. Just give me all their full names.' Howard looked at him darkly. McMillan burst out laughing.

If Howard thought he had steered successfully through these treacherous channels, he turned out very quickly to be wrong.

'Come round to dinner in Putney,' Mac said a week later. While Carolyn, who was also now apparently a civil servant of some kind, worked on the sweetbreads, they went for a stroll around the Common.

'Now', said Mac, 'Graham Plinston. Whatever you do, keep away from him. He's bad news, really bad news.'

'What do you mean, Mac?'

'Frankly, I hadn't realised he was as heavily involved in drug-smuggling as apparently he is. Major drug-smuggling. The police have a massive file on him. He is a very senior figure in the world of drug-dealing, and I don't just mean in Britain. He's actually served a prison sentence in Germany.'

'I don't quite know how to react to this, Mac.'

'I rather had the impression you were a bit of a dilettante in that drug world, but he is a very dangerous character. And dangerous to you, Howard, as someone who is helping us.'

'Oh that's a shame. I mean I thought he was rather a good bloke.'

'Well that's as may be. But you do have to make a choice.' He pulled out a photograph from his side pocket. It was obviously a recent shot, and equally obviously taken from a window with a telephoto lens. He handed it to Howard. The picture had a line of italic typescript at the bottom. It said 'James McCann'.

'Oh-oh', thought Howard, 'They did know it was Jim all the time.'

'Is this the man you were with?'

'Er, yes it is.' Howard had wavered across the line, and was definitely an informer. He had confirmed to these people that the Amsterdam Irishman was indeed the fugitive McCann. Howard frowned, and decided it probably did not matter. It was obvious they knew already. That's why the photograph was labelled up.

'Has he been in touch with you again yet?'

'No, not actually yet, no. But I expect he will.'

'OK. Let's eat. But do remember what I said.' They sat down to eat. Howard toiled through the sweetbreads, and was too pre-occupied even to try and charm Mac's wife. He did not feel much like a playboy. But he noticed something. Just before they sat down, Mac excused himself and slipped into his study. When he came back, he had his hand in the same pocket from which he had earlier taken the photograph of McCann. His nerves as taut as guitar strings, Howard felt an intuitive rush. Mac's hand was making an unconscious gesture. It was talking to him.

Mac had gone to put the picture of McCann in some hiding-place in his study, having taken it out for the confrontation.

Howard knew this was true. His mind raced. He was being forced into a corner. They were making him into a spook. He had thought he was using them, but they were using him in the end. He daren't tell either Graham or McCann himself what was going on, because they would suspect he was a genuine MI6 informer. He had no way of proving to them the prior depth of MI6 knowledge. And already, he had done something which he would not dare tell Plinston – let drop to MI6 that they were close, even partners. He had aroused the interest of Mac's 'office'. And God knows what fantasies about guns and terrorists and Provisionals they would dream up as a consequence. 'I wanted to be a spook', he thought. 'But I didn't want to be a spook against my friends, against people I like.' His imagination moved rapidly: he saw that he was beginning to slide, into a position where he would do things which afterwards he would bitterly regret. Howard saw with sudden clarity, how secret agents were hooked by the British, the Russians, the Americans – everybody, he supposed. You were drawn in, ever so lightly, into a lobster-pot. Or rather, you swam in of your own free will at first, thinking you were going to get some tasty morsel for yourself. You did things to get it; then they reminded you, gently, that the very fact of dealing with them made you suspect in the eyes of your friends. The only way to keep afloat would be to help them some more. And that made it even harder to withdraw. Eventually, you were thoroughly trapped, a puppet on other people's wires. It felt like blackmail, but really you had only yourself to blame.

'Yes thank you,' he said. 'I will have some more pudding. It's really very nice.'

He thought about the picture of McCann. It was proof that MI6, or at least the Dutch police, already had McCann under surveillance. If he could somehow get it, get the picture, he could show it to Graham. It would be proof of his bona fides, prove that he had done something against THEM. The ground was slipping under his feet: he had to get back to his friends.

'Excuse me, Mac. Would you mind very much if I used the phone? Thanks. It's in the study is it?' He stared around, a little madly. There was a desk, drawers, nothing on the desk-top. Three rows of books above it on shelves. IT WAS IN THE BOOKS. This was insane: but there was nothing to lose. He stared passionately at the books. There was one there called *The Unconscious Mind*. It had a pink paper cover. It seemed to be a fraction out of place. He reached up, grabbed it, rifled through the pages. There was the photograph. He slipped it into his pocket. Was this a dream? It was lunatic. Was his predicament giving him extra-sensory powers? Superman, half-closing his X-ray eyes, flung back his cape and returned to the dining-room. Mac and Carolyn began to discuss the Cod War between British fishing trawlers and Iceland. Then they talked about the old days in Oxford.

'Do you ever see George? Laurie? Old whatsit?' Superman could take it no longer: 'I'm sorry, thank you for a very nice dinner, I've had a few late nights, I really must be going now, really nice to see you again Carolyn.' He flung himself into a taxi and ordered it across London to Plinston's Maida Vale flat.

Graham Plinston exhaled smoke from his lungs and passed the joint to Howard.

'Yes, this is interesting', he said smoothly. 'I feel this connection will do us nothing but good. Such a find, to get MI6 on our side.' He tapped the little photograph Howard had given him: 'What if we were to co-operate with them, just as they want, and tell them all about Jim. Well, not all about him, but certainly about the bits that don't concern us. All this madness in Amsterdam. Tara Engineering and so forth. His addresses, the Belfast contact and so on.' Well, thought Howard silently, one reason is because you don't know they've got a lot on you too, mate.

Aloud he said, 'I don't really agree with that. I like Jim.'

'But you're the one who's always saying what a pain in the ass Jim is. Look at the way he tries to rip us off all the time, and rings up in the middle of the night with all this crazy stuff. I'd sacrifice Jim for the political health of our future business.'

'Yeah, but it's not just a question of slipping them info. I don't want to put Jim in nick. Jesus, you don't know what they do. This Irish business is very heavy. I don't want to get Jim killed, for God's sake.'

'Hmm. Well, that's probably right. I think it would probably be most prudent if we didn't say anything to Jim, though. It might upset him. Let's just string along your friends in MI6 for a bit.'

'Well, I'm not too sure how I can do that. This thing's putting me under strain, Graham. It's no fun at all – and heat from the police everywhere.'

'It'll all come out fine. We'll both end up with a pile of gold bars in a Swiss bank, don't you worry. Now, how are all our various irons in their fires? Blazing away?'

Howard tried to crisply review their trading position. The Shannon scam from Moone had been successfully concluded. All the money had come in from the wholesalers, and from Ernie in California. Howard had personally flown to Amsterdam and paid off McCann.

The Great Mediterranean Fiasco in which they had invested £100,000, of real money, was a different story. It was almost impossible to make contact with Doctor John in the Italian villa. The Italian phones were never working properly. He was having a long, but nerve-wracking free holiday. Sailor Jo, after an inexplicable and worrying delay, had finally turned up in Beirut to load the hash with Larry. His only explanation over a roaring phone-line, had been 'Ran out of fuel'. He was due to put to sea any moment.

The prospect of a third deal had come up in northern Italy. The Dutch dealer, Arend ter Horst, who had come over to London as promised, had a round of meetings with Charlie Ratcliffe and the other boys, and was a good contact. He knew a man in Genoa, who could get stuff out of the docks. Howard had flown over to Amsterdam yet again, for a 'summit' conference with Arend and Fred, who got Lebanese supplies, to see if this second shipment into Europe could be organised.

'There's another piece of bad news, though,' said Graham. 'Lebanese Sam and Ernie Coombes have played a bad trick on us. Sam has sent a huge tractor crated up back to the US – labelled it returned for repair or something. He's sent the thing direct to Los Angeles, to Ernie. They've cut out *everyone*.'

'That's bad, Graham. You and Ernie are supposed to be partners.'

'Yeah, the bastard. You can't trust anyone these days. And my girl's cleared off, you know. She's running around in Ibiza with this Californian dealer called Skip. I don't really care. She's so spaced out these days, there's no dealing with her.'

'I haven't heard from Rosie since she went back there either. She's probably running round with all kinds of guys. I wouldn't blame her. I mean, I see chicks in London. We're definitely falling a bit apart. All this dealing's got on top of her. She really likes the peaceful life in Ibiza.'

'Well, well, Howie, why don't we both jump on a plane tomorrow and go out there too. Right now. Jim McCann's going over next month. There's crowds of people, a good scene. Everything's bad vibes in London. That Lebanese stuff on the boat won't arrive for a few days.' And so, preoccupied and fretful, London's two biggest dope-smugglers bought their sun oil and mirror shades, and headed south for their summer holidays.

# CHAPTER 6

# The Bust

Ibiza was seething, although Howard's summer there was not to last long. Nothing was lasting long for him these days. Plinston's girl was taking a lot of speed and sleeping pills. Sometimes she would hang out with Skip from California. They went off together to a hotel in Palma, Majorca. And sometimes she would just hang out in Ibiza town, talking wildly to whoever she met. Richard Lewis, Rosie's straight ex-husband, was due to come out when his lecturing term ended and was growing a beard for the purpose. Lady Beatrice Lambton, one of the disgraced Air Minister's five daughters, could be seen around town, although she was not a drug-smuggler, of course. So could 'Cherokee George' from London's East End. Arend ter Horst was back in his villa, flamboyantly snorting coke and drinking whiskey. McCann and his girl were expected daily. Patrick Lane's 19-year-old sister Judy was going to turn up with Lewis in his BMW. Howard was rather partial to her. Her former boyfriend Fred from Sussex University, the man who bought Howard's hash consignments in Beirut, also arrived. So did a big Dutch dealer called Hugo and a crowd of dealers in the inferior green Moroccan dope which was purchased by those who knew no better. Sardines and marijuana, prawns and cocaine. Rosie Brindley was living as calmly as she could with the children out at Santa Eulalia, away at least from the madness and dangers of Howard's smuggling activities in London.

'Hello', she said. 'It's nice to see you. I'm glad you've come out.'

'Yes,' he said. 'Let's be nice and peaceful together. Graham and Jim Morris and me will have a bit of a summit conference out here. But not until next month.' A week later, the vortex Howard always brought with him began to swirl. A telegram arrived at Santa Eulalia on 20 June. 'PHONE LONDON. STEW.'

'What's this, Howard?'

'I don't know. It's the Mediterranean business. Sailor Jo's shipload is supposed to be at sea. But it's been a fortnight without word. That's far too long for the sea trip to last. I've been trying not to think about it.' He found a phone at the Post Office in Ibiza town and called Mike Clark's London flat.

'There's an urgent message for me?'

'Yeah. You've got to go to Athens. There's a hotel. They'll be in the lobby every evening.'

'Athens? That's in Greece, for God's sake. What's the matter?'

'I dunno. Some kind of problem.'

He drove back to the villa with a low feeling.

'Rosie, would you like to visit Greece?'

'When?'

'Er, now.'

'Oh, Howard!'

They caught the evening Iberia domestic flight to Barcelona. It was a long haul. Howard checked them into a hotel and called the airport.

'I wish to travel to Athens as soon as possible. When is the first flight?'

'Tomorrow, Señor, there are no direct flights. But if you travel to Rome, maybe you can get a connection through to Athens.'

'Yes please, make me two reservations.'

'Señor, there are only first class seats available, I'm afraid.'

'First class is what I want.'

It took them the whole of the next day. They did not arrive at the expensive hotel in Athens until 6 p.m. There were Larry and Sailor Jo together, looking sheepish.

'What in the name of Christ are you two doing here? Where's the boat? Where's the hash? You're supposed to be in Italy!'

'Yes, calm yourself, Howard. It was the goats, you see. It's absolutely weird the whole thing. The one thing we didn't bargain for was the goats; it was all planned out very well actually. . . .'

'What goats? No, never mind what goats. Where. Is. The. Hash?'

'We had it all loaded on the boat, right, at Beirut? Everything went very well. It's a nice little boat, sails and that with an auxiliary engine. So we put out from Lebanon, Sailor Jo and me together. We're going to dock at Crete, clear Greek Customs there, collect some fuel and stuff, it's all organised – the only landfall before northern Italy. We've got this little Greek island sussed – it's completely uninhabited. Bob knows his Greek islands, don't you Bob?'

'Yes I think I know my Greek islands. Yeah, sure.'

'So we're going to unload the stuff on this uninhabited island, hide it, put into Crete for the formalities and come back to pick it up. Well, everything goes well: we find the island and we dump the stuff, hide it under some rocks, and off we go. But it turns out that, well we did think the island was completely uninhabited, but it turned out it did actually have a population.'

'Of wild goats.'

'It appears that the goats must have dislodged some of the rocks. Yeah, and there was one other thing. The island had a fresh-water stream. They're quite rare, you know, among Greek islands.'

'Yeah, you'd be surprised at the shortage of water on your Greek islands. It's quite a striking thing to find one. Of course we didn't know it was actually there, although I do claim to know my Greek islands. . . .'

'The thing was, it turned out, that the island was quite well-known to the local sponge fishermen as something of a water-source. They would put in from time to time.'

'Well, that's what we discovered later, because afterwards we asked around and lots of people said "Oh yeah, it's quite well-known as a fresh-water source".'

'Anyway, to cut a long story short, we're just coming over the horizon back from Crete, and what do we see but a crowd of sponge fishermen loading up our hash and sailing away with it.'

'Yeah, maybe they took it back to Crete to sell it. But anyway, they've got it. That's the problem really.' Larry and the Sailor Jo fell silent. Howard stared from one to the other, open-mouthed and thunderstruck. 'You mean it? That's what actually happened? You mean it's gone? I don't believe it.'

Eventually, he came to believe it. He and Plinston, the investors, had lost £100,000. Just like that. He called Patrick Lane in London – the man with the reputation for trouble-shooting.

'Do not worry. I'll fly to Crete and sort it out. Can't have these lads taking our stuff.'

'Yeah, great, Patrick.'

He knew that Lane really would go. But this was harder than collecting a suitcase from outside Hammersmith police station. He knew that Lane would achieve nothing, except to ensure that the whole of Crete learned he was representing some people whose load of dope had been ripped off. It would probably just draw heat. But he had to try.

'Well, it's no good glowering at us like that, Howard. It was a perfectly sound plan. It would have worked very well if it hadn't have been for the goats.'

'Uh-huh; listen Sailor Jo, I'll have to think about this one. In the meantime, would you please go to Beirut and pick up a suitcase of hash from the same place you got it last time. The stuff's available. And fly it into Genoa, like you did last time – can you remember last time you did something that worked? Dump it somewhere, and let me know. OK? I'm going to bed. Do you have any hash actually in your possession? I need a smoke. Oh shit, well I don't travel with it either. But I can't sleep unless I'm blasted. Can you get sleeping pills here? Good.'

With a handful of Dormadinas bought over a late-night pharmacy counter, and Rosie moodily lying beside him, Howard lit a cigarette and stared at the ceiling. The sleeping pills hit him. Forty-five minutes later, Rosie shook him awake. He had set the hotel bed on fire.

It was the end of a bad day.

Plinston was withering when they completed the long trail back across the Mediterranean to Ibiza the next day. He hated to see money thrown away, especially his own. His small frame quivering with rage; he reminded Howard that the whole Great Mediterranean Fiasco had been his idea in the first place.

'I never heard such a display of incompetence. And Jim McCann arrived yesterday, while you were careering around Greece. He's absolutely furious too, that you couldn't be bothered to be here to meet him.'

With Plinston in this sort of hostile mood, Howard wondered whether he might not rat on Howard to McCann about the MI6 business. Best perhaps to get in first. McCann, had arrived with a Dutch girl, Sylvia, who was obviously becoming the new woman in his life. Anne McNulty looked as if she was on the way out.

'Where the fuck have you been, Howard?'

'Sorry, Jim: listen, let's dump the chicks and go for a cruise round the bars. Bit of Spanish high-life.' They settled in a dim tourist cellar with fishing nets and wine casks, and fell to drinking. McCann rambled impressively on about how easy he found it in life to bribe and bend people.

'Remember this, Howard', he said thickly: 'Number One rule. Everyone is corruptible.'

'Oh come on, Jim, not absolutely everyone.'

'Everyone.'

'Yeah, all right, look you see that bloke over there on his own, you can tell he's English. Go on, corrupt him. Corrupt that man.' McCann pulled himself to his feet and moved across the bar. Howard watched him strike up some kind of talk, drinks being bought, a low murmur of voices, a steady tête-a-tête develop. It lasted for a good half-hour. Then he came back towing the Englishman behind him.

'This is Harry from Keighley: he's in business in the north of England. We've just arranged that Harry's to do a bit of driving for us, strictly on the side, help us with a spot of the, uh, contraband. That's right, isn't it, Harry?' Harry nodded and beamed.

'Um', said Howard. 'Well, we'll be back in touch later. Come on Jim.'

In the next bar, the conversation turned to the Provisionals.

'You know', said Howard. 'I thought when they seized that arms ship coming from Libya, the *Claudia*, that British Intelligence must have been behind it.'

'That's right, no mistake. Them MI6 boys are everywhere these days.'

'These MI6 men must be all very upper-crust, Oxbridge types.'

'Yeah – do you remember that time when you and Graham came out to Ballinskelligs?'

'Uh-huh.'

'I thought to myself, these Oxford characters, they're not the same as Marcuson and all them normal hippies. I wonder if they're MI6 men?'

'You really thought that?'

'Oh yeah. Lot of paranoia in my mind, of course, them days.'

'Well, they certainly do have MI6 people in Oxford. Matter of fact I even know one of them.'

'You do?'

'In fact, he's even asked me about you.' McCann was, for once, stopped in his tracks. He listened silently. Howard explained they had been seen together in Amsterdam, and that MI6 had asked him to set a trap for McCann. He stared at Howard, thunderstruck.

'I won't do it, though, I'm not helping them trap you.'

'No, no Howard, don't let them do that. Come and stay out here with me. We'll be safe out here, we will.' He seemed quite frightened.

'Don't get me wrong, Jim. I'm not bargaining for your life or your freedom. I don't want anything to do with those bastards. I'm just stringing them along.'

McCann looked at him rather strangely. It was one thing to set up a 'front' as a Provo arms-buyer; it was definitely another to be genuinely persecuted by British Intelligence.

But they were never to have the chance to discuss it calmly again.

'Look,' said Rosie. 'All this hysteria has followed you out here, quarrels and flying around half Europe, and everybody sleeping with everybody else. Now, take me and the kids home. Or you'll be sorry.' So much for Howard's holiday in the sun.

'Yes,' said Plinston. 'Why don't you clear off home? Maybe you could move a bit of dope for a change. Jim and I will just try and recuperate here and make the best of things.'

Howard plodded around London, working. He went to see a Pakistani called Shazan.

They agreed a price for 1000 lb of hash Shazan claimed he could shortly supply in Hamburg. And Ernie himself offered another 700 lb of top-grade Afghani hash coming immediately into Europe. If Howard and Graham knew of anywhere handy where it could be de-stashed and fitted into some more of Morris's speakers . . .?

'Yeah,' said Howard, brightening considerably. 'As a matter of fact I have a villa in Italy all fronted up with a worker in place. It's called Cupra Marittima.'

When the plane landed in Rome, Howard and Jim Morris drove a long way through central Italy to the coast at Ancona, and turned south. In the villa by the Adriatic, a large crowd of people were milling about, and the courtyard was full of vehicles.

'Hi, Dr John, what's new?'

'These are your blokes, with the Avis truck, aren't they? Ray, Vic. And this is my wife and kids – been enjoying the sun with me. This is Dave and Lorraine from California. Theirs is the grey Belgian camper out in the courtyard.'

'Hi Dave, hi Lorraine. Had a good journey?'

'Boy, it's some trip all the way from Kabul in one of these. The stuff is in the panels and under the seats and the floor. There's a bit of welding been done around the wheel arches too, some little compartments. But it's OK – you can get access to them now by way of the headlights.'

'Amazing. Who's that little dark guy with the beard?'

'He's one of Ernie's workers. Lives out on the Lake Tahoe shore on the West Coast. Quite a guy. He was in the Air Force and they wanted to send him to Vietnam. He refused to go and then busted out of a military jail, in the Sixties. Great days. Jim, c'mere, meet the visitors.'

'Hi, people. Like old times uh? I once did one of these overland runs for Ernie, you know. I drove a Chevrolet truck all the way out to Peshawar from the West Coast. It was a mother of a drive.'

'Yeah, I heard about that once. Ernie's girl told me. What brings you across now?'

'I've got a car outside with 100 lb in the doors. Just driven it down here from Vienna, Austria. It was left over from the last shipment. Ernie thought maybe there might be room to fling it in with this consignment.'

'Tremendous man. Ray and Vic can truck it all up to Rome Airport when they're ready: the paperwork's all done. Where's it going this time, Jim?'

'Pan-Am. Direct to San Francisco.'

'Great. Now Jim Morris and me have a little appointment in Zurich.'

Howard had brought about 15,000 dollars out in his suitcase. There was a lot of other cash scattered around, despite his losses on the Great Mediterranean Fiasco – a bank safe deposit in Oxford; another one in Brighton; a steel safe at Annabelinda, and plenty of money still due from the US. There was also £10,000 in notes secreted in the cottage at Yarnton. Maybe £100,000 of loose money in total.

Howard had never been to such a hygienic, expensive town as Zurich before: 'Hey,' he said to Morris after their night's sleep in the Europa Hotel. 'You can tilt the bed up and down electrically.'

'Yeah, it's got all these little gadgets. It'll vibrate for you as well. Now, my sister arrived before you got up with the name of a man we're to see at the Swiss Bank Corporation in Bahnhofstrasse – they do everything in four languages, German, Italian, French and English, so there's no communication problem. This is the score. Evading British taxes is not against Swiss law, although hiding the proceeds of other crimes is. The Swiss will disclose, if they're put under a lot of pressure, details of bank accounts. But only if it's proved they are the profits of real crimes other than tax-dodging. They're all numbered accounts, in the sense that only the number is used in inter-bank transactions to protect their clients' anonymity. They're very hot on bank secrecy. If you deposit money on handcuffs – for a set term – they'll charge whacking penalty interest rates for taking it out early. But you can have money on immediate withdrawal: they'll give you 4 or 5 per cent interest, except that the Swiss government takes a cut. They deduct 30 per cent Withholding Tax from the interest, on the spot. So you're only getting around 3 per cent. But it's denominated in Swiss francs, which are nice and hard. So you probably stay ahead. Now, I'm going to go in there and tell the guy that I'm in the pop business, and there's lots of undeclared cash flying around from my international pop concerts. You can be an associate of mine. I'll say we want to bank cash dollars, in two separate accounts, and that we do not wish them to forward any mail that comes in to our addresses in England. Right?'

'Sounds great.'

An hour later, Howard walked out of the Schweizerischer Bankverein with a piece of paper. As from 24 August, Mr D. Howard Marks of 6 Gloucester Street, Oxford GB, was the possessor of 25,000 Swiss francs in Investment Savings Account number 326,324 of the Swiss Bank Corporation, Cable Address 'Suisbanque, Zurich'.

'This is wonderfully corrupt,' he said to Morris as they headed for the airport.

'Yeah, Switzerland is a tremendous place if you like money. See you in London in a week or so: I'm going to fly through to Los Angeles and make sure the stuff gets through the other end. Bye.'

Hamburg. Rome. Now what about that Genoa business? Got to make the bread back somehow before Plinston and McCann come back from Ibiza. He called ter Horst in Amsterdam.

'No Howard, I'm not going to bother with that Genoa business any more. I do not need any more supply here just now. Do you know, the most enormous shipment of Leb has just come in, I will not say from where. Twelve tons. Ja, that is right. It is all we can do to find buyers.'

'Might be able to help you there, Arend.'

And so, the whole troupe careered over to Amsterdam to do it all again. They'd done it in Paris, Vienna, Dublin and Rome. At this rate they would cover every capital city in Europe except Moscow. Except that, they were, in fact, about to make a very big mistake.

Howard called Mac the Spy from the Okura – Amsterdam's big, high-rise Japanese hotel. It seemed a good moment to keep him warm.

'Hi, Mac. How ya doing?'

'Fine, fine and you?'

'Well, I just thought I should let you know. I'm in Amsterdam and I'm probably about to make contact with our friend. The new branch idea is going well too.'

'Um. Let me call you right back. What's your number?'

'I'm at the Okura.' Something in Mac's tone was not warm. And he did not call back. Howard placed the call again, the Okura switchboard clerk dutifully recording the number: 928 5600.

'Oh Howard, I was about to get back to you.'

'Well, I think perhaps we ought to meet. I'm in London tomorrow for the weekend.'

'OK. You know that place where our friend Bob Yeats from Oxford works – the blues freak.'

'Yeah.' He meant Dillon's bookshop, just by the University of London campus off the Tottenham Court Road. 'Meet you there. 4.30 p.m.'

The meeting was still slightly chilly.

'Howard, I have passed on the information that you are about to see McCann.' He paused. 'There is a feeling in the office about the recent Littlejohn embarrassment. As you know, although the extradition hearings were largely held in camera, he *was* sent back to Dublin for trial, and it was in the end necessary to admit that he had held various meetings with ministers of the crown and members of the office. This did not, frankly, do any of us a lot of good. It is very important that no one has any idea of how we work. And it is equally important that the general public do not get the idea we are employing criminal elements to do goodness knows what.'

'That was all months ago, Mac.'

'Um, yes, I know. But it has now been decided as policy not to proceed with anyone like yourself who may be involved with criminals and crime.'

'I'm not like the Littlejohns. I'm not a robber.'

'No, but you might just get into hot water and use us as an excuse.'

For the first time, Mac's solemnity cracked into a smile:

'So our advice to you is this. Keep away from Jim McCann. He's a dangerous man to know.'

'You mean, I'm not being used any more? Are you saying that if I acquire any information, I'm not to contact you?'

Mac burst out laughing again: 'No, of course not! And don't talk about the office.' Thus, Howard Marks's career as an MI6 agent was snuffed out. The shame of it was, although Howard did not realise it at the time, that he was just about to become very badly in need of friends.

He went to America. Jim Morris invited him over to the West Coast to celebrate the arrival of the Amsterdam consignment. California! San Francisco! To be there, where the 'Grateful Dead' had their beginnings as a band, where Haight-Ashbury was a real street-corner, where dope and sun and every kind of craziness ran amok. Where the houses were in canyons and the mushrooms were magic. It was terrific. Howard came down dazed from the sky into the hysterical bustle and sub-tropical heat of Los Angeles International Airport: even for a plane-hopper like him, 10 hours was a long trip.

He had a couple of chores to do on the way back. Plinston had returned from Ibiza the warmest of friends with McCann and was full of tremendous new joint dope schemes. He wanted Howard to go to Canada. There was a suitcase full of cash to collect from the Montreal gangster there. Durrani himself was to be contacted in New York – his girl, to whom he was devoted, had smashed her spine in a Californian car crash running dope for Ernie. She was paralysed and Durrani was picking up the New York hospital bills. But other than that – it was California and pure freedom. Jim Morris, 'Captain Flash', collected him in his Mustang and drove him to the chic film-stars' enclave of Newport Beach.

'My pad.'

'Lovely, terrific . . . Hey, when you pick up the phone, you punch the buttons and they say "Operator" just like that.'

'Yeah, the phone system's fast. That's the very first thing you notice about America, huh?'

Ernie arrived: Ernie Coombes himself, the transatlantic connoisseur. He was about Howard's age, skeletally thin in his jeans and T-shirt, with round wire-framed glasses and trailing blonde hair. 'Hi Howard,' he said in a high pitched voice. 'Good to meet you after all this time. Let me give you a ride to the Newporter Inn. We've booked you in. It's a pretty classy hotel. Hey, what do you like to do? We'll fix it up for you. You like riding? Biking? Surfing?'

'Well actually, what I like is watching TV, getting stoned, and listening to all those old rock stations on the radio.'

'Fine, fine. Run down to the LA warehouse on the waterfront tomorrow with Jim, and we'll get some floor-space cleared for the Amsterdam load. I'm going to go over to Vegas and ride shotgun.'

The next day, Howard luxuriously switched on the remote control TV and lay back on the hotel bed. A newscaster swam on the screen in poor colour:

'Hey one of you guys out there,' he said: 'You've just lost five million dollars.' Howard drew peacefully on his cigarette. A picture of a set of large loud-speakers at Las Vegas airport came on to the screen. Howard sat up rather sharply.

Later, the history of the Big Bust became clearer. The consignment of dope, 838.2 lb as Jim Gater had weighed it in on a set of bathroom scales in Amsterdam, flew into John F. Kennedy Airport, New York. There it was transferred for a connecting flight to Las Vegas. But one of the big matt-black speaker cabinets got left behind. It was sitting alone in the Pan-Am freight shed when the Customs came through on a routine patrol with a sniffer dog – most feared of all anti-dope weaponry. It sniffed. A Customs officer unscrewed the back and drew out from inside the fibre-glass containers slab after slab of cloth-wrapped amber-gold dope. They found the rest of the consignment had flown to Las Vegas, reassembled the cabinet, and set Special Agent Harlan Lee Bowe of the DEA to watch the Las Vegas cargo shed. When Gary Lickert, Ernie's delivery man, drove it away in a truck, Harlan Lee Bowe followed. Ernie Coombes, riding shotgun, followed in turn. When Ernie pulled sharply in front of the truck, and dropped a piece of paper out of the window, Gary Lickert sighed heavily. He knew what he had to do. He drove round and round for three-quarters of an hour until the DEA men realised he was not going anywhere interesting. Then they arrested him. Harlan Lee Bowe was furious.

Lickert was the merest junior operative. Cheated of the main American importers, the authorities delved into the paperwork. It took them a very short time to realise that the ATA Carnet system provided a complete documentary record of seven fake runs into the United States from 'Transatlantic Sounds' of London, England. They handed the case over to British Customs. And Gary Lickert started to talk.

Meanwhile, the Los Angeles area was emptying of people. Howard ran on the first plane to New York, picked up Mike Durrani at the

Hilton Hotel, and they flew out of the US the next day to the Sheraton in Montreal. There they met Rene the Montreal gangster.

'Sniffer dogs,' he said disdainfully. 'We know how to deal with them here.' He pulled out of his side pocket a newspaper clipping. It described how the corpses of the three sniffer dogs at Montreal Airport had been discovered, each with a bullet through its head. 'One of my men took in a gun and he shot them. How else would I have got your hash in through here? And now gentlemen, I believe I have some cash for you – for you, Mike, and for you, Howard.' He gave Howard a wad of one hundred Canadian thousand-dollar bills. It fitted snugly into his inside jacket pocket.

'Thank you very much, Howard,' said Plinston later, pocketing his share. 'It's nice to see you bringing some good news for a change. Now. The show must go on. That suitcase of Leb from Sailor Jo has arrived in Genoa. And Shazan's Pak has come down in Hamburg as promised. Ideas please.'

'I'll send Robin over to Genoa to drive the Leb into London. There's no point trying to fly the Pak into the US under the circumstances. I'll send Little Pete out to Hamburg – tell him to take it off Shazan's hands, rent a big car and park it all somewhere for a bit. OK? Now I'm going back to Yarnton.'

'I can't stand it, Howard,' said Rosie. 'I really can't. You turn up here and as good as tell me you're going to be arrested any minute. I'm getting out of here with the kids and going back to Ibiza.' A message came through to Little Pete's phone:

'I'm just a friend of Marty's who happens to be staying in his house. Somebody rang up and said it was vital this message be got through to this number: I don't know what it means. 'Vickers and White have been busted.' Howard and Plinston knew exactly what it meant. Alan White had been personally paid cash by Howard to drive Transatlantic Sound trucks. Vic Vickers had his name on all the ATA Carnets.

Little Pete's phone rang again. It was Vickers himself! 'I'm a bit freaked out: can I meet you?' Plinston was jumpy and suspicious. The Customs had him in their hands, supposedly. They arranged a meeting at the top of Primrose Hill. Vickers never came to the London park as they watched from a safe distance. They persuaded themselves he had really escaped the Customs. He rang again. 'I couldn't make the rendezvous. Can we meet at the Wimpy bar in the Strand?' Again, he never came. Charlene Colon, Jim Morris's American secretary and phone answerer, rang in. She had just been arrested, and then released. 'Who else have they picked up?' 'They've got Vickers. They told me.' It had all been a trap. Customs men had certainly been watching, and photographing. Now they would be able to identify the 'Howard' that White and Vickers knew as a man who ran a clothes shop in Oxford.

'They're closing in,' said Plinston. 'I'm going underground. I'll drive around Ulster for a bit, make my way into Eire, and lie low with Jim McCann in Dublin.'

'Don't panic, Graham. What about all this dope that's coming in? The show must go on, eh?'

'Yeah, well you do it. Bye.' Howard flew from Oxford, and checked in at the Holiday Inn in Swiss Cottage, near Regent's Park in London. He consulted a solicitor as to his position. 'Well,' the solicitor said. 'I would go home, destroy all documentary evidence, and quietly go about my business. That advice will be £20, please.'

Howard drove back to Oxford, not daring to return to the cottage, stuck his head into Annabelinda and said to his latest manager there: 'Harry, I'm in dreadful trouble. Will you go down to Yarnton, clear everything out. Especially get rid of all bits of paper.' He did not find out until much later that Harry had broken out into a panic, and immediately run away. Not only did he destroy nothing – he even left the lights on and the electric fire burning.

Waves of panic now began to assail Howard himself. 'Marty, will you go and sit in the International Hotel for me? When Ray brings in this Leb from Genoa, keep it there, and I'll arrange for a buyer to come round. Got to leave town.' He packed several thousand pounds cash into the door panels of his car. He drove west, at 90 or 95 mph, into Wales, with McCann's Irish 'Peter Hughes' passport in his pocket, reached the Fishguard ferry and felt suddenly, blindly safe when he drove on to Irish soil. He sank seven or eight pints of Guinness in the first Irish bar, one after the other, straight down like they did in the old days in Kenfig Hill. He got back in the car, swung away towards Dublin, rolled himself a fat Afghani joint, and drove straight into a wall.

When he recovered consciousness, he was lying with a joint hanging from his lips, the money strewn about the wrecked car, listening to Irish voices. They were saying: 'Is it a doctor he wants, or a priest, do you think?' He staggered to his feet, reassured his rescuers, packed up the cash from the doors into his suitcase, and started walking towards the nearest lights. Wincing at the huge bruise on his back, he checked into a small hotel, and called McCann at the house he was renting near Drogheda.

'Ah you fucking wanker,' snarled McCann. 'Bringing all this heat over here. Yes I suppose I will come and get you, you Welsh cunt. Don't think I don't know what you did on the last Shannon trip. Graham's told me all about it. Ripping me off on me own soil, you Welsh cunt. And Graham thinks the same, I can tell you.' Howard was too defeated to argue at the injustice of this.

He did not know that McCann had brooded on the island of Ibiza over the machinations of British Intelligence. He read of the August fire bombs going off in Harrods, and at the London Stock Exchange. An idea formed in his whirling mind. He would pull out of Amsterdam. But he would fashion a parting shot against the Brits and one that would cement his credentials as a Provo activist for good.

McCann flew briefly back to Loosdrecht. He called 'Black Peter', Peter Elia, the swarthy barman at the Pink Elephant, whom he so much enjoyed introducing as an Arab sheikh. He spoke in a hoarse whisper, his voice rising a little and speeding up, as his gesticulating hands flew in the air. He fetched a large bundle of Dutch guilders out of the wall safe and pressed them into Black Peter's hands. Then he left for Ireland, never to return.

Elia packed a bag and drove south. In the small town of Bergen op Zoom, he called on a young, but bearded 19-year-old chemist with a distraught manner. His name was Willem van der Klooster, and he made a living from constructing massage equipment. Then Elia got back in the car, drove across the border into Belgium and parked at a succession of hardware stores. He bought: some batteries; three alarm clocks; a coil of electric leads; three large 'Camping Gaz' butane cylinders; seven pounds of sulphur; and some sodium chlorate weed-killer. On Friday night, 14 September, German police patrolling near the British Army on the Rhine headquarters at Munchen Gladbach found a 12 kilo bomb dumped by the roadside. In case there was to be a terrorist 'action', the following night the audience at the civilian cinema on the base were sent home early. Two bombs indeed went off that night – one outside a school workshop and one in the deserted car park nearby. They made enough of a bang to break some windows.

The Munchen Gladbach police announced, in a slightly puzzled fashion:

'We have to be very careful. The bombs contained 2-3 lb of explosive but we have not yet been able to determine the type used.' They turned over the case to the Federal Police, the BKA at Wiesbaden. McCann got his headlines in the Reuters international news agency telex. It said, 'German police suspect IRA after blasts.'

Howard never knew about any of this. At the time the bombs went off, he had been in America, running away from Los Angeles as fast as he could, in the general direction of Canada. And so, now, sitting in Ireland shamefacedly nursing his bruises, he made McCann and Plinston a crazy offer:

'I'll go back to Germany and get that Hamburg dope for you.'

'Good man, Howard,' said Plinston: 'Jim knows a guy in Hamburg who will buy it: Jim's a partner in this deal now.'

Dublin to Brussels. Brussels to Dusseldorf. The train north to Hamburg, on the Baltic. The last time he was there, he had been visiting the family of Mac the Spy. Innocent days. In an expensively furnished room high in the Atlantic Hotel, a dishevelled but determined Howard is now holding the phone. He is trying to do two major dope deals at once. He calls Marty in the London International:

'How are you doing?'

'It's all cool here. I've got a sample of the Genoa product here in my room, and the rest's in a car.' Howard fingers the false identity in his hip pocket he has been building up with: the Irish passport; the new Dublin bank account; the club memberships; the card from the Dublin answering service engaged by 'Mr Hughes'.

'Fine,' he said. 'I'll send somebody round – Charlie Weatherley – I know he'll take 30 cwt now he's back in London.' He calls another London number, talks rapidly into it: 'Half an hour? OK fine.'

He decided to complete the London deal before making any more Hamburg calls. He gave Charlie time to drive across London, try a sample in Marty's room, order 30 lb, wait for Marty to go out to the car and fetch it, collect his purchase in a suitcase, and leave. While these events were taking place, Howard decided to have a leisurely bath. In fact, while he soaked in the tub, something else happened in London.

Marty did the deal, and waved goodbye to the crumpled figure in the leather jacket as he padded off down the expensive hotel corridors, suitcase in his hand. Marty felt better. He opened the hotel fridge, and poured himself one of the miniature whiskies stacked inside to tempt guests. As he lifted the glass, there was a pounding on the door. Marty froze. He opened it. There stood Charlie with his suitcase, grasped firmly above the elbow by the middle-aged man in a tired suit.

'Sorry to disturb you, sir, but have you ever seen this man before?' Marty said rapidly and clearly: 'I've never seen this man in my life.' Charlie's face screwed up in anguish.

'Thank you very much sir. That's just what I suspected. I'm the hotel detective, and I caught this man leaving the guest floors with a suitcase. He claimed he had been here on business and had, in fact, just held a meeting with the occupant of this room. In view of what you say, it's obvious he is lying. We get a lot of theft in a hotel like this. I'll take him down to my office and see what's in this suitcase. Sorry again for this disturbance.' The crumpled Charlie was led away. As he and the detective turned the corner to the lifts, the gangling figure of Marty Langford could be seen fleeing down the corridor in the opposite direction toward the fire stairs. He had just said, it occurred to him, very much the wrong thing.

By the time Howard had used up in the complimentary shampoo provided by the management of the Atlantic Hotel in Hamburg, the house detective of the International Hotel in London had opened the suitcase and put two and two together.

Howard dialled the number of Marty's room in London. The phone rang once. Twice.

'Hi, is it all cool?'

'Hello.'

'Who's that? Where's Marty?'

'This is Marty. What do you want?' It was not Marty's voice. The dishevelled figure of Howard Marks, in its turn, could be seen fleeing down the corridor of the Hamburg Atlantic Hotel in the direction of the fire stairs.

At Hamburg Airport they were just boarding the Lufthansa flight to Paris. 'Peter Hughes' breathlessly paid cash at the ticket desk and with no baggage to load, was allowed to trot on board, briefcase in hand. At Orly Airport, the immigration officials gestured at him to open the briefcase, rummaged through it and inquiringly held up a British passport with a missing photograph, in the name of Marks.

'I found it in a hotel. I've been trying to hand it in somewhere for days. Everyone says "Oh, you've got to take it to the Foreign Office in London". Can I give it to you? No? OK thank you.' His heart was thumping and racing and his face felt flushed. At the telephone cabins, Marty's phone rang unanswered. At the Iberia ticket desk, they sold him a ticket to Barcelona and back to the island of Ibiza. Rosie was confronted by a hollow-eyed, travel-stained figure when the white Seat taxi finally bounced to a halt outside her primitive 'finca' at San Juan, a small port at the far end of the island. Howard was nearly at the end of the line. 'They're after me,' he said.

'Who?'

'Everyone. Everything's falling apart. I think I'm hallucinating. The walls are moving. Help.'

'I don't think you should smoke any more dope. You'd better go to bed.' For some days, Howard disappeared into a delirious and fevered haze, emerging only from his bed to crawl out into the fields and crap. The 'finca' did not have a lavatory. He muttered disjointedly to himself in worried tones.

Back in the Republic of Ireland, Plinston and McCann waited intolerantly for news of dope. Howard seemed to have disappeared off the face of the earth. Days passed. A bedraggled Marty Langford surfaced in Dublin, very much on the run. He had two more of the Marks organisation Welsh staff with him – Mike Clarke and Little Pete. They were all fugitives.

'Where the hell's Howard?'

'We don't know.'

'Where the hell's all the dope?'

'The police found the London car-load at the hotel. I checked in under my own name and wrote down the car number. I've never done a deal before. Howard told me it'd be all right. We don't know what's happened to the Hamburg stuff. Howard never contacted your dealer.'

'The stupid Welsh wanker. Maybe he's been busted. Can we try and get the Hamburg dope anyway? Jim?'

'I do have somebody in Holland. I didn't want to send him into Germany, and I don't really trust him. All your lot are on the run now, so who the fuck can we send?'

There was always someone, of course. The 20-year-old blonde former convent schoolgirl Anne McNulty was endlessly loyal to McCann. As she said, 'I loved him when I first saw him, and I knew that wasn't going to alter regardless of what was going to happen to the rest of my life.'

'Anne,' said McCann: 'Here is a plane ticket to Hamburg. Here is a set of keys and the log-book for a Mercedes parked underneath the Atlantic Hotel. You're booked into a double room there. When you arrive, " Black Peter" – remember him? – will come and find you. He is going to sell some stuff in there to a man who will come to the hotel.

The stuff weighs 234 lb: remember that. Stay with him until he has sold the stuff: don't forget that either. Bring the money back. You'd better take the "Anne Bannon" passport.' Anne McNulty left on October 8. Only two days later, McCann's Hamburg dope-dealer never having been quite what he seemed, she and Peter Elia were both in jail in Hamburg, minus the dope, and the German police were methodically leafing through Black Peter's address book.

Howard probably made a mistake at this point when he lifted his head from a pillow on the soothing island of Ibiza, and decided that he felt a little better.

He started to make a few phone calls, in an attempt to trace the state of play among the executives of the Howard Marks Intercontinental Dope Combine. Nobody at all was answering their lines. Little Pete's answering service was dead. A voice on the line at the home of Plinston's accountant, Patrick Lane, said, 'He's left the country. He's decided to retire permanently to an old mill he's bought in France in the Dordogne. He's going to grow snails. Yes, it *was* a sudden decision.' Finally Howard called McCann in Ireland.

'Jim, it's me.'

'You roaring Welsh shit-eater, where the fuck have you been?'

'There's been a lot of heat, Jim.'

'Yeah, don't we know it, you Welsh fucker. You've got my girl arrested, you cunt, in the hands of the Nazis, that's what, gone out there to Hamburg like a lamb to the slaughter, poor young creature, locked up in solitary confinement, fucked the whole thing up. Now then, get your Welsh arse over to Dublin right now, or face the consequences!'

'Jim, I have got one last idea. I know where we can get our hands on the last 60 kilos available in Europe.'

'Crap, crap, all you talk is crap, you useless Welsh crap-hound. Where?'

'Amsterdam. It's in store from the last big run we all did. We bought it, but it wouldn't go in the speakers. I'll go over there, find Tahoe Jim, and arrange to have it driven over to England and sold.'

'Yeah, well, get on with it you Welsh dope-head, me and Graham have had about enough of your half-arsed whining.'

'Listen, I'm a wanted man.'

'Ah crap, they've got nothing on you: we're all wanted men.'

Howard began to think this might be true, when he flew effortlessly into Amsterdam, was greeted warmly by Arend ter Horst, and was told by the saturnine Jim Gater that Ernie Coombes himself was on his way into Amsterdam in the next week.

'Naah, he's not worried about the heat,' Gater said. 'He's coming over for a Swiss skiing holiday. Let's all stay cool.' Back at the Okura Hotel, Howard organised Larry in London to set up a Cornish de-stashing operation for the Gater load. 'It's just a question of self-confidence,' he thought to himself. 'I've still got the nucleus of a working pipeline – Arend, Ernie, Larry, Jim. I think I'll just go back to England soon and bluff it out.'

He called Plinston and McCann, to brief the fugitives skulking in Ireland. 'All under control,' he told McCann,

'Let me tell you, I'm going to declare a personal fucking war on Germany if they don't let my girl out, and they know it. I'm going to blow up the fucking German embassy in Dublin. And another thing: did you know they've got this fucking German consul in the north, big businessman. He'll get his too if they don't let that little girl out.'

'Yeah, yeah,' said Howard, and went to have dinner with Ernie Coombes. He had just checked into the Okura under the name 'Colin Henderson'. Tahoe Jim Gater left on a KLM flight into London to complete arrangements for the joint shipment into London. Howard opened up a safe-deposit box in Amsterdam with 60,000 spare US investment dollars in it, some of which had been contributed by Ernie's organisation, some of which belonged to him. Ernie listened sympathetically to Howard's stories of Plinston's hostile attitudes: 'Yeah, he turned pretty nasty, over that tractor business. And it stinks the way he's treating his girl.' He scribbled her a note, for Howard to hand on with 1000 dollars' worth of Japanese yen – 'Just loose currency, Howie, got to empty my pockets.' The sealed note said: 'I saw Howard last night and had dinner with him in Amsterdam. He told me that Mr P. has financially deserted you and your kids. I am giving this letter and 1000 dollars to him to send to you. If you want to write me back, mail your letters to Howard and he will get them to me. However, don't write any name on the envelope because my popularity has gone down in certain circles, due to British Un-Intelligence (no offence intended). I hope your kids are doing all right and I hope the money helps. Love always, Dr Foster.'

Actually, British Un-Intelligence was doing rather well. Two British Customs men, senior investigating officer Mark Elliott and investigating officer Robin Eynon, had been pursuing the ATA Carnet conspiracy with grim zeal, travelling halfway round the world in their efforts to stamp out cannabis. They had collected the US evidence and statements, and they had pinned down from the confessions of the arrested small fry a description of a Welsh 'Howard Hicks'. It was only a tiny step from there to Annabelinda and Yarnton. They raided Yarnton, and found a mass of incriminating bits of paper in the deserted – and unsterilised – cottage. They ripped all the children's stuffed animals open in the hope of finding more evidence of the drug menace. They had built up a general picture of the most recent ATA Carnet run, via a rented house at Maarssen near Amsterdam and involving one 'Tahoe Jim' Gater, known to be travelling as 'Tyler'. On 14 November, when Howard waved goodbye to Tahoe Jim at Schiphol, Eynon and Elliot promptly picked him up at Heathrow and locked him in a room.

'I didn't want to go to Vietnam,' said Gater hopelessly. 'I have lived outside government rules. I have been honest to friends.' Then he told them all about Arend ter Horst and all seven ATA Carnet scams. It was 2 in the morning by the time the interrogation was completed. By the end of the following afternoon, a crowd of six Dutch policemen had been assembled to go and arrest Arend ter Horst at his Reguliergracht house. They were pleased and intrigued to see that a social call was taking place at the time, and that the caller in question was a tall, dark Welshman. Howard Marks too, was placed under arrest.

# CHAPTER 7

# Under the Law

Her Majesty's Customs won the first few rounds, hands down. Howard was dishevelled, exhausted and scared. He also discovered very quickly that the 'Aliens Detention Centre' in Amsterdam was not a nice place. The Dutch narcotics police found a small piece of hashish in his top pocket given to him by his old friend Lebanese Freddy in the Oxshoodt Club the previous night.

'Can I make a phone call?'

'No.'

'That piece of hash isn't mine.'

'It doesn't matter. We can arrest you for not having a residents' permit if we like.'

'Can I see the British consul?'

'Plenty of time for that tomorrow. Now, what do we have here? Address book, ja? Passport; credit cards; Dutch currency; English currency; Japanese Yen! Interesting. A statement from the Swiss Bank Corporation in Zurich: also interesting. A letter. Who is this from? Shall we see, perhaps? "Dr Foster", Hmm. And a set of keys. What perhaps doors and safes do they fit? Watch. Cigarettes.'

'Can I keep my cigarettes?'

'No.' Howard stared unhappily around his basement cell. It was covered from floor to ceiling in murky red stone tiles. A stool and table were bolted to the floor. In one corner there was a water fountain which dribbled continuously. In the other was a toilet bowl. It did not appear to have a handle by which it could be flushed. There was a light bulb set into the ceiling. It did not appear to have any switch on the cell wall. There was a bed let down from one wall locked in the 'down' position. It consisted of a single strip of cloth. There did not appear to be any blankets. It was dank with the early winter chill. There did not appear to be any heating either.

'Can I have my sweater from my suitcase? It's freezing.'

'No.' Howard sat on the bed, hugging himself with cold and nerves. He sat like that for most of the night. It was not possible to sleep. At dawn, the cell door opened and he was silently handed two pieces of thick dark bread, with bitter chocolate flakes between the slices, and a beaker. It was one third full of milk. Some hours went silently by, punctuated by tannoy announcements in Dutch. The door opened again and the guard handed him a piece of paper. 'If you want a lawyer, you tear off the bottom of the paper here and give it to me.'

Howard tore off the counterfoil.

'When do I see the lawyer?'

'As soon as possible.' More hours seemed to pass. The guard fetched him silently out of the cell and up a flight of stairs. 'Place your fingers on this pad. Here. Now stand here. You are to be photographed. Now turn to the right again, through 90 degrees. Ja.'

'When can I see a lawyer?'

'It is nothing to do with me.'

'Can I make a telephone call now?'

'No.'

Back in the silent cell, there was nothing to eat or drink. Once, a prisoner in the same block screamed out and started babbling. Then he too, fell silent. Howard felt his bowels loosen uncontrollably. He squatted on the toilet bowl for some time. There was no toilet paper. There was no paper of any kind. And the toilet could not be flushed. A little later, overwhelmed with fear, a sense of impotence and the stench, he began to retch over and over again. He banged on the door. 'Help me. I am ill.' There was no response. He banged again, again and again.

'What is the matter?'

'I am ill, I need help, I am vomiting.'

'Why, what is the matter, are you some kind of junkie?' Night had fallen for quite a long time when the cell door did open. He was taken upstairs again, and sat in a chair. Two Dutch Customs officers entered the room.

'We would like you to answer some questions.'

'I don't want to answer any questions until I have seen a lawyer.'

'This attitude of yours is unwise. You have only been charged with possession of 1.5 grams of hashish, which is not too serious. We merely

180

wish to establish what you have been doing here in Amsterdam, and then you will probably be released.'

'All right. I have a clothes business in England, in Oxford. It is called Annabelinda. I came here to Amsterdam because I am thinking of setting up a branch of the dress shop here. I have been forming a company and meeting people in the clothing business.'

'Yes, of course. But perhaps that is not the whole truth. We think you have been in Amsterdam before, and you have been dealing in cannabis. Why do you not give us some details about that?'

'I want to see a lawyer.'

'Take him back to the cell.' This time, the bed was locked against the wall for the rest of the night. There was nowhere to lie down. Cold, dirty, sleepless and hungry, Howard felt his morale plunge to a new low.

At dawn, they gave him again a piece of bread and chocolate, and a small beaker of milk. Several hours later, at 11 in the morning, they took their prisoner upstairs. By now, he was feeling like a worthless and forgotten scrap of human garbage: he had been 'sweated' to the point where his resistance to interrogation was limited. It gave Howard no pleasure, therefore to see two British Customs men standing cheerfully over him – the bespectacled Mark Elliott and the burly Robin Eynon.

'Hello, Howard,' said Elliott. 'You must be glad to hear an English accent. Have our Dutch colleagues been treating you well?'

Howard launched into a description of his sufferings: 'And I'm ill, I'm shivering, terrible cold, starving, exhausted. I can't think straight.'

'Oh dear. That sounds awful, I really am sorry. I can sympathise with how you feel. I'll definitely do what I can to improve things for you. First I'd just like to ask some questions.' In his briefcase he had a copy of the telex Deputy Chief Investigator Charles of HM Customs had wired off to the Amsterdam police at 1.26 the previous afternoon:

In relation to the man Dennis Howard Marks arrested on drugs charges in Amsterdam, I confirm that this man is involved in drug smuggling between England, Holland, Italy and the USA. It is for that reason that he will be arrested if he should return to the UK, by British Customs officers. I therefore request that you allow Messrs Eynon and Elliott to interview this man, and subsequently, through the normal legal processes, return him to the UK. I am at once putting in hand the proper legal process for extradition through the Director of Public Prosecutions in London, and it is hoped that the normal arrest documents will be produced to you within the proper period.

In fact, by this point British Customs had realised they were in rather a legal mess. These international conspiracies to smuggle drugs gave Customs men a logistic and legal headache. They had obtained draconian legal powers from a British Parliament which did not in those days include many MPs whose drug of recreational choice was cannabis. Howard and his friends had been smuggling dope from Holland and other European countries to the United State of America. It was not, on the face of it, against British law to smuggle cannabis from one foreign country to another. It was against US law, certainly, and it was against, for example, Dutch law when the base for the run was Holland, and against Italian law only when the dope was run from Rome. To get round this problem, the 1971 Misuse of Drugs Act provided for a novel form of crime. Under Section 20 of the Act, it was made a crime to plot in England to break the drug laws of other countries.

Thus, when the London-based ATA Carnet scam was broken, any smugglers the British authorities could lay their hands on could be prosecuted there in London. And they could be sentenced to up to 14 years in jail.

But there was a snag. Howard might have broken Section 20 of the British drug laws, and so might Arend ter Horst – the second man the Dutch police had picked up in Amsterdam. But it did not follow from this that either of them could be extradited back from Holland to London to face trial. Ter Horst was a Dutch citizen. He would be tried in Amsterdam for any Dutch laws he had broken. And Howard could only be extradited back to London if he met the one, strict rule of extradition law.

This says that people cannot be shipped back to their own country to be tried unless the offence for which they are wanted is a crime in both countries concerned. Thus, murder was a crime in both England and Holland. Howard could have been extradited for murder. But the Dutch did not have the equivalent of the draconian Section 20 law. It was not a crime in Holland to plot to smuggle drugs from one foreign country to another. So the truth of the legal position was that Howard could not formally be extradited from Holland to face trial in England for the ATA Carnet scam. He could only be tried by the Dutch authorities themselves for one of the runs – the Amsterdam run – which was harder to prove on

182

its own. It was a crime for which the maximum penalty was only four years, and the likely penalty under the circumstances a mild sentence of approximately six months in jail. Howard was in luck.

Or rather, Howard would have been in luck had he realised it. And, indeed, had he realised it, the next ten years of his life would have been very different. He said hopefully to Elliott:

'I keep asking for a lawyer. I want to know what my position is here. What is my position?'

'Well, let us see what you've to say first. Is this your passport?' Howard stayed silent.

'Look, we're Customs and Excise. We're not like some of the Drugs Squad. Customs don't plant evidence or do things in a corrupt fashion. Our methods are entirely straightforward.'

'OK. Go on.'

'When did you come to Amsterdam? Is the clothing business your only connection with Arend ter Horst? This letter signed Dr Foster . . . Is he an American? What is his first name?' Howard was lying as strenuously as he could manage:

'His first name is Colin.'

'Do you know an American called Tyler? Is that his proper name?'

'No. He has another name, I don't know what it is. He's a deserter or something in the States.'

'You must be a close friend to know that?'

'Not really. He's quite proud of it. Sometimes he's called Tahoe Jim.'

'You flew from London to Amsterdam, on KLM on 28 August with Jim Tyler?'

'No, you're mistaken.'

'Have you ever been to this house at Maarssen near Utrecht? Wouldn't it be an incredible coincidence if you and your friend Michael Clarke had both been there?'

'Yes, I suppose it would, but I've never seen the place before.'

'Mr Marks, we've been talking to you now for about an hour. I think much of what you've said is not true. We have been investigating the activities of various people including Tyler and Clarke for several weeks. I believe you have been involved in the organising and smuggling of large quantities of cannabis from Europe into the USA. I feel I should tell you that James Tyler, whose real name is James Earl Gater, has been arrested in London. Is there anything else you wish to tell me?'

Howard sat in silence for quite a long time, staring at the floor. Eynon said 'Do you know James Morris, Raymond Mayo or Richard Vickers?' Howard started to give a broad smile.

'All right. I had to try, didn't I? I'm not a prime mover. Can I tell you what I believe? Am I allowed to say this to you? I know your beliefs must be different to mine. I'm completely against cocaine and heroin, but I regard hash in a different light. I think it should be legalised. I've been sat downstairs knowing this was coming. I was wondering what to do.'

'So why tell lies at the start?'

'Well, I had to try, didn't I?' Howard admitted he had been running the hash from Holland. He asked again for a lawyer.

'Look, just answer our questions. Then you can have something to read in the cell – you can take my copy of today's *Telegraph* back with you, and something to eat. Mr Elliott's got a James Bond book. You can have that too.' Howard did not realise that a Dutch lawyer, van Bennekom was at that moment trying to get into the Amsterdam police headquarters and see Howard. One of Arend's friends had asked him to help. But there was no rush to admit him.

'I wish to see Howard Marks. You are holding him here.'

'You can't. He isn't here.'

'Where is he, then?'

'I don't know.'

'Last time I came, I was told he had been sent back to London already, but that is not so.'

'Perhaps he's escaped.'

Howard meanwhile was wriggling miserably. They produced a piece of paper from the raid on the Dutch loading bay:

'Is this some form of account for the hash?'

'Yes. It means Jim Morris 58,000 dollars, Plinston 29,000 dollars, Ernie 254,000 dollars.'

'But it doesn't say "P" for Plinston. It says "H".'

'Um, yes, that is me. But it was on Plinston's behalf.'

They produced the letters Howard had written from Ireland to Rosie, which she had taken home to Yarnton.

'Who's this Jim? Is that Jim Morris? What's it about – some kind of trouble with the shillelaghs, eh?'

'Look, it's very important I have a private word with you. It is a very important matter, really.' Eynon and Elliott adjourned to another room, out of earshot of the Dutch.

'The thing is, there are references in that letter – I know you're going to find this hard to credit – but I actually work for MI6.'

'Oh really? Fascinating. I suppose you supply them with dope.'

'No this is genuine. That's why I had to tell you in private. If you look at those phone accounts you've got there from the Okura Hotel you'll see I call 928-5600. That's my MI6 contact. I've been working for MI6 in Ireland and Holland, infiltrating an arms smuggler's organisation. He works for the Provisional IRA. He's called Jim O'Neill. That's the only reason I've become involved with this business to the extent I have.'

'Quite fascinating. Now, why don't we go back outside and you can tell us more about these other interesting people. Where exactly is Graham Plinston at this minute, for example?'

'That's what I'm trying to tell you. Anything Irish – I can't talk about. Look you can check. My contact's name is Hamilton McMillan. He's an MI6 officer.'

'All right, all right. We won't question you any further about Irish affairs. Now, I'm sure the Dutch police will be very pleased if you make a little statement about all these other matters.'

The statement, a rather muted confession, named Graham Plinston as chief smuggler, and cast Howard as an initially unwilling sorcerer's apprentice.

'Up to March 1970, my association with Plinston was purely social . . . asked if I was prepared to drive hash to England. I refused. . . . Graham gave me a few hundred pounds occasionally for my message services. . . . Jim told me about the system he was using to get hash into the USA. . . . Graham asked me to go to the States and pick up the money for the Dutch load. . . . I regret very much my weakness in accepting any role of involvement in this smuggling of drugs from Holland to the States.'

This document, which Howard rather hoped had minimised his activities in London at least, was written up by Elliott and Eynon. They added another slightly ungrammatical sentence of their own:

Having considered the matter I wish to state my preference to be allowed to return to England voluntarily than to await extradition formalities.

This was not Howard's idea at all. If anything, he was vaguely aware that Holland took a more liberal approach both to cannabis smuggling and to the length of time they locked people up in jails; he wanted to be tried in Holland. But by now it was 9 at night: his interrogation had lasted more than 10 hours. Despite being offered fruit and cheese once he started to talk, he was too distraught to eat. Several times he had been allowed to stagger to the toilet and was sick into it. He had not slept for two days, although they were giving him coffee and cigarettes.

'I don't want to sign this.'

'The only way we can help you is if you sign this statement. Then perhaps you can come back to England if the Dutch let you. Otherwise you could get four years here, and then afterward we can extradite you to England to be tried – and maybe the Americans will extradite you there first for their charges.'

'I don't see how I can be deported back to England for trial after I've actually served a sentence here for it.'

'Oh yes you can. It's Section 20 you see. But if you come back to England, you can apply for bail, can't you? You'll be in Brixton remand prison. They let you see your family every day, you have your own food, books, a radio – you'd be in there with your friend Jim Gater.'

'Well I want to consult a lawyer.'

'Be reasonable. It's Saturday night. We can't get a lawyer over the weekend, and we've got to get back to London. It's now or never. Of course, we really don't mind what you do. Just trying to help you, Howard.'

Howard signed. They gave him an orange, Eynon's *Telegraph* to take back to the cell, let him keep his sweater, offered him a meal and unlocked the bed in the cell. Howard fell into an exhausted sleep. They gave him Sunday off. By Monday, Howard had pulled himself together somewhat. His Dutch interrogators said:

'Relax Mr Marks, you will see the Assistant Prosecutor today. He will confirm to you that you can be tried both here and in England, if you do not return.'

While the Assistant Prosecutor was reading out to Howard some complex statutes which seemed to imply he could indeed to be sentenced in Holland, then deported to the US and then deported to England for successive trials, the lawyer van Bennekom finally managed to get access to his client.

'You have been held already for the maximum four days,' van Bennekom told the prisoner. 'You must be immediately charged or else released. No, you certainly cannot be extradited to the US for a hashish offence, and I feel sure you cannot be extradited to England either. But if they say you can be, then I must go and obtain definite information.

'I will be back as soon as possible, Mr Marks, after the necessary research.' Van Bennekom made for the door. The Dutch Customs men put Howard back in his 'Aliens Detention Centre' cell. Barely had he climbed on to the shelf bed than they pulled open the door again:

'Collect your clothes and your possessions from the upstairs office with us, Mr Marks. You are going to the airport.'

'I don't want to go anywhere. I'm waiting for my lawyer to come back. He's bringing me important information. I can't go now.'

'Yes, yes. Come with us, please. And now step on board this police van. Schiphol Airport at once, please, driver.'

They locked Howard in a room at the airport. After a couple of hours, the next plane to London began loading. When all the passengers had boarded, two Dutch Customs men unlocked the room, took Howard by the arm and walked out across the tarmac. They climbed the airplane stairs, and gestured Howard into a seat at the back. Limply, he buckled himself into the seat. The Dutch Customs men walked up the aisle and got off the plane. The stewardess pulled the heavy passenger door closed behind them, and the plane taxied towards the runway, gunned its engines against the braked ground wheels, and took off.

'Would you like a drink, Sir?' the stewardess said. Howard looked round the plane, listened to the steady roar of the engines, and fingered his grubby, vomit-stained clothes. He shrugged resignedly.

'Yes please,' he said. 'Champagne.'

But Howard never stood his trial. Indeed, he made fools of them all in the end – policemen, spies, Customs officials, politicians and judges. So, if it comes to that, did the shameless Jim McCann. They gave Howard bail eventually after three weeks in Brixton. It was an odd business. At first, the Customs men told the magistrate there were strong objections to bail.

'It is a serious charge, your worship. This man has a Swiss bank account, and his co-accused, Gater, has a false passport.'

Four days later Elliott arrived in his cell.

'Will you make a sworn affadavit for the use of the Dutch police about your activities in Holland? We would like you to co-operate.'

'Yes, I'll co-operate. Anything you want.'

'And um, are you intending to use anything of that certain private matter we discussed in your defence?'

'Oh, no, definitely not.' The following week, the objections were entirely dropped. On swingeing conditions, that he lived in Kenfig Hill with his parents and put up £50,000 bail – a very large sum – they let Howard out of Brixton Prison. Howard put up £10,000 of his own, and the rest was guaranteed by his father and a family friend, David Rhys. Rosie, who had rushed back from Ibiza on hearing of her man's arrest, camped gloomily with him and the two small children in their parents' South Wales back bedroom. Things did look pretty awful. It at last dawned on Howard, when he saw the committal papers, that the authorities had a mountain of evidence against him. As Bernard Simons pointed out, 'They can give you 14 years under Section 20 just for making a phone call.' Howard was the only one of the real smugglers who had been caught. He had the embarrassing job of contacting Ernie Coombes, leaving him a call-box number 'Kenfig Hill 455', to ring back from the US.

'Look, Ernie, I'm sorry, but I thought it best that you knew. I've made a statement, and said some things you might not be happy about. And I've found out that Jim Gater is thinking of going over to the Feds, and testifying against you.'

'Well, shit, don't worry too much, Howard. Life is hard for you, I know. I'm going to lie low here for a bit. My girl might come over and stop by to visit. I'll deal with the Gater thing. I'll get somebody fairly heavy to go over and talk with him – I've got to send to Europe anyway to collect my share of what's in that Dutch safe-deposit box. Who's your English attorney, Bernie Simons? Put him in touch with my attorney in LA and we'll see what my position looks like. Stay cool, now.'

Howard cabled Arend ter Horst's lawyers in Amsterdam:

'Affadavit I have sworn I now retract. Was only made to get me bail.' Ter Horst was eventually acquitted.

Jim McCann phoned. Typically, Howard was summoned to the Labour Club in Kenfig Hill to take the call.

'Well, you fucked up pretty thoroughly and no mistake. You Welsh shit. It's a good job there's me over here to look after everyone, isn't it? We'll all come through. I'm thinking of moving me business operations to Canada in a few months. Lots of opportunities for import-export. But I've got one or two strokes to pull first. Who's the Customs man in charge of your case?'

'Man called Mark Elliott.'

'Right, my Welsh friend. Just keep your mouth shut about Shannon Airport, eh?'

McCann's world, too, was getting very hot. Two weeks after Howard was bundled on to a plane in Amsterdam, the Dutch police picked up the half-crazed chemist, van der Klooster, at the German BKA's request. He started to babble not about cannabis but about McCann's bombs:

'I only did it to prove I could make bombs. I insisted that no one's life should be endangered.' The Germans announced that McCann, in Holland, had masterminded both the big Hamburg hashish deal for which they arrested his girl, and also the Munchen Gladbach bomb at British Army HQ. The London *Daily Telegraph* sent over a man who came back with a graphic tale, full of police material, about the gun-running dope-fiends of the Provisional IRA.

It was the first of many lurid half-truths that were to appear from now in the newspapers of Europe, and the angle was: 'Depraved International Terrorist conspiracy.' Poor Anne McNulty became 'An important member of McCann's Provisional IRA smuggling ring on the Continent . . . an extremely pretty blonde specifically sent to organise the supply of arms for the gunmen in Ulster.' McCann became 'A free-spending member of the Provisional IRA . . . using money from hashish sales to buy guns.' McCann was appalled. Although the newspapers and the police still had no idea of his Shannon hashish scam, or his partnership with Howard Marks in the ATA Carnet scam, this was shocking publicity. The Provisionals would be furious at being 'smeared' with drug-dealing.

McCann promptly organised some Public Relations of his own. He offered a reporter from the Dublin *Sunday Independent* an exclusive interview, driving him blindfolded, at high speed at night, to a room outside Dublin. There McCann unveiled himself. He was equipped with a pistol holster on his hip, an Armalite rifle leaning against the settee beside him, and a Landmann machine pistol lying on the opposite chair. Denouncing all talk of drugs as 'A British black propaganda exercise', McCann told one of his tremendous stories, which the paper printed at length as a front-page splash article.

'I admit I've been running guns to the North,' he said. 'But I've never touched dope. I don't approve of it.' He described vividly how he and his men had robbed a Hamburg arms dealer called Otto Schleuter of £30,000 worth of machine pistols, because the Irish government had secretly paid the man in 1970 for arms that were never delivered. This was total fiction. He added for good measure what Howard had told him, with his own embroidery: 'A British Intelligence Irish entrapment organisation works out of a special department in London', and includes both men from MI6 and Customs officers 'under the control of a man name Mark Elliott who has phone tapping and computer facilities at his disposal'. Anne McNulty was innocent, he said, and merely being held in cruel conditions because of her links with him. 'I will do anything to get her out of prison,' he added grimly.

A number of people around McCann wondered uneasily at this period about the mysterious kidnapping and disappearance a few weeks earlier of the middle-aged German businessman and honorary consul in Belfast, Thomas Niedermeyer. McCann, after all, had mentioned the 'German consul' when he first talked about his private war to get Anne McNulty released. A group of Provisionals from the Belfast Brigade had in fact kidnapped Niedermeyer, meaning to ransom him for release of their own British prisoners. They had then managed to suffocate him in the course of a struggle, panicked, and buried his remains in a Belfast rubbish tip where they lay hidden for more than seven years. Who had given the Provos the idea of picking on the German consul? Whom would Provo war-like 'actions' against prominent Germans benefit? Only McCann. It was McCann who rang up the Hamburg juvenile detention centre where Anne McNulty was being held, a few weeks later, and hoarsely threatened Provisional 'armed action' in Germany itself if Anne McNulty was not given a light sentence. One of the reasons for his heated feelings of obligation about Anne McNulty was that, in her enforced absence, he had abandoned her for Sylvia, the Dutch girl with whom he was to live for the next decade. 'Absence', as he would have no doubt said had Howard Marks been in a listening mood, 'makes the heart grow fonder.'

And indeed she was given a light sentence. The Hamburg judge said she had 'no serious criminal motivation'; he was not completely satisfied she knew it was drugs in the car, and he would treat her use of a false passport as a juvenile matter. As she had been locked up alone in a foreign prison for the last seven months, she was now free to go home to England. Jim McCann, satisfied, decamped to Canada with Howard Marks's smuggling team. Plinston went to San Francisco and teamed up with the fugitive Jim Morris. It was business as usual for everyone.

Except Howard. Howard was not very interested in McCann's menacing antics. He was wondering whether the hints to him to keep quiet about MI6 implied enough official embarrassment to do him any practical good.

'Well, you'd better make a separate statement all about it,' Bernard Simons, the lawyer, told him briskly. His parents, to whom he explained he was an MI6 agent, reminded him of the existence of his uncle Mostyn, former chairman of Glamorgan County Council, and a power in the Welsh Labour Party. 'Mostyn's arranged for you to go to London and see the Aberavon MP, John Morris. He's Secretary of State for Wales, now Heath's out and Labour's back in. He's a very important man.'

Howard drove down to London in his BMW and went through the St Stephen's entrance to the Houses of Parliament, and into the high, octagonal central lobby with its Post Office for MPs and its tailcoated attendants. No one was there.

A secretary finally arrived. 'He's not very well. You'll have to go and see him at his house. It's just on the other side of the river.' Howard went round and he made his pitch.

'I was working as an agent for MI6 all this time, you see, and that's how I got involved. It is going to be hard to present my defence, or my mitigation in court, without bringing them in, and making it all public, now I face these charges. What do you think I should do?'

'Oh dear. I'm afraid I can't have loyalties both to you personally as a constituent of mine, and to the government of the country, which of course I now work for. Who's your counsel?'

'Er, George Shindler.'

'Well, a very good man, very good man. I'm confident he will be able to do what's best for you. Thank you for coming.' After Howard had gone, Morris picked up the phone and called the Security Service, MI5, who always visit new government ministers to give them lectures about security and not being brought drinks by blonde Russians. 'Yes, it's John Morris, that's right. I've just had one of my constituents in, told me a story I think you ought to hear.'

MI5, as it turned out, were fascinated. It looked as though they were going to have to pull another one of MI6's chestnuts out of the fire for them. They always enjoyed that. Howard, frustrated, tried the direct approach. He wrote a letter to Mac McMillan, and sent it care of Bob Yeats, their mutual friend at Dillon's bookshop:

There is a slight overlap, as it were, between my work for you and the events that led up to my arrest on this cannabis charge. The case is proving difficult for me to defend, but I wanted you to know that I am not going to publicly name MI6 in my defence and cause embarrassment, although of course I suppose I could do so. I am at home now, in Kenfig Hill.

There was no reply. There never was a reply, in fact, ever again, from Mac McMillan.

Abandoned on all sides, Howard set out to save himself unaided. First, he got the bail transferred to Oxford, by embarking on a strenuous course of post-graduate study. He was allowed back, on condition he reported twice a day to police, and kept away from Annabelinda.

Fanny Stein was delighted to see him back in town, especially when he and Rosie moved into a rented room in a house owned by her acquaintance Kate Collingwood, only four doors down Leckford Road in north Oxford. She was separated from John Stein, her husband, and Howard would frequently arrive at her rather Bohemian premises in the daytime, a bottle of vodka in his hand.

'What are you here for, Howard?'

'A drink! A drink!'

'Do you know I've just had the biggest motoring penalty in the history of British justice for hitting that stuff? They fined me £800, banned me for driving for FIVE years, AND made me sit another driving test. I cannoned into the odd parked car or two. Not for the first time, I suppose. That Duncan Kilgour, Kate's prissy little lawyer friend, charged me £60 too. Get a couple of glasses. You are a poor thing aren't you? You must cheer up: there's definitely something about you, Howard, that makes ladies feel protective. Why don't you come round to this party at St Anthony's College. Raymond Carr, the Warden, is giving it. He used to be in MI5 too, you know.'

'Rosie's feeling a bit miserable right now. She doesn't want me to go to prison. She says it'll make me even more hard. And my daughter's only 18 months old. Rosie's had enough of my antics, really.'

'Oh Rosie! She spends too much time messing around with that ouija-board of hers. She's getting terribly introverted. What you want is a bit of life!'

Ernie's girl, very bubbly, said much the same thing when she popped over from Paris, to explain that Ernie's 'representative' would shortly be in town. Howard began to perk up. Dining with Kate and Duncan Kilgour in March after a prosecution the solicitor had done for the local police, he became irritated with Kilgour's air of small-town *savoir faire*. 'As a matter of fact, the whole reason why I'm in court myself is because I'm an agent of MI6. I've been working for them for Northern Ireland. Arms smuggling, you know, and drug smuggling, and the IRA. Course, I was working for both sides at once.' He smiled enigmatically, appreciating the effect.

He said similar things to quite a number of his Oxford friends that spring, with various embroideries. After all, if MI6 weren't going to help him, why should he help them? What the hell?

At the end of March, Howard had something of a shock. A low, gravelly transatlantic voice said on the phone: 'Ernie sent me. I'm at Room 804, the Hyde Park Hotel in Knightsbridge.'

'Give me two hours,' said Howard, and climbed into the orange BMW. Once in London, he sidled cautiously into the hotel room. 'Hi, I'm Bert,' said the owner of the gravelly voice, his unopened suitcases on the bed behind him. Bert had a tight double-breasted suit, was rough and heavy, though short, and in his sixties with nasty eyes. Howard listened intrigued as he ordered a room-service risotto over the house phone in that crushed stone voice. 'I'm going to see Jim Gater in Brixton about his scheme to go home with the Feds and testify against Ernie. I'm going to persuade him otherwise.'

Howard gave him a letter of authority and details of the safe-deposit box in the Amsterdam Algemagne bank. He did not have the key – he had last seen it waved inquiringly at him by the British Customs. 'I'll fix that problem. I'm going to Milan first, collect some of my friends. We are the Family. You know who I mean, don't you?'

Howard was impressed.

'As well as the 60,000 dollars, there's a small packet of about 3,000 dollars that's all mine, and some documents that might be incriminating about air freight. Can you drop them back to me here?'

'Sure I'll call.' One day later, the phone rang in Oxford.

'Call you in five minutes,' said the gravel voice. Howard trotted out to the pre-arranged payphone in the street. 'Everything is good. I want to see you.'

Howard drove to London. In the hotel room, Bert shook his hand again. He was wearing a trilby, like Humphrey Bogart wore. He had in fact, also flown to Amsterdam the previous day, wearing a huge false moustache, a wig, and a heavy fake Italian accent. He was a hard-working actor. 'Sit down, Howard. Like a Camel?' As Howard stuck it in his mouth, Bert lit it. Then he hit Howard rather hard on the side of his face, with a closed fist. It was a hard thwack.

'You're a liar. You're a cheat. The money's not there. You've ripped off Ernie's money – my God, you'll be sorry.'

Howard was scared, especially when Bert offered to throw him down a liftshaft. And even more especially when the bathroom door opened, and four very large men filed into the room and folded their arms. 'How theatrical can you get?' thought Howard. 'I wonder if I should start screaming. Or will that make them kill me faster? There's not much to be said for them killing me slowly, come to that.'

'Look,' he said. 'Phone Ernie, for Christ's sake. I'm not ripping off. Half the money was mine anyway. We're partners. The Customs must have got it, had the money. Please, please, just phone Ernie before you kill me.'

'OK, smart guy. I'll phone Ernie. And then I'll kill you. I want 10,000 dollars for my expenses as there was nothing in the box. I will give you four hours to get it. And be back. Don't think you can get away. We'll kill your family.'

Howard raced down to the lobby, and called his father. 'Please don't ask questions. The Mafia want money they say I owe them. They beat me up. Please get the suitcase from under my bed and drive as fast as you can towards London. I'll meet you half way at the Severn Bridge. No, don't go to the police. They'll kill my family. Please, please, just do it as fast as you can. If you don't hear from me by 5 a.m. call the police.

When he eventually arrived back, trembling, at the Hyde Park Hotel, with the cash, Bert was alone, all smiles. 'I didn't realise you and Ernie were partners. Ernie had just said get the money from this guy. Very, very sorry. And Ernie says to leave you a few thousand dollars out of this. If you decide to jump bail, you know, I can help. The Family, yeah? Just go to Italy. Go to the Palace Hotel, Piazza del Republica, Milano. I can give you protection there. And here's the name of a lawyer in Milan if they bust you. OK? Good to meet you. Ciao.'

'Oh, er, yeah. Right. Ciao.' He called his father, to say he was still alive, drove back home shakily, and banged on Fanny Stein's door. It was 4 a.m. He had to smoke a couple of joints before he could go home and talk to Rosie. Some of life's events were really quite terrifying. The next morning, he walked to the police station to report in once again. As he passed the canal, some police were hauling the corpse of a man out of the water. He was fully dressed and his face was mottled blue and green with putrefaction. Death, police, prisons.

'What I want', thought Howard, 'is a bit of life.'

He added up his cash resources. Without selling the cottage, they came to rather less than the £50,000 his family had at stake with his bail. He couldn't imagine where it had all gone to. He worked his way through the National Council for Civil Liberties manual on arrest and bail. It said bail was always forfeited unless the absconder was either dead, or abducted.

The next day he called up Dai, an old Welsh friend. They had once worked together years ago. He had offered to help Howard somehow in his plight. They met in a pub in the East End, near his friend's flat in a tower block down by the old London docks, in the Isle of Dogs; and they had a long talk and a lot of beer. A week later, Howard deliberately drew less than £20 out of the small £80 savings account he had opened in Oxford. Then he made an appointment with Bernard Simons, his lawyer, for the following week.

He was too pre-occupied even to notice that another intelligence agency scandal was brewing. Kenneth Lennon, who had just disclosed to the NCCL that he was a Special Branch informer on the IRA and was scared, was, a couple of days later, found shot dead in a ditch. 'So perish all Brit spies' was presumably the IRA's intended message.

On Friday morning Howard arranged to look after the landlady's children at 11 a.m. while she went to the dentists. He said to Rosie: 'Now go out shopping. And don't come back for at least 1½ hours.' Rosie left, stifling a sob. Howard carefully spread out on the desk his academic work, and a half-typed lengthy defence statement.

At 10.55 a.m. a large man in a raincoat knocked at the door of Leckford Road. When Kate Collingwood opened it, he said, 'Does Mr Marks live here?'

'Yes he does.'

'I'd like to see him, please.'

'Howard!' she shouted up the stairs, and as Howard, carrying his baby, emerged, the man said loudly 'Customs and Excise. You'd better come with us.' Two minutes later, Howard thrust his baby into his landlady's arms and said 'Can you look after her? I'm sorry but I have to go.' 'Is it very bad?' Kate asked anxiously.

'Yes it is,' he said solemnly. He looked close to tears and was trembling.

'Are you coming back?'

'Yes, I'll be back. Tell Rosie I'll be back . . . as soon as I can. I don't know when.' The large man loomed after him out into the street, the two of them turned the corner, and disappeared. In fact, Howard disappeared for six years.

When the phone rang exactly 33 hours later, Detective Superintendent Phil Fairweather was spending a peaceful Saturday evening at home in his Oxford suburb.

'Mr Fairweather? I'm sorry to disturb you. It's DI Cussell, Duty Detective Inspector H division, at Cowley police station. I thought we'd better ring – I don't know if you know Duncan Kilgour, the solicitor; he's a partner at Cole & Cole. Does quite a lot of prosecutions for us, I'm something of an acquaintance of his. He's a very solid bloke. Well he's just told us something rather peculiar this afternoon. We decided you'd better handle it.

'We've got a bail absconder, name of Howard Marks. He's a Customs case. It's a big cannabis-smuggling charge abroad, nothing to do with us really, but he got his bail transferred here. He didn't report in at Oxford station on Friday night: we called up the City of London police who were supposed to be doing his bail conditions. They said, "See if he comes in this morning". Well, he didn't, so a PC goes round to the house. The landlady and his girlfriend are there and they say "Oh, he's gone off with the Customs Officer". We tell the City boys; next thing, Customs ring me up at Cowley and say "We haven't got him. Would you look into this?"

'I go round to the house again with DC Bedwell, and get statements off the two women. The girlfriend tells a story about mysterious phone calls from the American end of this drug-running plot, and how Marks was beaten up in a London hotel by one of them over some money. Then he just disappears, she said. I go through his room and grab this great long defence statement off Marks's desk with masses of names. The girlfriend gets upset at this, and won't talk till she calls his lawyer in London, and tells him we've got the statement. Then the landlady gets all aereated too and she calls Mr Kilgour to come round – they see each other quite regularly it would seem. Well, of course, we greet each other like long-lost friends, and he says – well he says, "I think you should confidentially know this man told me he was an MI6 agent to do with the Provisional IRA". And then he says something about drug-smuggling and double agents. Well, this is out of my league, Mr Fairweather.'

'I'll come round to Cowley nick now, and you can fill me in. I'd better take charge of the case. There's not much we can do tonight, but I'll tell the Assistant Chief Constable.'

The next morning, even though it was Sunday, Fairweather took himself personally round to Leckford Road in north Oxford. He wrinkled up his nose at No. 46. The whole area seemed to have gone down these days: the big houses were infested with university types in little rooms. Fairweather didn't much care for dirty students and their cliquish dons, and suspected they didn't much care for him.

'Look at this,' he said to the fingerprint man. 'What a scruffy, hippy sort of place. You'd better try and get some prints. The landlady says this "Customs" bloke put his hand on the wall. And I'll get her to try to do a Photofit, while DC Bedwell is knocking on the neighbours' doors, see if they saw a car or anything.'

He grilled the two women, and went back to Cowley police station.

'Hello, Customs Investigation Branch? Mr Eynon? Well, the two women appear to be telling the truth as they know it. They both seem reasonably intelligent – the landlady went to university, and the Brindley girlfriend's the daughter of a rich businessman. Her brother is a director of Courtaulds. They're not idiots. Can DI Cussell and myself come down to see you in London tomorrow and get a briefing on the case? Thanks very much.'

'Special Branch? DCI Boyt please. Hello, it's Phil Fairweather here. Look I've got something that might have a security angle. Can you get on to your Security liaison in London and ask them if they know anything of Dennis Howard Marks, born 13.8.1945, CRO number 129408/73, commonly known as "Howard". No aliases we know of. Ta.'

'Mr Kilgour? Detective Chief Superintendent Fairweather here, Thames Valley police. DI Cussell told me about the matter you two discussed yesterday. Would you be available if I came to take a statement from you? I shall be accompanied on this occasion by the Assistant Chief Constable (Crime), Mr Smith. Fine. See you in 30 minutes at your house.'

First thing Monday morning, Fairweather took Alan Cussell with him on an expedition to London. They arrived at the Customs investigation branch HQ, in the office block at 14 New Fetter Lane, just behind Fleet Street.

'Good morning gentlemen. This is my senior investigating officer in our team handling the Marks case, Mr Mark Elliott. This is our boss, Mr Charles. He handles all the drug cases we do here, cannabis, heroin, LSD, the lot. And this gentleman here is Detective Chief Superintendent Coppeck, your opposite number from the City of London police. They are, of course, technically in charge of the Custody and bail arrangements in this matter.'

'Well, I think the first question to decide gentlemen, is just who will handle this inquiry. We at Thames Valley only come into this by accident, as it were.'

'Well Mr Charles thinks, and the City police agree, that, as Marks has disappeared from Oxford itself in this way, and your men have done the initial work, that this whole investigation ought to be conducted by Thames Valley. If he doesn't turn up for the trial next week, the court will need a full report from someone.'

'What's he like, this Marks?'

'Very highly educated. He was at Balliol, you know in the Sixties. Bright bloke. But he's like all these student types – scruffy, hippyish. Mucked about without a proper career, had some interior decorating firm, property speculating, stamp dealing. Doesn't seem to get anywhere with them. Now he's mixed up with this boutique in Oxford, Annabelinda. Wouldn't have said he's ever made any money out of business. He's got no nerve – remember when we were grilling him in Amsterdam, he was scared to death. You wouldn't go tiger-shooting with him, but he loves intriguing, deviousness, being mysterious. Walter Mitty kind of character really.'

The phone rang in Charles's office. 'Yes, Charles. Oh, I see, Right, right. Mr Fairweather – it's for you.'

'Mr Fairweather, hello. This is the Security Service here.'

'Um. Hello to you.'

'We would be glad if, when you have completed your meeting with Customs, you would just come over here and have a brief word with our legal advisor. His name is Mr Bernard Sheldon.'

'Yes, of course. Um, sorry, but where exactly do I come?'

'Oh yes, I do apologise, silly of me. It's Curzon Street House. Just on the corner of Curzon Street and Berkeley Square. Doesn't have a name on the door, but it's one of those big war-time government blocks. Used to be the Department of Education. You can't miss it – there's a sort of concrete verandah over the ground floor: it's a blast screen. Just come through the revolving doors at the front. There's a uniformed man on duty there.'

Fairweather knew something about MI5, of course. The local Special Branch were the ones who MI5 normally rang up when they wanted somebody arrested, or when they wanted to consult their diligently compiled local files of photographs of demonstrators; car number plates outside CND meetings; or signatories to anti-apartheid petitions. But he did not know that much, and he knew next to nothing at all about MI6, the espionage service. They were still trying to remain in the background, while their dirty linen was so embarrassingly washed.

Sheldon was the only regular liaison man with the outside world:

MI5 did not talk even to policemen on the 'outside' if they could help it. And Sheldon was quite clear about what he wanted Fairweather to do. He wanted him to hush the thing up.

'We've known all about this Marks case for some time, of course. We generally do get to know things, you'll find. Marks told Morris, the new Welsh Secretary, about it. Very patriotic, some at least of these Labour chaps.

'Now, the thing is, he *was* actually working as an MI6 agent for a short time last year. One of his student friends at Balliol became an MI6 officer and he did get hold of Marks. His dress shop, what's it called, Annabelinda? This certain officer thought he could use the Annabelinda branch they have in Amsterdam as a "cover" for his own activities.

'Well, um, it is also slightly more involved than that. This officer came to realise that your Mr Marks was engaged in, let's call them, "certain activities". I don't want to go into this too much, but he asked Marks to acquire information for him and his superiors about the Provisional IRA. It concerns a man we know as McCann, alias Jim O'Neill, who has been smuggling arms from Europe for the IRA. He's something of a well-known character. Nevertheless, and I have been asked to stress this, this officer's superiors instructed him to sever all contact with Marks last September. And they told him to have nothing further to do with him.

'It does seem, doesn't it, that Marks has already been talking his head off? The last thing any of us want is for this to turn into another Littlejohn. And I'm afraid it might. Marks could use this small but true involvement with MI6 as a defence for his criminal activities in drug-smuggling. And then, just as there was with Kenneth Littlejohn, there would be the most appalling publicity.'

'I see, Sir. Well, I can assure you that I will keep my investigation as discreet as I can. I'll give it no publicity whatever.'

'Yes, splendid. Look, would you let me know at once if any of the newspapers show any interest in this disappearance? And I mean at once. We may have to take steps. This is my home phone number.'

'We've already got hold of Marks's draft defence statement, Sir, that he was apparently doing for his solicitor when he disappeared. It doesn't seem to say anything about MI6.'

'We have as a matter of fact been running a few things through our files. I may as well tell you. His solicitor Bernard Simons is on our books as a committee member of the National Council for Civil

Liberties. And I don't need to tell you about them. So, don't trust him. We're worried about that. And there's another solicitor who's on the NCCL Committee, name of Henry Hodge. We have him down as a colleague of Mr Marks at Balliol. Be very careful.'

Fairweather went back to Oxford, greatly impressed. Alas, although neither he nor Shelton realised it, they were already too late. After the solemn visit to Kilgour from Asst Chief Constable Smith, and the taking of statements from Kate Collingwood, it had not required long. Just as Shelton was in Curzon Street speaking, the phone had began to ring at the Oxford home of a tough middle-aged reporter from the *Daily Mirror*, called Eddie Laxton. He knew a lot of people in Oxford and round about, especially lawyers and policemen. It was his patch.

'Laxton here. Oh, hello, how are you? No, haven't heard from you, have I, since you put me on to the big car crash? MI6 . . .! Blimey, this sounds good. What do you think, abducted by the IRA, just like Lennon? Be found dead in a ditch tomorrow? All right, I won't overdo the IRA bit. Fairweather eh? I know him. And a copper called "Smith". Ok, thanks very much. I'll get down to Leckford Road. You think the landlady might co-operate a bit do you? Say no more.'

Fairweather, all innocent, assembled a team. He had Cussell, a sergeant, two constables and Inspector Mick Strutt from the local drugs squad: 'Yes, I'll give you a hand. I remember doing Howard Marks for dope when he was an undergraduate. And all the Graham Plinston business. Why don't I go and talk to that blonde piece. Belinda at the boutique – I met her when Customs were grilling everybody down here and I've been cultivating her a bit.'

Fairweather stared at him. Strutt blushed. 'As a possible informant, Sir. Naturally.' Fairweather said:

'It is extremely important that the nature of this whole case be kept secret. You are not even to tell other police officers anything about it. You must never mention to anyone we question that it has anything to do with MI6. If they volunteer anything just find out what they know.'

The policemen toiled down to South Wales, where an anxious Mr and Mrs Marks told them about Howard's tangles with the Mafia; and his work for Mac McMillan 'trying to find which Continental banks the IRA were using.' They spent a ludicrous afternoon trying to persuade Redmond O'Hanlon to abandon his Darwinism for long enough to answer the door. He retailed a tremendous tale Howard had told him about being blackmailed by MI6 to work for them against the IRA, and how it was MI6 who had secretly arranged Howard's bail. Rom Harré, Howard's tutor, told them about Hempel's Paradox, and other maths problems; and said Howard was resigned to a studious prison sentence. Rosie Brindley told them all about Graham Plinston, Jim O'Neill in Ibiza, the visit of Ernie's girl, the beating up in the hotel and her belief that Howard, though pre-occupied and worried, 'was reconciled to the fact he would be imprisoned, and was preparing to face it.' They discovered that burly Bert from California really had stayed at the Hyde Park Hotel, visited Amsterdam in disguise and threatened Jim Gater in Brixton prison, saying, 'You'll be dead if you don't co-operate. I'm from the Family, and you can have 20,000 cash dollars and come and work for us in Italy if you get out.'

Duncan Kilgour, the solicitor, was tremendously helpful. 'It's been the subject of quite a lot of talk you know, in university circles – I move in them a good deal actually – that a former student from Balliol has been recruiting for MI6 agents. I'll tell you this: if Marks told me, when I'm just a casual acquaintance, he'll have definitely told the Steins as well. Probably told them more. John Stein's a fellow of Magdalen and his wife Fanny, well they're separated really – she lives just a couple of doors down from Kate. We're great friends, you know. She's the daughter of the Master of Balliol, of course.'

Fairweather became quite excited at this. He cautiously asked Rosie about Fanny. 'What's she like? Well – promiscuous in my opinion. Goes to a lot of parties. Course, I'm prejudiced: I think she rather had designs on Howard.'

He decided to consult MI5 once again. 'I think these Stein people and the University crowd might have heard about the MI6 aspect.'

'Leave it with me.'

Sheldon called back: 'We've got an extensive file on Christopher Hill, the Master of Balliol. Left-wing activity. And this John Stein is thought to have left-wing tendencies himself, although there's nothing definite. And there's one other thing. You said his parents are pillars of respectability and completely reliable. Well our chap from MI6 says there's reason to believe the father must have turned a blind eye to all this drug-smuggling. He's got a house in his father's name, bought with drug proceeds.'

Fairweather made a mental note to see the parents again, after he had bearded Fanny Stein. It turned out to be a dead end. Fanny, wearing rolled-up jeans, a lurex jumper, and enormous pink-framed spectacles, rattled on cheerfully:

'Well, I don't know what happened the day he disappeared. Frankly I'd been celebrating a bit the night before and I was dead to the world.'

Fairweather sucked his pencil and jotted down 'Early thirties. Obviously well-educated. Semi-hippy type.' He stared at Fanny's jolly clothes and added 'Appearance – Tarty'.

'Yes,' said Fanny. 'Known him since he was a student. Knew he was in trouble. He came round to a couple of parties here. What, Howard and me? Well, he's very nice, I won't say he's not attractive, but tremendously loyal to Rosie, you know. Lovely man, really. Oh, is that all? Bye then.'

'You didn't ask her about MI6, Sir,' said Cussell afterwards.

'I decided, DI Cussell, that in view of her unsatisfactory reputation, I would not mention the subject. For reasons of security.'

The MI6 tip about Howard's parents was a dead end too. He went and saw them again. It was quite obvious that MI6 didn't know what they were talking about. The Marks parents were as honest as the day was long, and did not own any suspicious property.

There was only one apparent break in the clouds of disinformation and misinformation in the world of Howard Marks. Chief Superintendent Holdaway of the Hampshire police rang up. 'Something here Customs thought you might like to see. Can you come down?'

When he arrived in Winchester, Holdaway had a sheaf of Dutch Special Branch reports on the surveillance of McCann, Plinston and Howard in Amsterdam. They depicted Plinston as one of the world's biggest drug-smugglers, but also (quite wrongly) as an active Provisional IRA arms-smuggler. Most interesting were the details of a statement of a man in a Dutch jail that Plinston had been smuggling drugs into England from Dublin, via Winchester, with a tall Welshman. It was Dutch Pieter's delayed revenge.

'Thought you'd be interested.'

'Yes, he's got some funny connections. His lawyers aren't the easy type, either.'

'Who are they? Bernard Simons and Shindler? Very interesting. Both of them defended the IRA in the big bombing trial we had here. Makes you sick.'

By the time Howard was due to appear for trial, Fairweather was, all in all, not much the wiser. His only firm convictions were that he was surrounded by unsympathetic hippies and lefties, and that the Secret Service had some very peculiar ways.

Howard did not turn up for his trial. The others pleaded guilty and most got four-year jail terms. Fairweather considered gloomily what he would say in his report for the judge, on the bail money.

And then the most terrible thing happened, the thing that so many of them had been dreading. Eddie Laxton of the *Daily Mirror* rang up. Fairweather did not know Laxton had spent the previous week up and down Leckford Road, interviewing Rosie at length, trying to track down Hamilton McMillan, and waiting to see if Howard would actually turn up for his trial when his disappearance would go on public record. Now the trial was over, and there was no need to hold back from publication for fear of contempt of court, Laxton was off the leash.

'Hello, Mr Fairweather,' he said. 'Hope you're still keeping well. I hear you're investigating the disappearance of a man. My office say they've had a report saying so from their Belfast man who knows IRA people. Can we meet urgently?' This was all a cover story of course.

'Call me back at 8 p.m.' said Fairweather, and dialled Sheldon of MI5 at home.

'Yes. Oh dear. Glad you called. See Laxton, yes. Find out what he knows. But don't tell him anything.'

They met secretly at 8.15 p.m. in a layby by a shopping precinct at Summertown, in Oxford. 'Before we say anything, you tell me what you know,' said Fairweather. Laxton reported his Belfast IRA cover story and went on: 'Howard Marks. His landlady has reported him taken away. He is coming up at the Bailey on a big drug-smuggling charge. He is an MI6 agent for a known MI6 officer.'

'You'll appreciate Eddie, that I can't tell you anything about it.'

That was excellent confirmation for Laxton. His story was obviously true. He told Fairweather he was going to print it the following night. The phone wires between Fairweather and MI5 hummed. Sheldon got on the line to the *Mirror* the night they published, but his remarks about the 'national interest' only succeeded in getting the piece toned down a trifle.

The next morning, Howard Marks, as he had thought he always wanted, became world famous. He was lying in bed at the time, in the Isle of Dogs, concentrating hard on growing a moustache. He had stayed there for most of the previous ten days, arranging to post a letter to Bernard Simons which said, 'I have gone away voluntarily with some people I injustly implicated in my statements. I am well.' He hoped it might let his parents at least know he was alive. He worried about them; but he didn't worry about anybody else. Being disappeared was very soothing.

Then Dai came in and woke him up. 'You're on the news,' he said. 'They talked about Nixon. They talked about Harold Wilson. And then they talked about you. It was something about the Secret Service. Tell you what: I'll go and get the papers.'

Eddie Laxton had told his news editor: 'This story's got everything – drugs, the IRA, the secret service.' In the atmosphere of Kenneth Lennon's 'execution' the month before, it was a peach of a tale. It covered the entire front page of the *Daily Mirror*.

*Mirror Exclusive*

Police hunt for drugs man who was a Secret Service informer

**WHERE IS MR MARKS?**

Detectives told: He was a link with IRA

A man who vanished before an Old Bailey drug-running trial has been named to detectives as a link between an American drugs ring, the IRA Provisionals and MI6 – the British Secret Service.

The story spoke of a 'top-level secret inquiry'; and said 'Marks has almost certainly been abducted'. It had the two contradictory implications – that Howard had joined the IRA; and that MI6 had sent Howard to his doom.

The *Daily Mail*, frantically following up the story late at night, had an even crazier front-page splash.

> Marks, the son of an Army officer . . . had been working for MI6 obtaining information about IRA activities. Police were last night investigating the possibility that Marks had been executed by the IRA.

Jim McCann's Green Card and Howard Marks's MI6 card had taken off together into a surreal and melodramatic world of their own, with Ernie Coombes's Mafia card floating close behind.

Reading all this, Howard was so terrified he retired to his bed with his moustache for another fortnight. The scheme had got completely out of hand. The IRA may not have been after him, but Fleet Street and the Secret Police certainly were. HM Customs, who knew only slightly more about the Secret Service and the IRA than did the ordinary general public, were almost equally terrified by reading their *Daily Mail*. On the morning of 6 May, at 9 a.m., the group of investigators gathered at Customs HQ, an hour before sentencing was due to start at the Old Bailey. It was an emergency meeting. There was Sheldon from MI5, Fairweather from Oxford, and the head of the Customs investigation branch in person.

A scrap of message paper was produced. It was an anonymous phone call to the Special Branch police HQ in London, of an Irish nature, threatening to execute the chief witness in 'the Old Bailey drugs case'. Scotland Yard had passed it to the Thames Valley special branch. They gave it to Fairweather, Fairweather called up Mark Elliott of Customs in London to tell him; and Elliott and his superiors remembered with alarm McCann's 'exclusive interview' in Dublin, naming Elliott as the head of the British undercover IRA machine. IRA executions were definitely Flavour of the Month.

'My chief has decided,' said Elliott, 'that the safe thing to do is to send me away into hiding for a week, accompanied by my family. He has decided to send Mr Eynon into hiding for the same length of time. He will also be accompanied by members of his family.' It was certainly the first time McCann had managed to frighten anybody quite that much.

'What about this leak to the *Mirror*, Mr Sheldon?' said Fairweather: 'Maybe that Bernard Simons, the NCCL lawyer, is behind it.'

'Oh yes, solicitors of that type certainly do deliberately leak matters to the press. I've known it happen in similar cases.'

Fairweather threw himself into the task of hounding Simons. That weekend a piece in the *Sunday Times* about Simons's firm caught his eye. He sprang to the phone. 'Mr Sheldon, it says here that a lawyer called Muirhead in London is working on the defence of Malcolm X, the coloured political extremist in Trinidad, Sir. He's under a death sentence for murder. This article goes on to say "The firm is taking up the fight for the innocence of Michael X because they believe in such causes". Well, Mr Sheldon, it's Bernard Simons's firm that is – "Simons, Muirhead and Allen".'

'Yes, mm. I wasn't aware, I must say, that Simons had set up his own firm and was a partner. Thank you for this information, Mr Fairweather.'

Fairweather wrote a 32-page report for Judge Edward Clarke, who was due to call Howard's parents up to forfeit their bail. The report was not brilliant. He hinted heavily that Bernard Simons was behind the press leak 'arranged in the hope his father will not have to estreat the bail, and also as a kick against the security service and the establishment in general'. This was quite untrue. Bernard Simons had behaved throughout with the utmost propriety; had immediately forwarded the only letter he had from Howard to Customs; and had nothing to do with the leak at all. Nor did any of Howard's friends. Fairweather was dazed by his prejudices against the lefties and hippies. On the other hand, he never raised the question of whether Rosie Brindley might be lying to him. Perhaps he was reassured by her relationship to a director of Courtaulds, and her possession of a private income.

Fairweather's conclusion was subtly wrong. Howard had not been abducted and murdered, he said. But nor had he straightforwardly jumped bail. He had jumped bail 'under a certain amount of pressure', from the American drug-dealers. There were other more bothersome conclusions which Fairweather was anxious to insert in view of the leak. He did not want to be suspected for it. 'The fact that he was an MI6 agent, he did not keep secret. He even told casual acquaintances. . . . The people he told in Oxford are unreliable people who live in this semi-hippy world which now exists in Oxford among many of the intellectuals. . . . Marks had clearly toyed with the idea of running the defence that he was not a criminal, but an MI6 agent. He told his parents too,' and they, said Fairweather – again quite untruthfully – had 'Well and truly broadcast the fact to far more responsible people in his home town . . . to them, their son is a hero who was doing his duty.'

Judge Clarke did not penalise the hapless Marks parents further – just yet.

'It has been brought to my attention that his failure to surrender may not be his fault,' he said, and postponed the bail-money forfeiture, provided his leniency was kept a secret. This was clever. Howard might yet be levered back into court by the threat hanging over his parents. And his parents would have no motive for talking bitterly to the Press about Hamilton McMillan. But there was no denying the fact that in his struggle to retain his freedom against the massed ranks of the British authorities, Howard had scored at least a draw. And he had by now finished growing his moustache.

# CHAPTER 8

# On the Run

The *Cutty Sark* is an elegant old British sailing clipper, preserved intact with her sleek black hull and her maze of rigging, in a little dry dock by the pier at Greenwich. Up hill on the park behind is the Royal Observatory and the impressive porticoes of the Royal Naval College, with cannon on the lawn. The easiest way to reach here, if you are not in any hurry, is by the Thames launches that run every hour or two just round the corner from Big Ben, under Tower Bridge, chugging through miles of East End, derelict warehouses, green, decayed dock entrances, acres of broken windows at Limehouse, Wapping, Rotherhithe, and the massive loop round the silent and abandoned cranes of the Isle of Dogs. It is a long way from modern London.

Here, on a spring afternoon, an odd figure emerged on to the small piazza, at the mouth of the tiled Victorian foot-tunnel that runs underneath the Thames from the Isle of Dogs on the north side. He wore cavalry twill trousers, a Marks and Spencer's cardigan, brown suede Hush-Puppy shoes, black spectacles, and a moustache. He sat down on one of the benches beside the ship, and looked carefully around. After a while, he spoke to the tall man sitting next to him in a sleeveless T-shirt. It was the stylish Dennis Irving.

'Hi Denny. Good to see you! Brought the bread?'

'Yep, lots of cash. And the birth certificate in the name of McKenna. And this FO-style embossing stamp from the artist guy in Oxford. Where'd you get those amazing glasses from?'

'You know, if you smoke a lot of dope it's supposed to affect your eyes . . . I smoked so much of this Afghan I could hardly see, and I went to an optician in Oxford. Before I skipped. He gave me a prescription; said I was long-sighted. Don't you think I look like a geography teacher?'

'Amazing. Been seeing anybody?'

'Yeah, Rosie, the kiddie, Robin, Larry, Sussex Fred, a few friends. Now things have quietened down, people have been coming over to the pub across the river, couple of times a week – the Waterman's Arms.'

'What, you all just sit around drinking?'

'You'd be amazed – it's got some social cachet being invited for a drink by the mysterious Howard Marks. Half of them think this stuff in the papers must be just the tip of the espionage iceberg. And you pull chicks too. Got this chick Sheila, knew her at Brighton. She's coming with me.'

Howard started working again, using the remains of his organisation. Sussex Fred and Arend ter Horst from Holland came round to the Waterman's Arms and offered Howard a cut if he could put them in touch with one of his big London wholesalers. They had a yacht captain who was going to bring in 1,000 lb of Moroccan to the south coast. And Larry and Sailor Jo were talking endlessly about another huge smuggling ploy in the Mediterranean:

'What, you mean like the goat saga? You're kidding.'

'Well, it'll be like the goat saga, Howard, but without the goats. If you're going to go and set up residence in·Italy and make like the Mafia, we could do it together. Sail it into Greece this time – that'll be much simpler. Then go and fetch it from Italy on the Brindisi car ferry or something. Listen, I'll buy a big camper, one of those Winnebagos, if you put up the money. Let me know when you're installed over there, and I'll bring it across.'

Howard refined a devious scheme for emigrating to Italy, where he had a vague hope burly Bert might have been serious about protection. 'Dai,' he said, 'Buy me a Mini Clubman. I'll drive off to a Post Office out of town and get a British Visitor's Passport, using the "McKenna" birth certificate and some phoney address. That'll get me out of England. Then I'll take over your identity in Italy – it's ready made, as you exist already. You go off and get a BVP too.'

'But I don't need a visitor's passport, Howard, I've got a full passport already.'

'Exactly. You're going to go out to Genoa, rent a nice little villa in your own name, and leave that full passport behind. I'm going to turn up with Sheila, and just step into your shoes. Give you lots of money.'

Two weeks later, Howard did just that. It was easy when you had friends, and very few of his friends wanted to do anything except help Howard survive. Nobody thought there was anything wrong with dope-smuggling. It was the counter-culture in action: what an older generation would have called 'fellow-travellers' and what Fairweather called 'the semi-hippy world'. Mr McKenna, ill-dressed geography master, with a chick by his side, took a train to the port of Harwich on the coast of East Anglia. He somehow didn't like British airports any more. They boarded the ferry to Esbjerg in Denmark. He didn't feel like taking risks in countries unless they had civilised penal policies. Denmark was reputed to be awkward about extraditions. With £200 in traveller's cheques and a guidebook to the Tivoli Gardens, Mr McKenna and friend booked into the Copenhagen Penta Hotel for what was obviously a geography master's dirty weekend. Then they went to the airport, and flew south.

Freedom! August 13th in high summer in the fashionable little resort of Pineta di Arenzano, a few miles north of Genoa on the Italian Riviera. In the Via di Erica, the millionaires' holiday complex with its own smart shops and its own beach, an anonymous bronzed figure ran from the elegant villa at No. 41, snorkelling gear and flippers in his hand, Sheila in her skimpy bikini by his side. It was Howard's birthday. He didn't really like swimming, considering it dangerous to his person. But on a day like this. . . . They plunged into the warm blue water, and swam with lazy strokes to the raft moored offshore. Donning his mask, Howard thought 'Happy birthday to me!' and dived gracefully in. He immediately hit his head on a rock, and felt himself beginning to drown. Much later, he came to on the beach, Sheila energetically pummelling his chest. There was an extremely large crowd of holidaymakers gathered interestedly around. So much for the anonymous millionaire.

But his disguise did not really come unstuck until well into the Autumn. The affair with Sheila rapidly collapsed and she went home. After a few weeks of jogging daily up and down the beach and working on his Italian, Howard began to pine for a social life.

From a phone-box in Genoa City he issued a stream of invitations. 'Come to Italy. Meet me in the Piazza de Ferrari in Genoa.'

The friends of Howard Marks turned up in the usual droves. There was Dai from the Isle of Dogs, who brought his wife and children out for a free holiday; Rosie and the baby. . . .

'Look at this,' said Rosie. 'I drag myself over to see the fugitive and you're living in a beautiful villa. This living-room's the size of a ballroom. You always have more money than everyone else, don't you? Still, I suppose it's a karmic necessity for you to live abroad like this, sort of the ultimate test of you as a person. I'm glad the horrible time me and your parents had was worthwhile for you. I'm going to live with Julian Peto and his family for a bit in Oxfordshire, out at North Leigh. I don't plan to see you for some time.'

Larry turned up with the Winnebago:

'Here you are Howard. Keep it parked well away from your place, won't you? But you can always loon around and pick up a few dozen hitchhikers in it: sleeps six, got its own shower, and an 8 track stereo. Nice, eh? Oh and I've brought you across a little piece of dope.'

Mike Durrani, Howard's biggest Pakistani supplier, accepted an invitation to stay overnight at the villa on his way to do some deals in Rome – he at least did not regard Howard as an unworthy person to do future business with. That was good. Hearing that Julian Peto and his brother Richard, the two Oxford cancer researchers, were attending a Cancer Congress in Florence, Howard fetched out the Winnebago and drove off to Tuscany. They were entertained to see their old friend arrive, with a conference badge he had got somehow,

Howard went to the English language lectures – it was always a subject that interested him – and joined the conference guided tour of the Uffizi Gallery. He regarded the solemn Botticelli gazers with genuine suspicion:

'Honestly now, which would you rather be doing? Looking at that, or having a shag?'

When his sister Linda was accepted for a language teaching job at Padua, in northern Italy, Howard was delighted. He arranged for his parents to fly out to Milan to visit her, and intercepted them at Milan Airport. There was a tearful reunion. It made him over-confident. When they left, he checked into the Palace Hotel. (He would occasionally register there, in the name of McKenna, in the faint hope that Bert's Mafia friends might take a protective interest. He never heard anything from them.) From the Palace, he decided to ring up Rosie almost direct in Oxford, and tell her about the reunion, try and mend fences.

'Fanny, is that you? This is Howard. Yes, I am alive. I've been alive all the time actually. Look will you run round to No. 46 and tell Rosie I'll call here again in 10 minutes?'

Fanny was flustered, banged on the door, and babbled to the first person that opened it – 'It's Howard. He's alive, he's just rung, he wants to speak to Rosie.'

A couple of days later, Eddie Laxton of the *Mirror* was making his regular check calls around the former neighbours of Howard Marks. Laxton was working overtime on the story. 'Any developments on the Marks business? What, he phoned! Think he's in Italy, do we – and the sister's out teaching in Padua. Oh ho.'

Laxton soon screwed a few facts out of Fanny, Kate, and one or two others, and caught the first plane for Milan. He did his best to browbeat Linda Marks. He wrote her a note when she wouldn't see him:

Linda, I give you the same guarantee as I gave your parents on Tuesday night – I am not interviewing you. Your name and the *Oxford School* – do not interest me in any way.

But you are a LINK to Howard. It is Howard I want to see, privately – secretly – any way you say. If I write what I know now, your parents' £40,000 is obviously endangered.

I want to avoid that, and want to avoid that, but only with your co-operation. No one knows I am here, Customs or police, I promise you that. I can give any guarantee you like to name.

My interest is in Howard's story and that is the only *sure* way he can influence the court if he ever intends to return OR if ever he is picked up. I don't have to use PADUA or any other definite clue which could lead to Howard. All this I can amplify. All I want is a few minutes of your time TO LISTEN. If I do write now then I name Padua, Rosie and your parents' involvement. That settles the bail question and Howard will have to start running again. I am being as reasonable as I know how. I am not about to double-cross anybody.

Remember I didn't start this. I only reported what I was told by many, many people. I want to expose the way Howard was used, then left to fight his battle alone.

If Howard goes back to England without telling his story first, he is facing a longer jail sentence and the estreatment of bail will still be made.

Ten minutes listening, that's all. LAXTON.

Laxton went home frustrated. Before he published, he called up Fairweather to pass on his information. The *Mirror* was a responsible newspaper, after all. Also, Fairweather had passed him a lot of material. Laxton had by now pieced together both hints about 'the Family' and Howard's links with Jim McCann, 'the Provisional IRA officer'. It was Laxton who gave Fairweather the first real break he had ever had on the case. He went around in Laxton's footsteps, and intimidated the same people. Fanny came clean; Rosie did not say much, but Mr and Mrs Marks were entirely truthful, and prepared to co-operate. He found out about Milan, and Linda. Fairweather was so pleased at the prospect of flying abroad and entrapping Marks, that he recommended their bail be not forfeited.

A moustachioed, bespectacled figure was in fact, at that very moment staggering off the British Caledonian lunchtime flight from Genoa to Gatwick Airport. He was weaving drunk, and clutching in one hand a carrier bag full of bottles of Sambuca, and, in the other, Dai's British passport with his own disguised photo clumsily glued and embossed in. He had left, stuffed in some horror down behind the airplane seat, the *Daily Mirror* British Caledonian so kindly put in the cabin when the plane set out from London first thing on Monday morning.

It was another front-page Eddie Laxton spectacular. He had been as good as his word.

### HE'S ALIVE!

The Mirror finds man they feared was dead.
Mirror Exclusive WHY THE MAFIA HID MARKS
By EDWARD LAXTON
In Padua, Italy                         IN THE MIRROR
                                        ALWAYS THE BIG
                                        EXCLUSIVE STORIES

Mystery man Howard Marks is alive . . . and living in Italy as a 'guest' of the Mafia. He was smuggled out of England . . . living under cover as a student in Padua . . . he was the man who knew too much . . . Linda, who teaches English at a private school, arranges all contacts for her brother. She told me 'Please go away and forget us'. He certainly did pass information to MI6. Papers and letters found in police raids prove he infiltrated the IRA gun-running operation. But the Mafia overlords thought an open trial might expose too much . . . the price Marks must pay: a life in the shadows . . . visits by Marks' parents and girlfriend Rosie.

212

Passport control at Gatwick waved through the 'man who knew too much'. He ordered a taxi from the Gatwick Airport phone and muzzily told it to drive the 25 miles into London's East End.

'Hello Dai,' he said. 'I've come back. They'll never think I've flown into London. Open a bottle of Sambuca. I can't take it any more. Wherever I go, journalists, coming after me, chasing my family, finding out, and the final bail hearing tomorrow. My money's low. If I go, they'll find out again. . . .'

'Yeah, mate, that's what it says here. "The price he must pay – a life in the shadows". It's a great read.'

'Oh shut up. Listen, I think I'm going to give myself up to the police. I want to see Rosie and the kids one more time.'

'You're in no condition to drive, I'll tell you. Me and my mate'll drive you up. We can have a few drinks on the way.' Eventually they reached the Victoria Arms on the corner of Leckford Road in Oxford. A gang of Howard's Oxford friends were there. They laughed uproariously, and waved copies of the *Mirror*. They drove on out to North Leigh in search of Rosie.

'Oh my God, it's you, Howard! Do you realise I've just had Superintendent Fairweather around here all morning grilling me again? I can't stand it. Why do you come back? Look at me, I'm so thin, and worn down. I told you it was over, why do you come back? You can't stay here.' She burst into tears. Howard collapsed on the bed and passed out.

The next day, to his astonishment, he discovered Judge Clarke had not forfeited the bail after all. He held a hearing in camera, saying the police had certain leads, and that it would not be in the public interest to announce just where Marks was exactly. Fairweather's new report said:

'The parents at once admitted to me that whilst on holiday in Italy, they had seen their son in Milan.'

'You have a moral obligation', Judge Clarke lectured Mr and Mrs Marks, 'to tell the police when you next hear from your son.'

It was obviously an omen. Howard would cheat Fairweather out of his prey. He went and spent the night at the house of a girlfriend of a friend. Then Judy Lane, the accountant Patrick Lane's sister, arrived with her Anglo-Irish good looks.

'Oh, Howard,' she said. 'Hello. Have you escaped again? I thought you were leading a life in the shadows.'

'Yeah, I'm feeling no pain. I'm just on my way back to London, dropped in to pay a few calls round here. Can you give me a lift?'

'Great, I'm going back to Brighton. Where are you staying in London now?'

'Oh, uh, here and there, you know.'

'Secret is it? I just want to know where to call or contact you again.'

'Well, I'm not exactly sure yet.'

'You haven't *got* anywhere to stay, have you? At all?'

'No. Tell you the truth, I'm a bit on the floor.'

'Well. I've just got back from Gibraltar. We were sailing this yacht back from Ibiza – a lot of storms. It's a long story, but my father's got this huge house in Brighton where I'm camping all alone. I'll harbour you for a bit.'

From now on, the extraordinary Lane children were to be the backbone of Howard's new life.

Kenneth Lane, their father, was a Midlands business executive with a Daimler and a swimming pool.

Patrick, eldest son of the family, was a romantic poser with a plausible upper-class manner and dry wit. At trendy Sussex University, he shot himself full of heroin; embroiled the family in a court case by jumping through a plate-glass window ('Police followed trail of blood' said the local paper) and ostentatiously broke himself of the heroin habit to become a trainee accountant with Price Waterhouse. He wore pin-striped suits, carried a rolled-up umbrella and a briefcase, and played the City gent. For 3 years, he had been handling Plinston's romantically dark flows of cash.

The best her teachers could find to write on Judy's school reports was: 'Carefree'. She hung around the Stafford coffee bars and parks with the aimless working-class town kids, truanting from school and wearing a mini-skirt. She blithely took her first acid trip at 13. They naturally smoked joints, these kids – they also took 'sleepers', 'speed' and cold-inhalers. Objecting to school rules, she got her class to go on strike and lock out the teachers. When she was ejected from the grammar school, her parents sent her to a nearby convent school. She got pregnant. The baby was adopted.

Judy rapidly stopped being carefree at an early age. Her mother began to die, slowly, of cancer. Her father was distraught. The younger children had to be looked after. (Natasha went to Essex University, met Anna Mendelsohn of the 'Angry Brigade' and eventually ran away from home with a highly 'undesirable' boyfriend. She ended up in a Mexican jail on a dope charge.) Judy stopped taking drugs and acid – although, like everyone else around, she smoked a few joints. When she first met Howard in a Brighton pub, she was doing 'A' levels at a Brighton tech, and her mother was dead. Howard was scruffy, yet glamorous. Rosie was just glamorous. Patrick was rather deferential to Howard and the other big dope-dealers, and always up at the Warwick Castle in north London, conferring with little Graham Plinston. He was disappearing to Ireland, too, so often that the family made jokes round the dinner table about 'Patrick's gun-running'. He bought the BMW. He bought the old mill in France. He pressed cash into Judy's hands: 'Go to Ibiza for a few weeks, take a rest from the family.' Judy slept with Howard a few times. She also had a longer affair with Sussex Fred. She was well into the 'semi-hippy world'. She thought the intrigue of dope-deals was quite romantic. And at 19, she was prepared cheerfully to try anything. She was tougher than Howard. She could cope with misfortune.

Howard needed a strong woman. No sooner had he recovered some of his bruised self-confidence and started to put together a few deals – than disaster stuck again.

Christmas Day, 1974, saw him in public having a slap-up turkey dinner at the Dorchester Hotel in Park Lane. There were five of them: Howard, Larry and his wife, Dennis Irving and his wife.

'Aren't you afraid of being grassed, Howard?'

'Don't call me that any more. My name's "Albi".'

'Albi? What's that – an anagram of BAIL?'

Howard giggled. 'It's actually after Albert Hancock, this ruffian I knew in Kenfig Hill. Always modelled myself on him.' He spooned Christmas pudding into his mouth. 'Apart from those two Customs men, nobody wants to turn me in.'

He was in the money again. The boat from Morocco docked and there was £2,000 a month commission flowing in from the sales. 'Ouncing it off' round Brighton to make a few more hundred pounds, Howard had picked up the threads with a lot of academic friends and made a new contact – 'Swede' the dealer, an old Hoogstratten rent-collector, fresh out of jail for posting in hash from Nepal, and then trying to collect it from the student pigeon-holes at Sussex University. Swede was selling him bits of 'ID' – stolen driving licences, old seamen's discharge papers – and he also knew a man in Southampton docks. True, Sailor Jo's project had collapsed as usual, with Sailor Jo arrested in Crete – somebody out there obviously remembered the goat saga. Howard flew Swede's own passport out to Heraklion, with a new picture glued on, and Sailor Jo escaped with it and went to ground. But you couldn't win them all.

Larry introduced 'Albi' to others of the New Vanguard of British culture and intellectual life. He was a visitor to Georgina Shaw's Islington flat in Thornhill Square, which she shared with Michael Fish, the fashionable Carnaby Street designer. He met Peter Gabriel, of Genesis; Jane Arden, the feminist who directed *Holocaust*, and Jack Bond the film-maker. He met Nik Douglas, expert in oriental art and Penny Slinger, the painter: 'She was a pupil of Max Ernst, you know, and Sir Roland Penrose of the ICA thinks a lot of her work. And this is Anthony Woodhead . . . oh, do you two know each other?'

'Er, yes, a bit . . . sshh! Come over here. What the hell are you doing? I thought you'd cleared off to Japan two years ago. My name's Albi, by the way.'

'Well, what the hell you doing here? Listen, you remember all that hydroponics stuff?'

'Yes, you ripped off my £100 for research.'

'Don't be like that. I'll pay you back. Right now. I've converted this massive attic in Wimpole Street to growing hydroponic dope and it's worked. I've got about 80 lb of grass ready for harvesting but I could do with some help finding buyers. I know you've got dealers at your fingertips. Cut you in 50/50 – you'll make about 5 grand. And another thing. I know a very big man in New York. If you know anyone who can do airfreight to him, he can get the stuff down at JFK airport. Via me, of course. There, now I've told you something worth knowing.'

The contacts multiplied. Dennis Irving came back from a sound contract for the Nigerian tour of Jimmy Cliff, the famous Jamaican singer of 'The Harder They Come.'

'Met a man out there. Called the Doctor. Can get Nigerian grass out through the docks. It's quite good stuff and cheap. Used to be a lot of it come through in the Sixties.'

Howard pondered these weapons at his disposal. At night, in bed, he leafed through a new hardback from Faber & Faber, called *Air Freight, Operations, Marketing and Economics*. There was a particularly gripping chapter, entitled 'Terminals, Handling and Documentation'. For light relief, he read Jerzy Kozinski:

'Hey Judy. There's a character in this book. He has three different identities, houses and things. But they all have the identical lock on the doors! So he only needs carry a single set of keys. What an interesting book.'

Both Howard's novel smuggling schemes went wrong. Dennis Irving caught typhoid taking out £5,000 to invest in Nigerian grass. The consignment got trapped in the notorious blockages at Lagos harbour and never reached Southampton.

The Southampton docker was a broken reed anyway. He ran in a consignment of his own in its place from Morocco, and promptly got arrested. Customs must have been watching him all the time. The New York collapse was far more serious. Sussex Fred had offered to organise a Beirut Airport pipeline, flying 'returned under warranty' machine parts, Beirut – Rome – New York. On the strength of this, Woodhead fetched 100,000 dollars cash investment over from his 'big man' in New York. He was called Don Brown. When Don Brown collected the crates off the plane, they were all empty except for one, single, toy wooden boat. The rage of all concerned was terrible. Don Brown berated Woodhead, who berated Howard, who berated Sussex Fred. Howard saw his career as a transatlantic middleman sinking faster than the *Titanic*, and said desperately:

'I don't know who did the rip-off. But I'm prepared to take financial responsibility. I've lost ten grand of my own, you know. I'll produce you another shipment, OK?'

Howard tried frantically to raise Mike Durrani from Pakistan. He was the only man he knew who would do big deals on credit. He didn't answer any of his phones, and never returned calls left with his answering service.

Finally the phone rang. 'Yeah. Yeah, it's Albi. Hello Dai, it's you is it? Sorry, I was expecting another call. Who? The *DAILY MIRROR*? Oh, Jesus Christ and all the Saints. Well, how the fuck did they get this address, if not off you? Grassed, eh?'

As Eddie Laxton and his photographer Eric Piper barged through the mansion swing doors, heading for his £90-a-week Regent's Park penthouse, Howard clattered breathlessly down the stairs, gnawing his moustache. He marched across the lobby past them, head down, as they spoke to the caretaker. The caretaker looked up and said, 'Do you mean him?'

'Excuse me, please. What's all this?'

'That's not him.'

'Not who?'

'Sorry to disturb you, Sir, sorry . . . No, Eddie, hang on a minute, I know my faces.' CLICK.

In a £4 a week Liverpool slum tenement, Mr and Mrs John Phelan stared glumly at each other over the kitchen table.

'You shouldn't have bought that bottle of wine. God knows it was extravagant enough to get a joint of meat.'

'Oh Howard, but it's our Sunday lunch. Come on, cheer up.'

'Shit, I can't stand it – the dirt, this filthy little bedsit. Do you know, when I went out to call Woodhead, I was worrying whether I could save money by putting 2p in the box, instead of a 10p piece. It's really destroying me.'

'What did he say?'

'He just screamed at me about "Where's the shipment? Where's Don Brown's money?"'

'It's just as bad for me you know. Worse. I've always lived in nice houses, and now we've got a dirty, stinking shared toilet where you have to take your own paper. What a grotty place this is.'

'Well, at least no one knows whether we're alive or dead. When I think of what I left behind for the Customs to crawl over – there was 8 grand in cash, you know. All those bits of ID in the drawer. The stereo. The electric typewriter. The digital clock. My whole record collection. . . .'

'Look on the bright side. If we didn't have that 100 quid from your family, we'd be sleeping in the park. Why don't you try and get Dennis or somebody safe to lend us £500? You could buy a passport, and if we got an old van we could go camping. It's summer, it'd be much nicer. We're only waiting, after all.'

'Yeah. It's all right for Durrani, isn't it: "Nice to hear from you Howard, but I don't think we ought to meet for a few weeks. Not while your face is so well known on the front pages." Huh! "The Face of a Fugitive." Very funny. That pig, Laxton. That fucking Laxton. Why has he got it in for me?'

'Come on. I'll take you for a row on the boating lake. That's really cheap. Anyway, you look nicer without a moustache.'

That was the bottom. But it got better. A lot better. The pair of runaways spent a hot, cheerful summer on campsites in Wales, Hampshire and the Isle of Wight at 50p a night. It was a healthy life, apart from Howard's insistence that they pitch camp near the toilet blocks. That was where the payphones were, and he was always leaving

218

messages for contacts to call. Eventually, he persuaded one of his Sussex University friends to risk going out to Zurich with a signed note. From Annabelinda's address, directed to the Swiss Bank Corporation, it said:

Please pay the bearer of this letter the balance in full of the sums in my account No. 326324, after having deducted whatever charges are due to yourselves.

Yours faithfully, Dennis Howard Marks.

With £6,000 cash, they rented a flat in South Kensington, Durrani finally came across, and it was agreed to smuggle 700 lb of the best Black Pak via a dhow from Karachi to Dubai in the Persian Gulf and Rome Airport. This time, the dope arrived. Judy Lane came back from New York with a small suitcase of dollars and they picked a pleasant Suffolk inn from a Good Hotel Guide for a little celebration. It was the Swan at Lavenham.

'I've left most of the cash as you said, to be looked after over there. You have made, Howard, after clearing that debt to Don Brown, slightly more than 80,000 dollars.'

'Oh good, let's do it again.'

They did. Four times in all. And then, when Don Brown got jumpy about more cargo from Dubai, they did number five via Japan Airlines in Tokyo. That one was one whole ton. Don Brown in New York was delighted with Howard and their relationship matured.

Mike Durrani became a warm friend. Predatory in pursuit of unattached women, he was gentlemanliness itself to Judy Lane. The three of them would yarn for hours in Durrani's new Trevor Square flat, close to Harrods.

'Howard, do you know I was a policeman in Hong Kong for 11 years?'

'Well, you must have learned a bit about corruption there!'

'It is true there was a certain amount of vice. But there was a Welshman I worked alongside. His name was Evans and he was a good friend to me. I think it is from him that I get my affection for the Welsh. I was educated at a British-run school in India, you see. They were better schools than you could find in Afghanistan. And naturally, I went to work for the British. You know Howard, what I would like very much – you were at Oxford, were you not, a graduate of Balliol?'

'Oh yes, a Balliol man, Mike. Through and through.'

'It would give me great pleasure if my son were to be able to study at Oxford. Do you think you could bring influence to bear?'

'Um, yes, I'll do what I can when the time comes. Don't you ever get nervous wandering around with suitcases full of bent money like that?'

'Oh no, Howard. There is nothing to be afraid of in this business. I rarely worry. I just never write down phone numbers on pieces of paper, that's all.' These were the good times. Howard stacked up approximately one million dollars, about half of it safe in the US. Even by the mercurial standards of the dope business, he was doing terribly well. He turned to dabbling in his hobbies. At this point in his life, Howard had three. The first was financing ludicrous projects; the second was inventing telephone equipment; and the third was constructing false identities.

He sank about $50,000 into a glossy art publishing scheme.

'Hi, Albi. Penny Slinger and I are very close. My name's Nik Douglas. You want to try some of this Nepalese? It's hard to get. Heard you were looking for a place?'

'Yeah, I like to move around a bit.'

'Why don't you take over our flat in Gledhill Gardens for a bit? Penny and I are going off to the States to promote an amazing set of Tarot cards we've designed. You don't mind having Eastern statues around? I've spent quite a lot of time in Nepal and Tibet. I directed this film *Tantra* backed by Mick Jagger: years ago, I was road manager for "The Cream", but I've composed a few books since then.'

And so, *Sexual Secrets* by Nik Douglas and Penny Slinger, a lavish illustrated production by Hutchinson at £8.95, billed as 'The definitive study of sex and mysticism', came to have a small acknowledgment in the Foreword:

'Albion Jennings, for support and good advice.'

'Jennings' was one of Howard's running jokes. He developed a passion for the American country singer Waylon Jennings, one of whose songs was 'Lonesome Outlaw'. Howard had a vast collection of his records, and he eventually went to some trouble to equip himself with a full-scale false identity as Waylon Albion Jennings. He told Judy 'People should be helped to exploit their fantasies – including me.'

Howard could also be seen for days on end, in clouds of strong Thai fumes, dismantling telephones and trying to put them together again. He acquired an American paperback: *Telephone Accessories You Can*

*Build* by Jules H. Gilder, and frowned over the instructions for scrambler machines, auto-diallers and automatic tape-recorders. *General Principles of Telephony* went on the bookshelves alongside the freight manuals and the ABC *Airways Guide*. 'Dennis,' he said. 'You're doing all that work on synthesisers with Mike Rutledge and The Soft Machine. When you're not hang-gliding, that is.'

'Right.'

'Well, I think I've invented an amazing telephone machine. It just needs somebody practical to build it. I'm not good at soldering and manual things, and besides, it's not actually quite invented yet. . . .'

Dennis Irving worked on it for weeks, constructing circuits. The problem was this: dope-dealers use telephones all the time, often making international calls. But they have to do them all from coinboxes for reasons of security. And they frequently change their contact numbers, and use a variety of answer services, lines at friends' houses and so on. Most British coinboxes at the time would not even direct-dial at all to the US, and when they did, impossible sums of money had to be fed in. Foreigners did not understand British coinbox tones, and would frequently put the phone down when they heard the 'beep-beep' signal. There was no doubt that, on balance, the anonymous global direct-dialling system that was coming into general use was a major boon to international dope-smugglers. But there were specialised problems peculiar to the trade.

'What I want you to invent', said Howard, 'is a machine using two telephone lines, with a black box between them. When anybody phones up, from anywhere in the world, the machine will automatically dial them through to the number I am at, anywhere else in the world. And I have to be able to ring up the machine myself and feed it new numbers where I want it to route calls, using a hand-held bleeper code.

'Also, I want to ring up the machine from a coinbox, and have it dial me through on my own line, to wherever it is in the world I plan to call.'

'Oh fantastic. So you can change the number you're at every half-hour if you like! Mind you, it's not totally secure. If you knew the set-up, you could put a tap on, and listen to the auto-dialler routing calls through.'

'I'm sure it could be refined. And you could built in an auto-destruct device, so if anyone interferes with it, it blows up.'

'Truly amazing. I'll get to work.'

221

Irving actually designed a prototype that functioned. The portable tone-coder was a bulky briefcase full of wiring, and the black box was a mass of silicon chips, capacitors and circuitry about three foot square on a large piece of board. But it worked. Then Dennis crashed Ernie Coombes's hang-glider on the Sussex Downs.

When they finally switched the life-support machine off, Howard gave Irving's wife and his six-week-old god-daughter practical support. But every time he looked at the Amazing Telephone Machine he felt too sad to go on with it.

Howard continued to work, however, on his identity problem. He was buying passports at £150 a time from Swede, who was a useful source of underworld material. He bought one as 'Goddard' and another as 'John Hayes'. He also rented a nice house at Charlbury and installed one of his Oxford friends there for free, as a small token of appreciation. It was from the Charlbury address that he successfully applied for a provisional drivers' licence as 'Waylon Albion Jennings'. That was easy.

But his long-term plan was to get out of Britain with Judy, and go to America. The Don Brown connection was coming on well; the money was piling up there waiting for him; and the ruthless Woodhead was showing signs of emigrating to Dubai, where there was gold and falcons and some interesting dope connections he might make. If he was in America, and Anthony Woodhead was drifting away, he could move in directly on the US connection. But the travel arrangements made him nervous. Howard Marks might well be wanted still for the ATA Carnet scam, which had been the downfall of his last US project. And he could not get in without a visa.

A friend of a friend knew a courier who took a sheaf of oil company passports round to the US Embassy in Grosvenor Square every week, for those of their employees who were travelling across the Atlantic. The embassy stamped them in a routine fashion. Howard bribed the courier to slip the 'Goddard' passport in. It came back with a single short-term entry visa.

'I don't like it, Judy. I've never felt comfortable about this "Goddard" one, it's only a brief visit allowed, and there isn't a false passport for you.'

'I'll go out under my own name.'

'No: too many people know about you and me. I'm going to try and get really well fronted up and start again.'

Howard acquired two real passports for a husband and wife via an ingenious scheme of his own invention which he convinced himself was foolproof.

He found a couple who had never been abroad: a TV engineer called Rudcliffe and his wife. There were a surprising number of youngish Britons who had never owned a passport.

'Now, I'm going to give you quite a lot of money. What I want you to do in return is this. Make an application for two passports. That's all. Fill in the forms just like it says, get some photographs to go with them, and ask your doctor or someone like that to certify the back of the photographs. Then give the lot to me. If anyone ever asks you about the applications, say they were lost or stolen. You haven't done a single illegal thing.' Howard rifled through the completed forms with satisfaction. The only problem was the doctor's rubber stamp. He ordered half-a-dozen different rubber stamps from branches of Rymans, each containing useful bits of the doctor's name and address. He razored them off, and glued them together again in the right sequence. Now he had a doctor's stamp, that no one could ever testify he bought.

He collected two more blank sets of application forms and he and Judy carefully filled them in, in his own handwriting, and sighed them 'Rudcliffe'. Then he asked someone else to copy out the doctors endorsement signature onto the backs of photos of himself and Judy. He carefully pressed his home-made rubber stamp over them, and posted the lot off to the Passport Office in Petty France, near Scotland Yard. Back came two perfectly genuine passports.

'And if they ever checked,' he said to Rosie: 'The doctor would confirm that he endorsed some photographs for Rudcliffe: and the Rudcliffes are perfectly real. Clever, isn't it?'

But the plot did not stop there. Mr 'Rudcliffe' needed an employer. Howard went to the trouble of sitting a driving test, and getting 'Mr John Hayes' a full driving licence, at the address in South Kensington he had vacated some weeks before. (He had kept the key to the lobby, so he could collect mail from the flats. He always kept copies of all his old keys.)

'Mr Hayes', armed with driving licence and address, went to Ewell, in Surrey, just outside London. Swede had some relations there who were paid to set up a 'Hayes' answering service. 'Mr Hayes' had some stationery printed up declaring himself to be the director of 'Insight Video', of High Street, Ewell. And 'Mrs Hayes' opened up a bank account in nearby Epsom.

Then the phantom Mr Hayes launched a provincial branch of 'Insight Video'. He rented a suite of offices in New Street, Birmingham, from a secretarial services company. He filled up the offices with video catalogues and trade fair brochures. The secretaries there could observe his TV engineer employee, coming in to work each day. His name was 'Rudcliffe'. (Howard paid a friend to sit in the office for eight hours a day, pretending to be Mr Rudcliffe.) And naturally, 'Mr Rudcliffe' needed somewhere to live in his new job. Howard rented a cheap flat in Moseley, the Asian immigrant area of Birmingham where few questions were asked. It had a mailbox in the porch, with a key.

And now came the finale. 'Mr Rudcliffe' applied to the US Embassy in London for a pair of visas to travel to the US. He enclosed passports for himself and his wife, and a letter from his employer, a Mr Hayes of 'Insight Video' in Birmingham, outlining his employee's plans to buy some video equipment in the US. He enclosed the first-class return air tickets already bought. A couple of weeks passed. Two perfectly genuine Rudcliffe passports dropped into the Moseley mailbox, with two perfectly genuine sets of 'Multiple Entry, Indefinite Validity' US visas stamped inside them. Howard was on his way. He went with Judy to Birmingham – it was, after all, the 'Rudcliffe' family home – and flew from the airport there to Brussels. No one had anything against him in Belgium, as far as Howard could remember.

He decided to go to Zurich to deposit some loose money. In Zurich, there was a family reunion with Judy's big brother Patrick. He had fled during the 1973 Big Bust to the Dordogne to grow snails. Wolfing a grand dinner in the Nova Park Hotel, they posed like mad.

'It's very nice, Howard, but it's not as good as the Dolder Grand. They've got some very decent rooms at £500 a night there.'

'Get another bottle of champagne and stop complaining. I tried to book us in the Dolder Grand but they were full. How's the snail farm?'

'Bit of a drag. The snails ran away one night. But I've turned "Le Moulin" into a centre of ethnic art. I knock off about 10 little oil-paintings a day, and flog them to the tourists who come through Molières. And I grow marrows.'

'Aah, it's borin', playing at being a fugitive from justice. It's not even as if you're really a wanted man.'

'We're not all as good as you at life in the shadows, old chap. I've been writing a screenplay actually. It's all about us, and the IRA and the PLO, lots of conspiracies.'

'We didn't have anything to do with the PLO.'

'You've got to have an open mind about our sort of business. Anyway, Sussex Fred and some of the others got a bit hostile when they saw the typescript.'

'Shame. What were you going to call it?'

'Great Title! "The Politics of Pot in Paddy-Land".'

'You need an occupation in life. Come up to the room. Let's send for some more champagne and I'll put a proposition to you.' Before they drank themselves unconscious on the Nova Park champagne, Patrick Lane agreed to become Howard's personal money manager. He left town with a stack of books on offshore banking, to begin his research.

Howard did not want to try to fly into the US direct from Zurich. It might raise an eyebrow somewhere. With uneasy memories of the ATA Carnet scam, he decided against going to France or Italy either.

'It's years since I did anything in Germany,' he said to Judy. 'Let's go to Frankfurt. But we'll go on the train.'

From Frankfurt, they only had economy class seats available to New York.

'Good,' he said. 'It's anonymous. But if it works, we'll never fly economy again.'

The plane touched down at John F. Kennedy Airport. Howard gazed curiously at the fork-lift truck drivers, wondering how many of them worked for Don Brown. They queued up at Immigration. And they were in. Howard picked an anonymous cheapish hotel -- the 'Executive' – from the airport hotel reservation desk, and called up Don Brown, from a payphone.

'What are you staying at that scruffy place for?' he said nasally: 'Go and get a suite at the Waldorf Towers. You'll find it's really nice.'

In Vancouver, in the wintry far west of Canada, there is a Planetarium of which the local tourist authorities are very proud. One snowy evening in 1977, it was showing a new programme: 'Mountains and Volcanoes of Hawaii'. There were two single men in different parts of the auditorium, which was not crowded. Throughout the one-hour show, they cast sidelong glances at one another. One was lanky and balding, the other short-haired, tanned and prosperously dressed. At the end of the show they moved together slowly, then suddenly threw their arms round one another and shouted uproariously.

'Marty!'

'Howard! You old bastard! Here, at the ends of the earth!'

'Are you living in Vancouver? My God! Come back to the "Bay-shore". I've got a suite.'

'You're in the money. I heard you were on the run, but you look so rich!'

'I'm so rich I don't know how to spend it. I've got a wall safe stuffed with dollars. I'm buying $80,000 of real estate near Aspen, Colorado. They're going to build a Holiday Inn on it. I'm working with all these big New York dealers. We've got a Miami condo down in Coconut Grove. It's got a TV intercom so you can see who's at the front door. All the New Yorkers have one. We're right on the shore, and it's got a gym, swimming pool, tennis courts. I've bought a pale green Cadillac Seville and I met these amazing guys – there's one called Cuba knows all the hit men in Detroit, and this guy, Charming in New York: he made a million dollars before he was 21, but he's just so *nice*! – he's got a sports shop on Madison Avenue, he finances these Paris designers and he collects Art Deco. His brother's got his name on the moon: he's a NASA scientist. They really know how to live, these people. You know, I'm getting fitness conscious. I've bought all these tracksuits, I take tennis lessons, I belong to a sports club in Miami with jacuzzis and saunas and that. I go shooting with Cuba at a range – I'm good at it, I'm really good. You take your own guns. And I play some golf too. They don't have caddies; you get a dune buggy of your own. . . .'

'Slow down, this is too much. The new *sportif* Howard, eh?'

'All the fruits of crime, Marty! How about you?'

'I'm here with The Man. Jim McCann. He's running his interests out of Vancouver. He's got a company called "Ashling Multi-Media". Spends a lot of time hanging out with movie actresses down on the West Coast.'

A few hours later, McCann himself turned up at the hotel.

'How's British Intelligence?'

'Fuck off!'

'You Welsh fucker, you always fall on your feet. Tracked me down, have you? I suppose you want something?'

'Leave off the bullshit, Jim. It's pure coincidence. We took a trip out of the States because my entry permit was going to expire, and thought we'd come back down the West Coast. I enjoy plane travel: first-class only of course. Come downstairs to Trader Vic's and let's have dinner.'

McCann was flying high. He had an office floor in the Guinness Tower, talked lavishly about his oil interests in Venezuela, claimed to

226

be putting finance into the film *Equus*, and spoke of his warm friendship with James Coburn. The hotel staff treated 'Mr Kennedy' with great respect, as of a man accustomed to disburse huge gratuities. But his smuggling seemed to be in a curious lull:

'Ah, there's been some ugly incidents in that business. I brought a container into Oakland, outside San Francisco. Somebody got shot.'

'How's Graham Plinston?'

'That tiny fucker. He's turned into a poof. They're all poofs in San Francisco! You did well getting clear of that MI6 business the way you did. I just might come down to New York and see you soon.'

Howard never quite found what was at the bottom of this cagey talk. But the truth was, McCann had made himself notorious in San Francisco. It seems McCann never much appreciated the art of pricing in the dope trade. His idea of doing business was to set dealer against dealer; to sit on stocks and force up the price; and to offer sudden cheap bulk deals. Wholesale dope needs to be marketed down the line at a predictable price – smoothly and fast. Instability, recriminations and rip-offs lead to trouble: and trouble is dangerously uncool. Plinston also seemed to have neglected Business Rule Number One: never let McCann owe you money.

Ambitious as always, Howard tried on the strength of this situation to invent a grandiose smuggling system to solve the importing problems of the jittery Donald Brown organisation. Donald Brown and his men were basically bootleggers from Queens, trying to do for themselves what an earlier generation of piratical New York families had done during prohibition. Like all smuggling firms, they were loose: connections came and went. But although they had an Irish flavour, they would not do business with the IRA; and they kept well away from heroin and the Mafia. It was a life of endless opportunism, revolving around Kennedy Airport. They had been bribing and suborning airline freight handlers for something approaching seven years, having grasped the fundamental principles of air-freight when German-based GIs started shipping in suitcases of dope through Frankfurt Airport at the end of the 1960s.

But they were in a state of running war with the Drug Enforcement Agency – just about the only New Yorkers who still regarded dope-smoking as a disgusting act. The DEA knew very well that the main man behind the endless JFK airport scams was the hyperactive red-head who held court in his London-bought Turnbull and Asser shirts in Nicola's restaurant in East 84th Street on the Upper East

227

Side. Describing his early life as a high-school drop-out, Brown said, 'I took the back roads. Not the highways. The back roads.' He was another pirate, like McCann and Howard: he loved scams. He used to boast that as a graduation present for one of his youthful Queens friends, he borrowed his beat-up Cadillac, fitted it with false licence plates and took it to a garage for a full set of repairs. He then simply stole it back and presented the renovated machine to its delighted owner.

Brown used 'straightened' freight handlers at Braniff, Alitalia, JAL and Pan Am to divert cargoes and siphon off their contents as they were labelled for transhipment through JFK, largely to fictitious importers in South America. The DEA had two sniffer dogs, called Smack and Brandy, a computer called TECS, teams of agents, and an increasingly sophisticated 160-page printed manual on how to detect discrepancies, fictitious shippers and consignees, and suspect countries of origin on the fundamental air freight document – the Air Waybill. If a shipment came from a hash-producing country, such as the Lebanon, Morocco or Pakistan, the DEA were increasingly likely to spot it. If it was heavy, vaguely labelled, and had unusually precise requirements as to which airlines should carry it, and which routes they should fly, the DEA men started to get out the Criss-Cross telephone directories: was the contact phone number listed as that of a recognised importer? Did trade association directories in the country of origin list the shippers' name? Did the plane's cargo manifest show any interesting items marked as 'off-loaded prior to arrival at JFK' or 'Not loaded'? Was it worth doing a full visual check with the manifest as the cargo came through the plane doors? Was it worth opening up a couple of crates?

Both sides used dirty tricks. The DEA arrested Don Brown associates on cocaine charges, and persuaded them to become spies. Some of Brown's men bribed DEA staff to get working manuals, and computer print-outs of individuals and methods under suspicion. They also learned to vacuum-seal slabs of hash, and wash them down with petrol.

This war was why Howard had been a welcome appearance on the scene in 1975. A PIA shipment of 400lb loaded in Damascus ostensibly for Quito, Ecuador, had been accidentally routed to London and discovered by HM Customs. Don Brown escaped by the skin of his teeth. A shipment from Pakistan coming via JAL in Tokyo to disguise its origins, had shuttled about the world for weeks, pursued by frantic phone calls, because JFK was not a logical routing for it to take to South America. Brown was hearing a whisper that the DEA were curious about these new Alitalia shipments from Dubai. Was there another new routing anyone like Howard could dream up?

Three men sat round the six-foot-square Oregon pine coffee-table in the new luxury 10th floor apartment in Pavilion Buildings, while Judy busied herself as a good dope-dealer's chick should, preparing the Sunday lunch and not interfering with business. The 200-dollar-a-week apartment on 62nd Street near Maxwell's Plum, that looked so chic with its built-in bar when Howard and Judy first arrived, had soon come to appear embarrassingly tacky, when he learned now rich people could really live in that town. He did a 'front' deal with Rico, one of his smoother friends from Sussex, for his video company to lease this East 77th Street riverside pad which Howard would periodically occupy. He stocked it with a sumptuous bed, an enormous desk, a glass-topped table, a remote control TV, an expensive tape-player, and the latest British invention: a record-player which would play designated tracks by an infra-red remote control switch. He loved gadgets.

At the moment, Howard, quietly dressed, sat with his feet up on the Oregon pine. He had a shoe-box lid of tobacco and cigarette papers in front of him. Mike Durrani, dark, lean and aristocratic, had a crystal glass of whisky, and a pencil in his beautifully manicured hands. His brown eyes were frowning at the sheet of paper lying on the table. Jim McCann, a little fleshy these days behind his tinted glasses, lounged in the deep leather sofa.

'No, Jim,' Howard said. 'There'll be no necessity for you to meet Don Brown. I know his terms and I think we can agree on this. He gets 25 per cent personally. His airport crowd get another 25 per cent. You and Mike will get 35 per cent between you for bringing the stuff through. Two tons will leave Karachi as "transformers" to an Irish company and it'll re-emerge from Shannon on Aer Lingus to New York as, what? Something fragile – Irish coffee glasses. Guinness glasses! Yes, and 15 per cent for me, for masterminding. Don't worry, I'll do my share of the work.'

Six weeks later, Howard sat alone in the flat. On the Oregon pine table was a bowl of disinfectant for his hands. They were black and filthy. He was surrounded by video-recorder cartons and suitcases full of used 20-dollar bills. He had been counting money for almost eight hours continuously. It added up to 5 million dollars. Mike Durrani and Donald Brown came round personally with empty suitcases. McCann said: 'Get a chauffeur-driven limo, and deliver it round to Olympic Towers. That's where I'm staying, with Jackie Onassis and Adnan Kashoggi. It's very nice, overlooking St Patrick's Cathedral. I'm looking down on what I looked up to all my life before.' Howard took three-quarters of a million dollars and put it in the safe deposit of his own New York bank.

There followed a period of crazed celebration. Howard could be seen driving round New York in an enormous limousine with a black chauffeur called Harvey. He would go out with Harvey and send him in to pay his electricity bill. Rico, who sold cocaine and heroin to playboys, brought round famous girls who did not know who they were meeting: Sabrina Guinness and her sisters; Jane Bonham Carter; Lady Antonia Fraser's daughter Rebecca. Charming, the young impresario, took him to the fashionable nightclubs – Regine's and the briefly notorious disco, Studio 54. At a private Studio 54 party thrown by Charming, he met Bernie Cornfeld, the controversial financier. He was frequently seen at Nicola's restaurant, where they did not take notice of anything but cash, and handed out backgammon boards at the close of meals, drinking champagne among the folksy Germanic decor, with the gangsters, actors and CIA men. Run by the former headwaiter of Elaine's, the well-known actors' haunt at 88th Street, Nicola's used to be written about in *New York* magazine. The magazine's journalists would make such remarks as this:

'Nicola's had become a focal point for a new class: a bit raffish, very preppy, and with a strong admixture of the *émigré* European rich, fleeing socialist depredations at home.'

It was arguably one way of describing Howard Marks.

Unfortunately, there were to be no repeat performances. When McCann returned to Vancouver in triumph, the Canadian Mounties came round to his wood-and-glass mansion in Brunswick Beach by the side of the Pacific and took him away. They said a 'confidential source' had handed them a drinking glass with his fingerprints on and he wasn't 'James Kennedy' at all.

'Let me do a deal,' said McCann. 'I'll leave voluntarily.' He said: 'If you arrest people like me, the effect will be like a stone dropped into water. The ripple will have you peeled like an apple.'

He was in fine, crazy form, playing the Green Card for all it was worth. When immigration officer Jack Betteridge said they thought they might deport him back to Ireland, McCann riposted, 'Mr Betteridge, you are an enemy of the Irish people and will be tried in front of an Irish tribunal. You are also a fucking fascist pig, and justice will be served on you.'

McCann hired the country's leading lawyer, former MP John Taylor, who launched a battery of appeals, submissions, applications for bail, representations to the federal court, habeas corpus actions, pleas for stay of execution, and claims to political asylum. McCann announced, variously, that his fingerprints had been forged by British Intelligence; that he had unearthed a Protestant Ulster gun-running plot in British Columbia; that Cathal Goulding of the Official IRA and Michael Murphy of Ballinskelligs would vouch for his true identity, and that he had been a member of a Sinn Fein delegation to Cambodia and Vietnam between 1966 and 1968.

He whipped up a media storm. The *Province* and the Victoria *Daily Colonist* interviewed his Dutch wife, Sylvia, holding their baby. It was called Ashling. They probed, unsuccessfully, into Ashling Investments, registered in Curaçao. They quoted film producer Elliot Kastner saying 'Kennedy' certainly did not finance *Equus*, and contrariwise, CKVU executive Norm Klenman saying he certainly did buy a package of films and TV shows from Kennedy. 'He was a most charming and personable man. I would swear he is Jim Kennedy,' he said. 'Mind you, I live in a world of Hollywood hype and nothing would surprise me.'

Aki Lehmann, wife of the prominent New York banker Robin Lehmann, who McCann had met in Paris, said innocently: 'I regard him as a very close and dear friend.' Kennedy she said, seemed to be the backer and distributor of a number of Hollywood big-name productions. 'He's dynamic, extremely intelligent, sensitive and very human. He is generous to a fault. I don't mean financially, though he doesn't hesitate to spend money – but in his dealings with people. I cannot believe that a man as gentle as Jim could be a terrorist.'

Various hoarse telephone calls were made by the 'Irish Republican Army' to the Canadian missions in Dublin and Belfast, threatening dire consequences if 'Kennedy' was not treated right. The Federal immigration Department wrote a bail report saying:

The protection of the public demands the detention of the applicant. He has escaped custody twice, he has enormous financial backing

231

and is an international fugitive. He is a public menace whose threats to public officials cannot be treated lightly.

They also quoted rather embarrassingly from the early McCann police record at Scotland Yard.

Whirlwinds of confusion were sown by Jim. When it transpired that on first arrival he had been known not as Kennedy at all, but as 'Kingsley', he said it was his mother's maiden name, which it was an old Irish custom to use in conjunction with one's own. He produced a birth certificate for 'Joseph' Kennedy, and explained that 'Jim' was an old Irish abbreviation for Joseph. He announced that the British had confused him with the IRA commander Joseph McCann who had been supposedly shot dead in 1972, but had not, in fact been shot dead at all, through an old Irish ruse. As the Federal lawyers stumbled and weaved under this barrage, the local papers began to write querulous editorials about 'incompetence'. The British announced they had better things to do than seek the extradition – awkward as it would certainly have been – of someone who was more a common criminal than a terrorist. In the end, after enduring three months of McCann mayhem, the Canadians relieved him of 5,000 dollars 'bail' and returned his passport. McCann shot out of the country like a hare, leaving most of his wealth behind.

Oddly enough, throughout the entire high pitched affair, no one mentioned dope.

Undaunted, Howard persevered with his trade. In the following 18 months he visited eight countries, changed his address six times and his identity thrice. He put together nine different smuggling operations, ranging in size from a carton the size of a suitcase to five tons of hashish. Five of the scams failed spectacularly, in one way or another, but he survived them all. He made about a million dollars. And he lost about a million dollars. It was a gambler's life, but he lived high while he was gambling. Howard was becoming one of the most hardened intercontinental dope-smugglers in Europe.

Had he been under surveillance – which would have been a most expensive operation for any national police force – he could first have been spotted in France, fresh off the Concorde waiting at the Meridien Hotel, on the Riviera in Nice, for Jim McCann. Of course, McCann never came. Howard drove to a luxurious villa in the Alpes Maritimes, and had a few bottles of champagne and a little talk with the owner –

Mike Durrani. He moved to the Carlton Hotel in Cannes with one of the guests he met there – 'Lebanese Sam'. And they had another little talk. He and Judy drove north to the old mill in the Dordogne where Patrick Lane was studying banking:

'I've worked out how to deposit and extract money in off-shore fiscal paradises all over the Caymans, Canada and the Caribbean. . . .'

'Here's 20,000 dollars, the keys to my New York flat and the combination of the safe. Go do it.'

They drove to Paris. Douglas and Slinger were holding an exhibition of Tantric Art, and Howard had it in mind to offer the services of his accountant in one or two joint company enterprises. He loved to have fronts. 'Let's stay in L'Hôtel. It's madly luxurious. Oscar Wilde used to go there.'

Dining at Maxim's, Howard was squashed by the black-coated waiters.

'M'sieu may be correct that the Chateau d'Yquem is on the wine list. But I am sorry, it is not available. We have only a few bottles left.' They knew a nouveau riche when they saw one.

Howard left for a little holiday in Albi, near Toulouse. The name made him laugh.

The next country Howard could be spotted in was Switzerland. In Geneva, Lane returned with his fiscal report, a courier came from Don Brown with a 250,000 dollar investment for Lebanese Sam and he bumped into Anthony Woodhead outside the railway station. (Dope-dealers are always bumping into each other in Switzerland.) They had a little talk about a man in San Francisco.

'I'd like to live in Switzerland,' Howard said to him. 'They don't make trouble about where your money comes from, and you can *work* from here. The trains run on time and you can direct-dial Bangkok from a coinbox on top of the Jungfrau.'

'My family live in Padua. I know a bit about this part of the world. Go and have a hunt around in Ticino. It's the Italian canton of Switzerland. You'll get the right combination of Italian dirt and Swiss efficiency.'

But Howard could suddenly be seen again in New York, talking in low tones to a grim-faced Don Brown. Before they'd even had a chance to try the new Trans-Mediterranean Airlines connection, Lebanese Sam had managed to get himself arrested in Beirut. 'Shit, Don. I've always had terrible luck in the Lebanon.'

He would now, equally rapidly, have been sighted back in Italy, where Judy was house-hunting. Not exactly Italy in fact. Not exactly Switzerland either. She had rented an apartment on the lakeside slope of an extraordinary little Alpine town. There, having installed a few necessities of life, such as the electric organ and the inlaid baccarat table, Howard sat with his binoculars on the window ledge, looking out across Lake Lugano or down the hill towards the cafes and the casino, past street doors with hundreds and hundreds of brass company name-plates affixed.

Patrick Lane, who rapidly also set up house there himself, wrote most lyrically about Campione in an anonymous 'Tax Haven Report' he compiled and sold off to surprisingly large numbers of shady subscribers.

Campione d'Italia is a unique tax haven. It is an Italian enclave on the shore of Lake Lugano, entirely surrounded by Swiss territory. It is about 12 miles from the Swiss/Italian land frontier at Chiasso. Sheep and goats used to be grazed all over the mountainside, but over the past few years, every inch has been developed for building. The Italian Lakes enjoy some of the best weather in Europe. The winters are mild, although the snow is plentiful enough for skiing. The summers are long and hot, with cool breezes from the lake. Of all the world's tax havens Campione is probably the most beautiful.

Since the time of the Romans, the rich and powerful in Europe have been building their pleasure palaces on these shores. The deep blue waters of Lake Lugano, the red-tiled roofs of the delicate Italian architecture, the timeless majesty of the Alps and the solid vaults of the surrounding banks, create an environment in which it is good to be alive.

Mafiosi, sports stars and actors come to live in Campione, Lane's Tax Haven Report explains, because neither the Italians nor the Swiss bother in practice to levy any taxes on resident foreigners.

Germans, English, Americans, French and other expatriates who have no commercial dealings in Italy live, to all intents and purposes, absolutely tax free. Campione is under Italian jurisdiction, but physically located in Switzerland. . . . Like Andorra, it is small and beautiful, hidden in the mountains and has a long history of proud independence. But where Andorra is isolated on the edge of civilisation, Campione is situated in the heart of Europe. The perfect business day starts at 7 a.m. on the jetty at Campione. The ten-minute ride across the lake gives ample time for a quick coffee. A short walk to Lugano railway station, where you can pick up the latest copies of the *Wall Street Journal*, the *International Herald Tribune* and the *Financial Times*. A journey on a Swiss train through the Alps, eating an excellent breakfast and reading the international press will put you in excellent mood for your late-morning arrival in Zurich for luncheon with your banker on Bahnhofstrasse.

Lane goes on:

A professional consultant, such as a major rock star or tennis pro, offering services all over the world, can have his fees paid directly into his Swiss bank account. If he chooses his bank very carefully, he can sit at home on his patio in Campione, and look at his money across the lake. Possibly the corporate structure best suited to Campione is the Sociata Responsibilita Limitada – private limited liability company. Unlike a Swiss A.G. it can be entirely owned and operated by foreigners, who also may choose to remain anonymous. As long as the company has no business dealings with Italy, the tax liability can be reduced almost to zero.

Howard could not, however, have been kept under surveillance long in Campione. The next sighting of him would have been in the maternity ward at St Teresa's private hospital, in the bourgeois south London suburb of Wimbledon. 'Albert Lane' was attending the birth of his daughter Amber. He always enjoyed seeing his children born, and besides, he did not want his baby to be stateless. England was best. And it was not that he had any ideological prejudice against the National Health Service. He just felt ill signing his name on forms. Naturally, it was the friends of Howard Marks who gave him the necessary references for a bank account in Twickenham, and a flat in Richmond. Then one in Chelsea Cloisters. Then one in Queensgate.

'Ray, are you still running that answer service for me in Epsom? Great. No, listen don't worry. It was a long shot sending you off to Kabul like that with a fistful of dollars to bribe the Intercon waiters. I just like Afghani very much. If the guy in New York never saw his box it's not your fault. You did your best.'

'Mike, you sound terrible. What's the matter? McCann made you give him my home number? Well I can believe it, he's very terroristic

235

at times. Don't distress yourself Mike, for God's sake. You sound as if you're actually crying. Yeah, I can do that: you'll get it down yourself in New York and give me 10 per cent to find wholesalers. Money for old rope, eh?'

'Yes it is me, Jim. Don't give me all that old bullshit. Why should I have to give you money? So you're broke in France. Whose fault is that? I don't see I could have done anything to help you more than I did.'

'Judy, let's move flats. McCann says he's going to blow up my parents' house and stuff like that. I'll get a new ID too, I think. No, it's just sour grapes, but with us having the baby, I don't want to take silly risks. We'll go and spend Christmas at the Metropole in Brighton. That's a quiet place.'

'Peter Whitehead – yes I remember you very well from the Sixties. You made the film of *Wholly Communion* at the Albert Hall, and *Let's All Make Love* in London. Great films. Yeah, Nik Douglas: I helped him set up this Caymans' company, "Sceptre Holdings". The position is this. If you're disposing of the Carlisle Street office, I'd very much like a West End address for my company, Worldwide Entertainments. It's registered in Liberia. Oh, films and things. I'm a pop impresario these days. The name's Donald Nice.'

When the baby was old enough to travel, Howard could have been observed moving his family back out to Campione with his new passport. In Paris, en route, he could have been seen in a phone booth, talking rapidly to Los Angeles.

'Oh no. Oh no! I thought you had these docks sewn up. That was five whole tons. What the hell made them open up the container – it was all labelled personal effects from Karachi wasn't it – tables, chairs . . . lampshades? What health hazard? "Camelskin Lampshades!" Oh, the fools!'

That summer, patient surveillance might have picked him out among the tourists in Karachi, inspecting ancient ruins and wolfing mutton moghai with a palate trained for years in the Pakistani restaurants of Westbourne Grove. He would certainly have been spotted at the airport there meeting another Englishman:

'Swede. Hi. You got out here OK? I'm having a great time. Bought a load of books, done all the trips. It's amazing you know, the poverty makes people behave differently. If you're handicapped or misshapen, they don't hide you away. Do you realise this is the first time I've ever visited a country where they grow dope. Amazing. I still haven't actually seen any. I'm kicking around here. The New York man said "Come out and make sure the wogs don't screw up again." He's been very All-American since we lost the Beirut load. But I want you to go to Thailand tomorrow. To Bangkok. There's a lot of tied-up Thai sticks been there for weeks. Need babysitting. I've got 100,000 dollars stuck in them.'

Had the DEA been watching the New York apartment at East 77th and York, they would have seen him back in residence later that year, with filthy hands and the bowl of disinfectant by his side.

'OK. That's all your suitcases counted. Thanks very much. We really needed a sweet 1500 kilos like that to come through. What complications! I was starting to sweat when we had to go to Basle, buy all the sewing machines and send the other stuff up under bond from Paris to be "consolidated" with them up there on TMA. I did fear Paris would do a Customs inspection once the routing fouled up like that. Do you really think you can get the Bangkok stuff uplifted this time?'

And had the American DEA been watching, they would have heard the New York apartment phone ring a week later, and seen Howard freeze at what he heard. They would have seen him pause only to pack a few cherished cassettes of WAMC radio station output, which he loved playing to himself. And they would have seen him run, leaving a deserted apartment behind. But the DEA would not have been watching Howard. They were too busy at that point systematically arresting 16 New Yorkers alleged to be at the centre of the Donald Brown organisation. The Bangkok shipment had really and truly gone down.

Howard just kept moving. He was doing the hippy trail, Howard Marks style, when next visible. He was cruising up the foothills of the Himalayas in a chauffeur-driven car provided by the Intercontinental Hotel. On the way to Murray Hill station, he stopped the car. There were wild grass plants growing by the roadside, just as he had hoped. There it was. Real dope. The humble cannabis plant, for which he was going to so much trouble, and which was making him so dangerously rich. It was, he found to his disappointment, a curiously emotionless occasion. He and these plants did not really have much to say to each other. He climbed back into the car, gestured the chauffeur upwards, into the Himalayas.

In the hills, he encounted an old dope-dealing Oxford chum – the way that Balliol men so often did, even in these late days of Empire.

'I been out of jail a few years now, Howie. I'm pretty desperate for money. You can't make any, dealing hash in London these days. I'm just out here, looking around, you know. Might run some heroin.'

'Don't do that. I'm out here on a big American scam. A guy says he can get a load down in San Francisco for me, so I'm doing the buying in Karachi. But I've got another scam in London soon, with any luck. It's a yacht. Judy's sister was out in Greece with this guy, learning to sail. He's going to bring in a lot of cheap Moroccan and land it in Scotland. You can wholesale it for me when it lands. That's OK. It's a pleasure.'

Howard could have been watched return to Europe on a classic dope-smuggler's itinerary. Karachi. . . . Pause at Zurich during banking hours. . . . Campione d'Italia. His hippy trip gave him dysentery. But his work was never done. There was a frantic phone call from Larry in London. Dysentery notwithstanding. Howard was to be seen, pale and sweating, not eating the excellent breakfast as the train rattled back through the Alps to Zurich Airport. This time he went to Spain; back to the Balearic Islands. There was the yacht *Bagheera* in the harbour at Palma, Majorca. And there was its bearded American skipper, Stewart Prentiss.

'Well, I'm not going to do it, and that's that. I won't collect dope on the Mediterranean coast and sail it through the Straits of Gibraltar. It's got to be delivered on the beach the Atlantic side, as we said in the first place. And your man was supposed to be producing four times as much as that. I'm going to continue sailing my normal route home. It looks better. So sort it out before I dock in Cadiz.'

Howard's next moves would have baffled a policeman. He would have been sighted in Germany, driving up the Rhine in huge Mercedes with Judy and the baby, clutching his stomach and groaning faintly. He booked them into the Swan hotel at Ostereich, and after a while, began to recover his spirits. It was purely a sentimental holiday: the Swan at Ostereich was where he had done his first deal.

And he flew back, this time to Cadiz, via Madrid. There was a lot of cajoling, arguing, consulting almanacs for dates of the full moon, trips to a safe-deposit in Frankfurt for more cash, quality sampling, promises about sales. A fellow yachtsman, let down in the Lebanon with a cargo, was making his way home empty-handed and desperate for business.

He agreed to collect the Moroccan dope, do a 'bottle job' through

238

the dangerous straits of Gibraltar, and rendezvous with *Bagheera* in mid-Atlantic. The dope would then proceed, as planned, to Scotland.

'Right, I'm glad you're all at it now,' Howard said. 'My San Francisco shipment's come in. I'm off to America to sort it out. They keep saying it's going to take as long as two or three weeks to collect in all the money from sales.'

He could have been seen at the Waldorf Towers in New York, pacing up and down. He could have been seen flying across to San Francisco, with an anxious expression. And finally, he could have been seen at the Japanese Centre Hotel in San Francisco with a private sauna in his room, storming at Cuba from Miami who had come out at Howard's request. For Howard's first thought had been – for once – violent revenge.

'Anthony Woodhead's gone to Nicaragua with all the cash, mine and the Pakistanis! A million dollars! The rat! He's sold a ton of hash and run away with the money!'

'Why did he do it? I mean, there's so much trust in this business. If he'd come to me with some cock-and-bull story, I'd have believed it, anyway. You know, when he didn't show, I thought – "Maybe he's been mugged by some 12-year-old black kid and he's too embarrassed to say." The little shit! I'll have to take full responsibility for the Pakistani money. It's the least that business ethics demand. They're my main suppliers. I'm going to have to give them at least something like 600 grand. What a rip-off! If things go on this way in the dope business, everything's going to turn into some crude cash-for-hash transaction. I mean, how vulgar can you get?'

'It's not much,' said Cuba. 'I know some guys who set fire to a $3 million Lear Jet just because it got bogged down in some mud. Now if you'd lost a *hundred* tons like we sometimes do on the Colombia runs. . . .'

Larry rang up from London. 'He's safely landed it all in Scotland. A ton.'

'Has he? Has he?' Disappointed as Howard was in human nature, Cuba had given him the germ of an enormous idea. He decided to cease his travels, and return decisively to England. There he would work on a project. What he was going to do was nothing less than the biggest dope-smuggling operation Europe had ever seen.

# CHAPTER 9

# The Great Big Monster

Death comes to everybody. That was how the crucial new connections started. Howard was at the Westminster Hospital beside Mike Durrani, descendant of Afghan kings and the most reliable smuggler ever to work out of Karachi Airport. Although only in his 40s, like so many busy men, he had had a heart attack. 'Howard,' he said faintly. 'Don't forget, this Dutch deal, I must have payment in guilders.'

'No, Mike,' said Howard. 'It will be all right.'

Back in Durrani's big flat near Harrods, waiting for bad news from the hospital, Howard picked up the ringing phone. It was Jim McCann.

'Ah, Howard,' he said, quickly. 'It's you, is it? I've tracked you down, that's it. Shame about Mike. How is he? Yes, well, I was a bit animated and under pressure at that moment, wasn't I? You're a cunt, yourself. All right, come over to Paris. I've got political asylum here, now. I'll look after you.'

He was, for once, telling more or less the truth. The 'flics' had picked him up in the club-house of a villa estate on the Riviera, near Cannes. 'James McCann,' they said. 'We know all about you. The German police would like to extradite you. A matter of an IRA bombing at Munchen Gladbach in 1973.'

They locked him in Les Baumettes, the Marseilles jail, and set about the contentious business of extradition. It was McCann's bad luck that the Provisional IRA had just started a new and genuine campaign of explosions at British Army bases in Germany, spewing his name on to the top of computer printouts throughout Europe, particularly in the Wiesbaden headqaurters of the BKA. It was McCann's tremendously good luck to become the darling of the French left. The Germans had taken a heavy-handed line the previous year, successfully forcing the

240

extradition of Klaus Croissant, lawyer to members of the Baader-Meinhof platoon of anarchists. Upset about the erosion of the French tradition of asylum, activists helped to defeat extradition attempts by both the Italians who wanted a supporter of the 'Red Brigades', and the Spanish, who wanted back one of the Basque guerrilla group, ETA.

The Marseilles lawyers in the ETA case, said they would take on McCann for 'idealistic' reasons. McCann strutted about Les Baumettes, announcing to the only English-speaking prisoner he could find – a German called Wolfgang Kustner – 'I'm James. I am an Irish terrorist.' It was an authentic McCann performance.

'They arrested me as Kennedy, but my name's McCann. The Germans and the French picked me up together and flew me here by helicopter from a military prison. A judge called Lucas wants me sent to Germany. He must be an Englishman. I'm a volunteer officer of the IRA, but I'm not a combatant. They're legal in Ireland, and I've been raising IRA funds in America. I'm over here to present an appeal to the European Court of Human Rights in Strasbourg about the torture conditions which Irish prisoners are forced to undergo.'

'What are you charged with, James?'

'Oh, various assassination attempts. And this bombing at Munchen Gladbach. The British Army has a computer with all the IRA membership lists. They keep it there, for security. It's a big building, three or four storeys. There was plastic explosive in holes drilled all up the walls. But I wasn't present myself, mind. Do you know what happened to my woman and the two children? Were they arrested? They'll tell the IRA; they use helicopters for escapes, you know. Or we take hostages. They could kidnap Lucas, and then they'd exchange him for me. And if they won't exchange me, they'll break his arm! And next, they cut off one of his legs! He should be liquidated, that Lucas.'

A full-page article in the Communist paper *Liberation* exhumed the memory of James 'The Fox' McCann, authentic member of the IRA's Belfast brigade, shot by the British in early 1973. He was the real McCann, they revealed: the other McCann was a harmless 'underground journalist' and besides, the man in Les Baumettes, was in fact, 'Peter Joseph Kennedy'. . . .

The Trotskyist trade union group, the 'Organisation Communiste Internationale', organised petitions in Marseilles for intellectuals and liberals to sign. The 'Comité pour la Liberation de KENNE-

DY/MCCANN' posted up handbills declaring 'Un scandale judiciaire et politique!'

## LIBÉRATION IMMÉDIATE ET SANS CONDITION DE KENNEDY!
## DROIT D'ASILE POLITIQUE POUR LES ÉTRANGERS!
## NON À LA CONVENTION EUROPÉENNE DITE ANTI-TERRORISTE!

McCann, the political prisoner, replied in shocking French:

Camarades. Je suis tres touché par votre solidarité . . . mes circonst-ances personelles sont le résultat d'une conspiration entre les services secrét anglais at allemands de l'Ouest, tumeur fasciste au coeur de l'Europe democratique. Yours in Combat, James Kennedy (McCann).

Just before Christmas, the French authorities, like the Canadians before them, wearily capitulated. McCann would not be extradited, a court in Aix-en-Provence ruled, because his crimes were 'political'. An elated McCann told sympathetic Paris journalists:

'Drugs? . . . It was a plot of British Intelligence to character-assassinate me. Let me tell you that I totally abhor any form of drug-taking. I would like to mention someone in connection with that situation. A gentleman called Howard Marks, an ex-Oxford graduate, a double agent for British Intelligence. He made an attempt to infiltrate an international revolutionary group I was involved with. He is the cause of the rumours that began about my character. My various victories overcame this.'

A few weeks later, at the lakeside casino at Enghien, outside Paris, there was a slightly less publicised meeting.

'Howard, have you got a source of supply? Let me tell you, Dublin Airport is finally under my grasp! You get all the European flights into there.'

'Jim, I'm working on the Great Big Monster deal of all time: and you can be part of it. But there's one we can try together first. Bangkok. Can you do it?'

'Into Ireland?'

'Yeah. I've had a guy out there. We've tried one kamikaze run into Heathrow with Thai sticks in bales of silk. But when the truck driver opened them up, it was peat. Must have been a bust somehow. Funny, peat must be quite a lot dearer than dope out there. . . . Anyway, what about a full-scale air freight scam? I do all the Thai end, the buying, paying off the Army to deliver, paying off the Customs to load. Comes in Philippine Airways, 'origin Manila'. It's a Thai Air, 'straightened' freight agent. And I sell it in London, after we bring it across in teams of cars. Like the old days. At Shannon. . . .'

It worked fine. Whatever nameless methods McCann had to make people do his will, functioned once more. Howard, unknown to the police of four continents, was back in Dublin, temporary proprietor this time of No. 24 Wyvern, a rather smart executive home in Killiney. It is questionable whether Killiney Bay in fact stands comparison with the Bay of Naples, as the local hotels are fond of claiming. But if it does, then Killiney itself is a kind of soggy Beverley Hills. Killiney Road is the Rodeo Drive of Dublin. Italianate mansions, with absurd ceramic tiles and swimming pools, lurk on the hillsides between the chi-chi shops. The Canadian ambassador to Dublin has his residence there. More to Howard's point, 'Fitzpatrick's Castle' and the baronial 'Killiney Court' have, among the suits of armour and the dungeon discos, a fair selection of payphones.

Eight cars went on the dope run. One got searched by British Customs at Liverpool; and then there were seven. The tiniest of paragraphs appeared in the *Liverpool Post* on 20 July 1979. 'Famous soccer star' Eddie Clamp had six international caps to his credit, the paper said. It added that he had been discovered in the passenger seat of the car a Wolverhampton man was trying to drive off Trafalgar Ferry Dock with 70 lb of compressed Thai sticks tucked into the bodywork. (They acquitted Clamp later and sent the driver down.)

That counted as success. Howard could shortly after have been briefly sighted in a bungalow on the teeming outskirts of Bangkok, setting up the second deal. He was in a bleary state. He had jet lag, and he had been visiting the massage parlours in his capacity as a 'fronted up' pop video salesman. There were couples having sex on customers' tables. There were nude women doing difficult things with ping-pong balls, and blowing smoke rings with their cigarettes. There was a young man on stage having sexual intercourse with a duck. The duck seemed heavily drugged. Howard had followed its example.

And now he was staring fascinated at the square 'ethnic' tables with inlaid chess sets, into which his expatriate Australian middlemen friends were forcing slabs of vacuum-sealed dope. He could swear one

243

of the tables was moving. It was moving. It exploded! When he opened his eyes, they said 'Yeah, It's the heat. There's a flaw in the packing method. They do that sometimes. But we'll get them to Oz in the end.' Howard groaned slightly and closed his eyes. He had better get back to the airport. . . .

At peace, Howard and Jim McCann later looked out over the silvery rocks of Ballinskelligs Bay. This was where their bizarre partnership had begun, eight years before. Now, their womenfolk and children could be seen playing on the see-saw below as they leaned on the balcony rails of the elegant Waterville Lake Hotel. They could look out towards the muddy little village of Ballinskelligs from this side of the bay – and they could afford the hotel. Howard was expecting to clear £100,000 once the Thai sticks were sold.

'Jim, I'm glad you still retain your grip! Let me reveal my Great Big Monster scheme. All the hash we move is just peanuts really. I saw that when I was living in Miami. The real dope industry is there. They smuggle literally thousands of tons of Colombian grass every year. It goes up the East Coast of the States into Florida. Shrimp boats, trawlers, yachts, tugs. They once bust a boat with 140 tons of grass on board. Can you imagine it? It's just so highly organised. Colombia is a country exporting nothing but drugs – coffee, cocaine, quaaludes, and the grass. The dope is all run by the Cuban exiles in Miami, and they wholesale the stuff off, Bang! Bang! Two or three guys buy it in a single day – they all carry huge stocks of cash. It's out of sight.

'Now, I think I've got the connections to do this. My friend Cuba started the Bangkok caper, and I'm taking him some of my profits over as a kick-back. A little thank you. He got clear of the Don Brown bust. I don't see any reason why I can't bring a ship load of Colombian back this way, over the Atlantic. Import it direct. Very popular stuff in England: fetches twice the price it does there.'

'A boatload, eh? Where do you land it?'

'Here. County Kerry. It's the ideal spot. Thought we could tour around, look at a few sites. It's isolated. I guessed you might be capable of organising a few people to land a really big shipment.'

'Of course I can, my good friend. His Nibbs can always do it. How much?'

'Forty tons?'

'Holy mother of God, you're out of your mind!'

'Well, those people won't sell in small loads. It's not worth their while. Thirty tons, at least.'

'It's a total Taff lunatic I see before me! I'll start investigating this autumn.'

'Yeah, right. Now in the meantime, this second Thai run. I'm a bit worried about the Liverpool bust. That driver knew me as "Albi". I don't want to do any more cars.'

'I can fix something with a fruit lorry. Got a few connections there. Send it up to the north, and over on the Larne ferry. They do a weekly trip.'

'Great, great. I do feel a bit uncomfortable being back in England. I'm picking up some attention. Did you know London Weekend TV were working on a programme about me? This guy Stephen Scott has some police report Fairweather did, when I skipped. I got my mate in LWT to pinch a copy of the script. Here. . . .'

He fetched it out of his briefcase. McCann chuckled as he read the choicer bits aloud:

. . . Smuggling cannabis from Holland inside Volvo cars. . . . Gone it seemed were all those dreams of riches and fame. . . .

'Ah, Howard, what a tragic tale . . .!'

He told his friends bail had been arranged for him by the Secret Service . . . the London Programme has documentary proof that Howard Marks was telling the truth.

'Oh ho!'

There was another Irishman in Amsterdam, British Intelligence were interested in.

'This is it. This is the Kid!'

McCann was in on Plinston's US drug smuggling operation.

'Hey, Howard, this is assassinating my character!'

'You read a bit further on. It's assassinating more than your character.'

James McCann claims, while he was on bail Howard Marks was involved in an attempt to assassinate him . . . a very good reason why Howard Marks *had* to disappear in April '74.

'Did I say that?'

'Apparently, Jim, yeah.'

'Hey, what is this?'

In September 1977 he turned up at a party at the Mirandy Gallery near Baker Street to launch a new book by Penny Slinger. . . . *Guardian* columnist Peter Hillmore says 'went to a party in London last year, several hundred people, Howard chatting to old friends, we even talked about having lunch'.

'Yeah, well, that's why I'm a bit bothered. I have been getting a little loose. Do you know, I saw my lawyer Bernie Simons across the room in the "Zanzibar" the other day? I'm sure he recognised me. And I went to this party of Henry Hodge's – he's a solicitor I knew at Balliol. He didn't know I was coming – I don't think he even saw me. But I was looning round saying hello to all my chums – I saw Kate Mortimer, she's in Lord Rothschild's Think Tank, and Chris Patten, the Tory MP, though I don't think he knew who I was. It was amazing, just amazing. That other Tory, William Waldegrave, spotted me once. He's the only one who ever did. He's married to Caroline Leith, Rico's friend. I was convinced he recognised me and called the Old Bill!'

'Ah you know all the right people don't you Howard? It's a wonder you don't march stark naked down Oxford Street banging a drum!'

'Yeah, but this script is really off the wall. Redmond O'Hanlon in Oxford said something. It was just a wind-up to get rid of them, about MI6 wanting him to keep his mouth shut – so now they're announcing I have special protection from the Secret Service! They cancelled the TV programme at the last minute, but this bloke Scott wrote a long piece in the *New Statesman* last month. So it all came out.'

'Ah, it's terrible: you can't believe a word you read in the newspapers, can you? Still won't do you any harm, will it? Bit of mysterification?'

'Naa – I'm not really worried. Got this very active front. I met Peter Clifton, who directed a film about Led Zeppelin. I'm sinking vast amounts of bread into a record studio called "Archipelago". See Peter Whitehead the film director all the time. He's very into falconry. You can sell falcons out in Saudi Arabia you know. Very macho stuff. He got fined once in Scotland for pinching baby golden eagles. Albi's a big pop impresario, isn't he? I meet P. J. Proby and Tom Baker – they don't know who I am – they're making this film called "Life After Elvis". And "Worldwide Entertainments" just loves the idea. So I'm tipping in loads of cash. It's a pretty ludicrous project. That's what I'm officially doing in Ireland now: looking for Elvis lookalikes!'

Early on a summer's morning the following week, Mr Tunnicliffe checked out of his Scottish hotel, and sat patiently in his rented car just outside the West Coast port of Stranraer. He was waiting for the fruit lorry. Further down the road, two of his workers sat in an empty van. Howard was going to have to wait a long time.

In the small hours a big articulated truck running north from the docks at Cork with a load of South American bananas had pulled into a layby on the main road just south of Dublin. A rented van was parked in the darkness. A courting couple were there too, at the other end of the layby.

McCann had been experimenting with cocaine, and was in an invincible mood. He banged on their window and jerked his thumb. 'You!' he said hoarsely. 'Out of here!'

The annoyed couple stopped at the first coinbox in the little town of Naas. 'There's some men acting suspiciously in a layby,' they told Garda Brendon McArdle.

A battle ensued in the darkness when the patrol car arrived. McCann waved a pistol, which was kicked out of his hand, roared off in a Hillman, crashed it, and was batoned to the ground while scrambling up a hill. The Irish Army bomb-disposal team blew open the truck doors when dawn broke, to discover to their surprise 21 tea chests full of Thai sticks. No one had ever seen so much dope in Ireland before. They were expecting IRA explosives.

Across the water, Howard continued to wait. No one answered the phones in Killiney. Then the lunchtime news came on the car radio. He swung the car round and braked by his waiting van down the road. 'They've been busted,' he said. There was a screech of tyres, and the van disappeared. Howard helter-skeltered back south to his current flat in Chelsea, just in time to switch on the evening news. The million-pound International Dublin Drugs Haul story did not, to his surprise, mention his name. He bribed a police constable in Fulham to look up his name in the Criminal Records computer. There was a downbeat note about an arrest warrant on a car insurance charge of

1972. Howard had never had any problems with car insurance, but the computer was clearly 'flagged' to ring a bell in the offices of the Special Branch. The PC found himself grilled the following morning.

'Where did you get that name from?'

'Oh, um, it was mentioned to me by a West End snout as somebody selling drugs.'

'Hmm.'

Howard had another friend, working in the office of the Director of Public Prosecutions.

'Yes,' he said. 'The name "Tunnicliffe" does seem to be known in this connection.'

Howard rapidly ordered a new passport in the name of 'Roy Green'.

It was tricky. They had locked up McCann and would be probing his foreign connections. And Mike Clarke was one of those arrested at the scene: he was one of Howard's oldest friends from Kenfig Hill. Cuba in Miami was waiting to close the deal on the Great Big Monster, but Jim was in jail. It didn't look as though they would let him out this side of the year 2000. But Howard did very much want to do his Great Big Monster. . . .

He summoned 'Crab' Prentiss, the 40-year-old US Navy Veteran who was running the yacht charterer's on his remote Scottish island. He wasn't as experienced as McCann. And he had a tiresome personality. But he had demonstrated he could land dope: and he knew that remote coast well. They met in Blake's Hotel, the stylish and high-priced spot in Victoria much favoured by big dope-dealers.

'Thirty tons? Don't be ridiculous. I can't land that. I brought the Moroccan ashore from Kerrera one suitcase at a time, you know. What about five tons?'

'There's room for discussion, Crab. My Americans have to work in big quantities. Just let's talk to the guy when he comes over, hey?'

In early November, Howard could have been spotted at sea. He was hunched miserably in the bows of a Shetlander launch as it lurched through the Firth of Lorn, the rainy mist down over the bleak West Highland mountains, and the Atlantic somewhere south and ahead through the wet chain of Inner Hebridean islands. He fully expected to drown. Since the boat had rounded the northern tip of Kerrera Island and ploughed out of the shelter of the Bay of Oban, the water had turned choppy. They were on the exposed side, between Kerrera and the Isle of Mull. Away on the right, a light flashed feebly through the mist.

'That's the lighthouse at Grass Point,' shouted Prentiss self-importantly from the wheel.

'Very appropriate,' bawled Howard over the wind. The third man in the boat, a short, dapper, New Yorker with a distinctive silver patch in front of his black hair, gave a mild smile. The boat grated on the rocks of a tiny creek and they stumbled ashore, sea-birds screaming overhead and Howard cursing and shivering as the ankle-deep water saturated his Italian trousers. To the right were a few tumbled, slimy stones of a long-ruined jetty. Ahead, up the muddy grass slope in a curve of the hills, was a small stone farmhouse, with a single-storey barn on its right, and an overgrown track winding upwards into the mountain. A long, whip, transmitter aerial curved over the roof top.

'Barnamboc!' said Prentiss. 'They blasted out a few of these rocks in 1760 and sailed cattle across from the Isle of Mull. They did a bit of salt-smuggling too, when the tax was high. They used to call it "one of the wildest and most dangerous ferries in the Western Isles". I got married here, out of doors, in the summer, and we've still got the lease on the place.'

They clambered back into the boat and pushed off. Prentiss worked his yacht operation from Mount Pleasant, the big rented house on the sheltered far side of the four-mile island, looking across the bay to the little Victorian resort of Oban. There was no way on to the Island except on Prentiss's boats, or the one-man ferry across the sound from Port Kerrera.

Back at Mount Pleasant Howard squatted down, gloomy and wet. He hated these nautical scenes. Prentiss seemed actively to enjoy living in draughty surroundings, surrounded by oilskins and outboard engine parts. The New Yorker fetched out a little bag of grains and substances. Howard stared, appalled, as he stirred hot water into his cubes and packets, and tucked in with a small picnic set he also produced from his attaché case.

'Miso,' the New Yorker said. 'I'm a Jewish Vegan.'

'No meat?'

'No milk either. And you can't rely on these supermarket vegetables. I carry my own food everywhere.'

'You don't look very fit on it. What about drink? You do smoke dope, don't you?'

'Oh yes, of course. Just pure sinsemilla weed. No tobacco. And maybe half an occasional glass of really good claret. All vegans have this slightly yellow complexion because they don't touch meat. But I jog every day. I can assure you I'm in the peak of physical condition. I feel tremendous.'

'Oh,' said Howard. Prentiss made him a Marmite sandwich. He took it without gratitude.

They argued all night. Prentiss made endless difficulties. Eventually they agreed to take 15 tons – half what Howard hoped:

'And I'll need two yachts for that. It won't be at all easy. I don't think you understand very much about life at sea. I'll have to buy a small fleet of inflatables to get it on to Barnamboc; it's too shallow for keel boats. And we need at least two other landing sites. Spread the risk. But I suppose I can find plenty of sites round this area. Even on the east coast if we have to. Sail right through. We should only do 5 tons per yacht, really. That's what I'd prefer.'

The New Yorker had travelled up with Howard via Concorde, Aberdeen Airport, and the Highland tourist exhibition at the Aviemore ski centre:

'I saw your "Scotsail" stall there, Crab. You've very adequately fronted up. My boys have got an ocean-going tug. Led a life, you know. It's coming over from Norway with a crew of sorts. The beautiful thing about salvage tugs is they have an excuse for hanging around anywhere in the ocean, and being vague about their destination. They're steaming across to Aruba Island, off Colombia. Cuba will arrange to load them. They come across here up the west coast of Scotland. . . .'

'I thought we could trans-ship the cargo here somewhere in the Firth and your tug can steam on through the Caledonian Canal, and out into the North Sea. As though it's proceeding back to Norway.' They huddled over charts. Then they started haggling about money. It took hours before Prentiss would grudgingly settle for 22½ per cent of the proceeds. Howard was to get 12½ per cent, plus control over the sales. 'Your credit's good,' said the New Yorker. 'Nothing in front.'

Howard was going to make a million pounds.

There was a lot of work to do. Much had changed in England in the fluid world of the old Oxford dope set. Some had taken their profits and gone into legitimate businesses. Some were sniffing small fortunes up each nostril: too scattered on cocaine to perform reliably any more. His wholesaler Charlie Radcliffe, who Howard had rather squeezed out of the original Shannon scam, seized the opportunity of Howard's emigration to the US. He had teamed up with the Dutch dealer Arend ter Horst – Howard's own connection. They were busy smuggling on their own account, running in tons of cheap Moroccan every spring on the Mediterranean sailing yachts. Radcliffe had been at it rather successfully for years now. A 'South African fisherman' at Falmouth in the West Country would one day chug quietly out to sea, and meet a boat. Or an overloaded yacht would start sinking off Devon, and a stream of launches would frantically roar ashore in the darkness into Hope Cove. . . . that spring he had sailed a whole ton into Beaulieu, on the south coast, and successfully trans-shipped another ton into an off-shore fishing boat in the Scilly Isles, beyond the far tip of Land's End. He was living down in Dorset, 'fronted up' as an antique dealer, and working on his own scheme to land a ton and a half on a north Welsh beach the following spring.

But Radcliffe's down-the-line distributor, Vic Grassi, was still available in North London. And Dave Pollard was still around in Kensington, running his little amateur LSD lab in Herries Road. There were plenty of dealers in the network. The loyal and long-serving Marty Langford was back in town too.

'James Goldsack will do the wholesaling for me,' Howard told Patrick Lane. 'He's a very calm, honourable, professional guy and he handled the Moroccan just fine. He's underground since he was bailed for having morphine. And you can do the subtleties with the sales money. Get one of those little two-grand computers; take my advice and find a mate to count the actual notes. It's a good deal easier now there's no exchange control. God bless Mrs Thatcher. We'll just set up some tax-shelter nonsense: pop groups, or Pakistanis sending their cash home – and then launder it through a few front bank accounts in the Channel Isles and off to New York. No more suitcases of notes, eh?'

Patrick Lane, joint director of 'Overseas United Investors Ltd' of Campione d'Italia, Switzerland, incorporated in Grand Cayman, nodded and inspected his well-manicured fingernails. When he flew first class with his accountant's briefcase, he liked people to look at his shoes and his fingers and see that he was genuinely rich. He was constructing a front for 'OUI Ltd' which mockingly parodied the real thing:

OUI is an international financial consultancy organisation, with representatives in the USA, the Caribbean, the UK and mainland Europe. OUI also has an excellent network of contacts throughout the world.

251

OUI offers advice and information on a multitude of financial subjects. Research is carried out on specific problems. . . .
OUI office and communications centre is strategically located in the heart of Europe. . . .
OUI is not affiliated to any government or official agency.
OUI is an independent, international organisation created to serve the individual in his struggle to preserve his capital and his independence in the face of growing bureaucratic restrictions and oppression.
OUI believes in the preservation of Capitalism, Free Trade, and individual freedom and initiative. OUI believes the individual should be free to reap and to garner the fruits of his own toil. 'Government is the enemy – Government is necessary, but it must be kept at bay': Senator James L. Buckley.

Howard had one major administrative problem. He needed a distribution system. The Great Big Monster was going to bring in enough bales of marijuana to comfortably fill a 38-ton articulated truck – he needed mainland landing quays, trucks and cars; at least three regional holding warehouses; a second London flat to use as a secure HQ; and a Scottish control centre for the whole landing and trucking operation. On top of everything else, it was winter. The roads were icy and night fell early. Prentiss came south to see him, embarrassed:

'The tug. They re-named it the *Karob*, built a big false cabin and gave it a new paint job to beat the US coast guard blockade. It's on its way. They're sending Crazy Alex over from Miami with the radio codes. But it's just too long. It's more than 100 ft. It won't go through the Caledonian Canal.'

'Well, we'll have to find landing sites on the west – and it can go back across the Irish sea, and dock somewhere over there. They've promised to send over some muscular New Yorkers to help with unloading.'

A secretary was hired – she was the daughter of a high-ranking Scotland Yard officer, but it didn't seem to worry her. She wasn't using her real name:

'I want you to write a lot of letters to estate agents, machinery manufacturers and people who sell cardboard cartons and those black polythene bin bags. We want warehouses out of town, and some vacuum-sealing gear, in case this stuff starts to deteriorate on the shelf.'

'Sure. No problem.'

'Would you start by taking this letter? It's on the "Worldwide Entertainments Inc. European Head Office" notepaper, and it's to the Lochaber Estate Agents, 38 High Street, Fort William, Inverness-shire:

Dear Sirs, During the winter period, our company will be producing a semi-documentary film located in the Western Isles, and set in the latter half of the last century.
We intend to rent a large lochside property capable both of accommodating the staff (about 6 to 10 people) and of featuring in certain parts of the set.
We would wish to assume tenancy by about December 1 of this year and stay for a minimum of three months. Adequate funds are available for the right property.
If you have anything which you might consider suitable for our purposes, would you please let me know as soon as possible?

And would you sign it: 'Yours faithfully, Donald Nice'?

The salvage tug *Karob* had been at sea for more than three winter weeks under the command of the 35-year-old Texan Randall Lacey, when the most enigmatic entries appeared in the ship's log. They read:

DEC 29 1979  23.30 NUMEROUS MANOUVERINGS
             00.00 WE'RE GETTING THERE
             01.00 INCREASED SHAFT SPEED TO 162

As the long black tug steered south again, her oilskinned crew heading for the stormy waters of the Irish Channel, Prentiss's two 40-foot yachts, *Bagheera* and *Salammbo*, slipped north in the maze of deep sea-lochs round the Inner Hebrides. They were low in the water. *Salammbo* disappeared in the direction of the Grass Point light, making for the channel between Mull and the mainland that would take her up towards the Ardnamurchan peninsula – a land of heather and rock, remote even by the standards of the Scottish highlands. *Bagheera* drifted up the Firth of Lorn, the crackle of her short-wave radio drowned by the scream of the wind, and the slap of the pitch black water. Two black rubber Zodiacs, that would carry 1½ tons each with their big 35-horsepower outboards, whined eastwards, heading for the cove at Barnamboc. On past the rear of Kerrera Island, the *Bagheera* turned north-east into the long fiord of Loch Linnhe, which pushes a 30-mile finger of water up as far north as Fort William. The *Bagheera* cut her engines off a tiny bay on the desolate, western side of the loch by an old boathouse. With whispers and grunts in the darkness, the crew bent and heaved once more. A third Zodiac, loaded deep in the water, grounded on the shingle by the boathouse in sheets of rain. Among the figures toiling in the night to carry the hessian bales onshore and into the waiting three-ton box-van was Howard. It was the supreme moment of his career.

The lorry jolted slowly back up a quarter-mile of track, a small timber bridge over the creek creaking ominously with its weight. At the mouth of the track, the lorry killed its engine, its black bulk invisible in the murk. Howard walked on ahead up the narrow tarmac road and round the corner. He passed Conaglen house, the baronial mansion full of rented film and lighting gear. It had been leased for £1,000 a week for a company called 'Worldwide Entertainments', and so had the cottage at the gates by the road, now full of sweating New Yorkers. Howard just wanted to be sure the truck was in no danger of attracting attention.

A police car was blocking the road. A uniformed man was climbing out. Howard's first impulse was not, in fact, to turn and run. He went up to him in the darkness.

'Hello, there. We're shooting a film out here. I was just out checking conditions for some dawn shots.' He gestured vaguely towards what might have been light meters hung around his neck. In fact, he was carrying an infra-red night scope and a CB radio transmitter.

'Ach well, I'm glad to see you. I'm on my way to Strontian, and I wondered, would you be having any petrol?'

'Yeah, sure. I can let you have a can. Look, do you mind not coming in the cottage – it's bound to wake up the others, and they need their rest. I'll just tiptoe in and get it for you.'

'Extremely grateful to you. Good night, Sir, and good luck with your filming.'

'Goodnight.'

He waited until the engine note of the police Hillman faded, and waved the truck out on the icy road. It would reach Fort William, avoiding the ferry, and taking the long, unfrequented northern route round Loch Eil, before first light, and there it would be left in the municipal car park, from whence it had come the previous night. Later, a driver who did not know precisely where the truck had been in the previous 24 hours, would pull the keys out from the exhaust pipe, climb in the cab, and drive south.

Everything worked. The whole 15 tons came ashore in three different parts of the West Highland coast. The yacht *Salammbo* landed her final cargo a few days later on the weedy shores of Loch Sunart, another long inlet to the north: and then she ferried some of the Barnamboc cargo, stacked on the deserted beach round on to the mainland at the same place. The dope was snug in four warehouses: Barnamboc itself; an Inverness-shire farm whose bearded Scottish tenant Prentiss had befriended on Kerrera; a barn in Essex owned by one of Goldsack's Oxford friends, the barrister Nick Cole; and, rented by Howard (through a front company), film-maker Peter Whitehead's falconry in Northamptonshire.

Howard had just successfully smuggled enough dope into Britain to make 20 million joints.

Mrs Thatcher was comfortably in power, and a brash Toryism was in vogue, dedicated to transforming the ambitions of the small businessman into social fact. Howard, who was to join the National Federation of the Self-Employed, felt a successful small businessman's triumph, and the stirrings of something even deeper. He set off round the Scottish Highlands on a 'front' holiday tour of the district's scenery, making bookings for a married couple. On the narrow road by the deep grey waters of Loch Ness, he parked Whitehead's four-wheel drive Lada and picked his way down to the water's edge. He unbuckled the £1,000 Jaeger le Coultre gold and lapis lazuli watch he had bought seven years before, on opening his first Swiss bank account in Zurich. He hurled it high into the mist and rain, and it sank out in the bottomless loch. It was a sacrifice to the gods.

Then came the feasting. He rented the biggest luxury flat he could find: a 5-bedroomed apartment in Hans Court, near Harrods. The rent was £500 a week, and Whitehead's film company 'fronted' the lease at Howard's request. He issued invitations to a small but lavish party there; Judy and he were getting engaged to be married. There was nothing to drink but vintage champagne. There was nothing to eat but unlimited quantities of caviare, from the Caviare Bar in Knightsbridge. The decorations were the most studied exercise in conspicuous consumption Howard could conceive. They consisted of numbers of large and romantically proportioned statues of swans positioned around the grandiose reception room. The swans were sculpted entirely of ice.

He said to Keki Mody, owner of the Jamshid where he and White-head so often dined: 'Come to an engagement party and bring your wife.'

'I can't. I'd have to close the restaurant. Lose a night's takings.'

'How much is a night's takings?'

'Oh, goodness. Maybe £80.'

Howard peeled off £80 from his wad of banknotes.

'Now come to the party.'

When the dancing started, Howard went upstairs and changed out of his quiet silk suit into one made of supple black leather. He wore it with a Blondie T-shirt.

'Like the gear, Albi.'

'Yeah. Designed by that Italian, Versace, got it at Harvey Nichols in Knightsbridge.'

'Cost a lot?'

'Yeah,' said Howard. 'About a Grand.' It was what most of his individual possessions seemed to cost.

Getting married was fashionable at the time. Peter Whitehead, the film-maker, had just consummated a whirlwind romance with the husky socialite Dido Goldsmith, former paid assistant at the recently opened London Regine's and former lover of Sir William Pigott Brown, described routinely in the gossip columns as the 'sporting baronet'. Pigott Brown went to Cape Town to forget, and was at that juncture awaiting trial in South Africa, charged with possessing cocaine and marijuana. (He was acquitted, and said he wished Dido well.) Dido, whose appearances in the tabloids revolved around discussions of her fieriness, her sensuality and the size of her breasts, was the daughter of the ecologist, Teddy Goldsmith, and the niece of Sir James Goldsmith, the tall, half-French millionaire businessman with the pale blue eyes whose libel suits against the magazine *Private Eye* had made him a figure of controversy. The wedding photographs of this moneyed crowd are remarkable for one beaming figure in the front left-hand corner, who wears a lop-sided carnation, an ill-fitting three-piece suit, and an unlikely moustache. This was the Best Man. Before going off to drink champagne with Bianca Jagger, Nicaraguan wife of the chief Rolling Stone, he was seen to sign the register: 'Donald Albertson'.

Some bothersome little things began to intrude that extraordinary spring. The stock was selling slowly. Goldsack would not push out more than a ton a month to the dealers, and the market became saturated with his cheapish Colombian. The down-the-line dealer Dave

Pollard was picked up by the Metropolitan police, shambling one night along Queensway, in Bayswater.

'What's this big bunch of car keys for?'

'Nothing.'

'Going equipped to steal, eh? Let's go and have a look at your house.'

After they found the LSD tablets in the lab, they patiently tried to fit Pollard's Volvo key to every likely car parked within a half-mile radius. It was good police work. It would have been magnificent police work had they gone on to deduce that it was one of Howard's cars they had found, and the 50lb of Colombian in the boot was from Howard Marks's Great Big Monster.

Vic Grassi came unstuck as well. HM Customs were targeting Charlie Radcliffe's yacht captain – the Moroccan scams had been going on just that bit too long. When the yacht *Elouise* slipped into the Menai straits of Anglesey one night, with 1.5 tons on board, an enormous project called 'Operation Yashmak' swung into gear. Coast-guard cutters blocked the straits, and the whole team were arrested on the beach. Grassi also had no less than 5 cwt of Howard's Colombian. He went to jail and stayed there, without ever mentioning this fact to his interrogators. Unfortunately, no one else knew where it had been hidden, either.

A big dope deal is like a wave. When it has rolled across the bay and broken, there is no evidence of its passage. When the boat has sailed away, the plastic bags have been burnt, the money banked, and all the dope smoked by satisfied customers, there is no longer anything to be seen. But while the wave is gathering and rolling, there is a great deal of dope-related activity, much of it visible, if not to the naked eye, then at least to the trained one.

So Howard's position was much more precarious than it might appear. This was the most dangerous time. There were little signs of strain under the festivity. He would peer round a room carefully, before going in. He would be peremptory with Judy. He needed to smoke bigger joints before he could slow down and sleep. He was feeding off the late-night adrenalin of a hooked poker player.

And Her Majesty's Customs were devoting a quite disproportionate amount of the taxpayers' money to hounding down the cannabis bootleggers. It was tempting for them, of course. There was so much cannabis flooding in for eager buyers, nearly as much as in the great revolutionary days of the Sixties. And cannabis was so bulky! All those crates and bales were easier to spot than little heroin packets of white powder sewn into the lining of a jacket. The Drugs Group of the Customs Investigation Division at New Fetter Lane had two branches, each headed by an assistant chief investigator. 'Branch 2' investigated heroin. It investigated cocaine. It investigated morphine. It investigated opium. It investigated amphetamines. It investigated LDS. It investigated all the other synthetic dangerous drugs. 'Branch 1' was just as sizeable but it exclusively investigated the smuggling of cannabis – a plant universally accepted to be much less dangerous than any of these others, and widely considered harmless.

Of Customs' 11 'drugs teams', each made up of four men, the cannabis branch had five allotted to itself. One, the least busy, did dope from Africa, the Caribbean and America; one concentrated on the Mediterranean dope countries; one handled purely India, Pakistan and Thailand. The two others worked on 'selected targets'.

Howard's phone rang. It was New York.

'I'm coming over. I think we need to talk.' He caught Concorde. 'Cuba's people are getting a little worried. They don't understand why these sales are taking so long. The money comes back fast in their business.'

'Everything's fine. It really is. This is a small country, but we're selling steadily.'

'Yeah, well, maybe there are dealers in this country who could work a little harder at it than your people. And I'm a little embarrassed to say this to you Howard – I know you're a man of honour, but Cuba's people want an inventory. Make sure all the "unsold" goods are still there, and the sales money tallies up. We did this deal on credit, after all.'

'Suit yourself. You won't find anything missing. I don't rip people off.'

'Now, I didn't say you did. I'm going straight back to New York, but my attorney's here, Joel Magazine. Treat him as you would me. And Walter Nath. He's coming out in 2 days to do the stock check.'

He did not mention that Walter Nath had already made one or two calls to old friends in Britain, to sound out the recruitment of new, possibly more efficient, wholesalers. One of those he rang was Ray Humphries, a yacht captain who had spent some time floating around the southern Mediterranean. Humphries was in fact quietly working on a scheme to smuggle a quarter of a ton of his own in that autumn, to the Devon coast near his home. Humphries also had a special distinction, one of which he was quite unaware. He was among the Fetter Lane cannabis branch's 'selected targets'.

Nobody arrested Ray Humphries for a long time. They watched him instead. When he travelled up to Paddington railway station in London, he was observed. And so too, when he checked in to the nearby Royal Lancaster Hotel, on the north side of Hyde Park.

'Walter, this is Dave. He's very optimistic of finding a buyer. How much of this grass is available?'

'As many tons as you like. 15 tons came into Scotland just after Christmas.'

'You got a sample?'

'Sure. I've been to the London store already. Let me know in a few days whether you two could find a buyer. And next time. . . .'

'Yeah?'

'Check into a different hotel. And use a different name. I like to be careful.'

Nath, a short Californian with a droopy black moustache, walked back round the corner of Hyde Park and down Park Lane to his own hotel. It was the Dorchester. Customs men followed, fascinated. They watched him meet a fat Miami attorney with small boyish eyes, and found they were both checked in the Dorchester under their own names.

Magazine and Nath collected their womenfolk and all four went off in a taxi late at night to Carlton House Terrace, to gamble at Crockfords. Senior Investigating Officer Terence Byrne, head of Drugs Team C ('selected cannabis targets') led his men into the Dorchester Hotel. They searched Nath's room and Magazine's suite, noting all the scribbled phone numbers and calculations they could see. What *were* they up to?

Senior Investigator Byrne was indefatigable at his work. At 7 a.m. he was on duty to watch a man with a moustache who looked remarkably like the long term fugitive Howard Marks arrive in person at the Dorchester. He saw him pick up Nath in a Rolls and drive him to Heathrow Airport to be introduced to 'Crab' Prentiss. A rather sulky Prentiss flew up with Nath to Glasgow to take him on a conducted tour of the northern dope warehouses. They drove off north towards Oban, followed by a bunch of Customs men in a car. Prentiss picked up a single radio phrase as they drove after him. It came through his dashboard cassette player. 'There he is!' He frowned. He suddenly braked and picked up a hitchhiker. He watched a car with men in it pass and halt further up the road. It had two radio aerials. His frown deepened. When they dropped the hitchhiker at Fort William, Prentiss weaved round the back streets of the little highland town. It was Friday 14 March. Prentiss ever afterwards thought of it as 'Black Friday'. There was no mistaking the situation. It was heat. They abandoned all plans for a stock check, and drove hastily back to Glasgow. Nath ran to a phone-box in the railway station:

'Start packing. The Eagle is blown. Get rid of those two pieces of paper.' He headed back to London. Prentiss called his wife to get out of Kerrera and head south. He called his workers at Barnamboc.

'Dump the stuff. Dump it in the sea if you have to. Destroy all papers.'

In the small hours, when Nath returned, Magazine and he both disappeared down to Howard's £500-a-week flat in Hans Court for a long and anxious meeting.

Next day, the Customs started to tap their hotel phones. Customs men, like British policemen, never admit they tap phones, and adjust the evidence they bring to court to disguise the fact. But they do, and they did in this case. The tape-recorders spooled slowly at $1\frac{7}{8}$ inches per second.

One of the first phone calls they picked up that night at the Dorchester was about a proposed council of war with Prentiss, who was making south hastily.

'How you doing?' said Magazine.

'Still nothing,' said the unmistakeable voice of Howard Marks.

'It has to be tonight. Where are you now?'

'At home.'

'OK, hold on a second. OK. Call me back as soon as you hear something. Does he know where we're going to meet? Just say there's a meeting and we're going to show up there, rather than tell everybody . . . you could just tell him I'm here in town, and I want to speak to him.'

'I'll just say you're anxious to have a word with him,' said Howard. 'Keep it at that level, OK?'

The tapes next picked up Magazine woken at dawn by a call from his daughter. She was calling at midnight, Miami time, from a car radiophone in Coconut Grove, for a little friendly *badinage*:

'Are you coming home today? Are you busy?'

'I'm not busy.'

'Why are you being such a bitch?'

'Why don't you do what I tell you for once, and stop being such an ass-hole? . . . Get some sleep.'

'I got some today – I'm sorry I woke you up.'

'I couldn't sleep. I've been under a lot of pressure. . . .' Magazine was still trying doggedly to find new English wholesalers: the Customs tape clicked, again that morning, and recorded:

'Yeah?'

'Boy, oh boy, I thought I was never going to get hold of you.'

'Really? Been having a hard time?'

'My home phone, I'm getting calls in still, but I can't get calls out.'

'No kidding?'

'I've got some real good. . . .' The caller checked himself, suddenly security conscious. 'Can you call me back . . . the same area code as my house but the number is 229.'

Magazine headed downstairs for a secure payphone. It was just as well he did.

The following evening, he called Miami to give a progress report on his trip. It was heavily coded, and very deliberately made no mention of the little burst of heat:

'Two things we had to take care of, right? Phase 1 was Junior's friend. Phase 11 was *yours*. You know, for commissions on both – you follow me? – two pieces of info I was waiting to hear about on negotiations for the club, whether it was going to be *with* the restaurant or not – and one was Junior's friend. Just a briefing on that. And the other was with your friend, your clients. Junior's friend I have *nothing* on yet. But *your* client looks like, real good – we might be able to reach agreement on price. It's difficult dealing with Europeans, they're so *slow*, they say "OK, we'll call you tomorrow!" it's really a pain in the ass. I don't like talking price when you're dealing in *gold* or anything, because of the switchboard's always listening in.'

'The first contract, with our original brokers: it's still being handled through his office?'

'Completely,' said Magazine meaningfully.

The Customs men listened to a long business discussion about a bar, 'The Happy Pelican' in which Magazine was involved as a partner.

'When I leave London, it might all change round thoroughly. I'm here doing some *heavy* negotiation. It's a pain up the ass.' And they had to listen to Walter Nath working his way through the Dorchester menu:

'Last name is Nath, NATH, I'd like sliced tomatoes vinaigrette, vichyssoise, Sole Eugene with lobster and cream . . . what's the soup of the day?'

Ray Humphries from Devon could not find a new buyer after all. The market, just as Howard had maintained, was flooded. But Nath disappeared off down to Devon to stay with him for a fortnight, until the heat cooled. Customs picked up on the tapes a series of calls from Nath leaving the numbers of local Devon payphones for Magazine to phone him back. They picked up his plan to move back to the Savoy for security reasons, and they tapped the Savoy. They picked up enigmatic arrangements:

'Any word?'

'No.'

'Son of a gun?'

'Joel, please, it's real important.'

'Yeah.'

'Can you come down to the Hilton right away please, right down the block. Either Trader Vic's or the lobby. I've got another call to make.'

'Do you need a jacket to get in?'

'No. Come by yourself. It'll only take a few minutes.'

'I was waiting for what's-his-name to call.'

'Well, he'll want to hear about this.' There were snatches of conversation from switchboard operators:

'If he dials out now, you've got no trace of it, have you?'

'He's not answering. . . .'

'Do you want me to switch that through?'

Customs learned a lot about the gold market from Magazine's stockbroker:

'Currencies up half a point. That's not *bad*, Joel. I got something going for you, you'll have to come down to Miami to talk about it. Currencies look good here: I'd be buying the Swiss franc if I were you.'

'What's the reason for the bounce in gold and silver?'

'Oversold. Way oversold.'

And just occasionally, they picked up a damning snippet, showing just how close Howard was to the centre of things. They would hear him arranging more meetings between Prentiss and the Americans – who were furious, and sceptical that he had really thrown a hundred bales of expensive marijuana into the sea.

'How you doing?' said Howard one night. 'I've just talked to Crab's friends. They don't reckon he'll be here until about 10.'

'OK.'

'So I thought I'd just let you know that, to save you hanging about unnecessarily. So at 10 they'll call, and I'll call you, yeah?'

And they heard him arranging for Nath to collect cash payments:

'Hello, how are you? I'm at home now. I have to stay for another two hours before I can leave. Could you get it collected here?'

'Maybe. Don't leave without calling me.'

It was tantalising for the Customs men. But they eavesdropped and they followed and they photographed. A lot of smugglers faded away while they tried to work it out. Captain Randy Lacey from Texas and his engineer dropped into the Ritz to collect their first pay-off for the run from Colombia – and out again. Magazine and Nath both slipped back to the US (if flying first class to Miami in your own name can be called 'slipping').

Alex, another New York emissary, came over from an indignant Cuba, got into a rancorous argument with Prentiss about who should pay for the dope in the sea, and went away again. Prentiss's yacht crews and friends slid out of Kerrera and left the country. Prentiss buried himself in London under the name of Paul Morgan. He wrote to his friends back in America:

Who put these people on to us? Lots of ideas, but at the moment nothing solid. WHO ELSE KNEW ABOUT 'SALLY'? All the 'ugly Americans' including Crazy Alex, Huey, Randy (the 'Nice' people are OK). All this trouble began with them raising hell and wanting an inventory. Alex smells. They all stink bad. (I can't leave now, so I might as well keep the pressure on Nice & Co and see if we can come out of this thing on top. I am winning the battle of money with the Yanks.

For the future, I don't know. It is most certainly wise to attempt to lay plans that would recoup our fortunes if this all turns out to be futile. I do believe that the UK is not the place for us now under just about any conditions. I'll be delighted to leave (and hope I can figure out how to do it cheaply).

I think we should fix 'Sally' up . . . ready to be used again if we so desire. There are other world possibilities. 'Baggy' must be sold, I think. Other suggestions should be to think about a farm in Canada and go back to the Pacific. Anything we do has to be done by the new rules, though we must think super carefully (cheers to paranoia and James Bond) and watch our step. Big Brother is really there, and everywhere.

So, God bless, keep the faith, and miss you all very much.

Patrick Lane tiptoed away to the Dordogne for a bit. Howard was left in there, doggedly selling his tons of dope.

The trial of Jim McCann opened in Dublin, a couple of weeks after 'Black Friday' in London . He had conducted himself in the usual fashion, shouting as Garda Dave Dowd thumped him with his baton on the night of his arrest: 'I did it for Ireland!' He had then slumped to the ground, apparently unconscious.

They had refused to bail him out of Portlaoise high-security fortress, patrolled by armed guards in the little town halfway between Limerick and Dublin. It was McCann's own fault: when he recovered consciousness, his first words were:

'My name is Mr Nobody. My address is the world!'

And a gang of Provisional inmates then decided to teach McCann a lesson for spending so many years pretending to be a member of the IRA. They cornered him en route to the prison library, and beat him up.

McCann recovered his poise. By the time of his trial, he had arranged for obscure legal reasons to be tried separately from the other three picked up on the layby. A quantity of the seized Thai sticks were discovered to have reached the black market through a suborned Garda: an embarrassing investigation began into that. The lorry driver and his colleague were acquitted on the grounds that they had no idea what was in the sealed metal containers found in the fruit lorry. Mike Clarke pleaded guilty and told the authorities the cannabis gang had been led by an Englishman. He got a light sentence of 12 months, refused to testify at McCann's trial, and, when threatened with jail for contempt, shrugged. McCann composed an entertaining defence. The drugs were being smuggled by Howard Marks, the notorious British propaganda agent: this was its central theme, and indeed, as far as it went, it was perfectly true. McCann, he planned to say, had tracked Howard Marks down 'for Ireland', producing out of a hat accurate details of Marks in County Kerry, in Dublin, and in Killiney Bay. Secret agent Jim McCann was infiltrating the Howard Marks MI6-backed dope organisation!

But McCann never needed to produce this creative defence. His counsel tied the prosecution up in sufficient knots about the dimness and darkness; the difficulty of seeing who had thrown a pistol to whom; the way McCann's fingerprints had been forcibly taken by 10 men; the question of what colour McCann's shirt had been; the sealed nature of the containers; the absence of corroborative testimony from Mike Clarke. To widespread interest, the judge directed that the prosecution had not made out a sufficient case in law. McCann was acquitted on the spot.

'His Nibbs triumphs again, eh?' said Howard on the phone, as McCann headed rapidly out of Ireland before the authorities could lodge their appeal against acquittal. 'I'll let you have some of my Colombian to sell, if you like. Oh no, it's the least I can do.'

Sitting in his mansion block at Hans Court, Howard fiddled with his expensive automatic camera. It had an infra-red remote control, and he set it up to take pictures of himself. They showed the same old Howard in some ways – nylon anorak, open-neck shirt flapping out of his trousers, the full lips, the wide grin and the shoe-box lid with its open packet of cigarettes, torn bits of cardboard filters, the rolling papers and a little lump of hash. But the eyes looked pouchier, the moustache more ratty, and the facial lines seemed somehow stretched. Howard was really under strain. He was handling a huge business operation with quarrelling partners, millions of pounds of other people's money, and the Customs breathing down their necks. Fishermen kept hauling bales of floating marijuana out of the sea off Kerrera, and the papers were full of Highlands 'Cannabis Galore' jokes. He dropped the price from £310 a lb to £260. By mid-May 1980, almost six months after the Great Big Monster had landed, he had sluiced two million pounds through his organisation, and paid off the expenses of the US investors. Walls of suspicion were beginning to build around him – galloping paranoia is an occupational disease in the dope business. He felt sure he was being watched. He inspected every face carefully in every bar and restaurant before he sat down, memorised every car number parked regularly in his street.

'Marty,' he said. 'I went to Brighton yesterday. And saw this big wheel on the funfair. It was going round and round and the lights flashing and the music playing it sort of loomed. And then it started coming towards me, and toppling over my head. I just started crying. I couldn't stop.'

'You're hallucinating, Howard. The more you smoke in those moods the more paranoid you get.'

'No, Marty,' he said sombrely. 'It's a premonition.'

He booked the family in for two nights at one of his favourite East Anglian hotels – the Swan at Lavenham. He thought they might drop in the next day and surprise his old solicitor college friend Henry Hodge – now married to the rising Labour politician Margaret Watson – at their weekend cottage in Norfolk. As usual, he inspected every face in the hotel lounge with meticulous care. He did so the first night. He even punctiliously did the same the second night.

He studied for a long time the faces of the two youngish men at the bar. They looked the type to be Customs men, if anyone was. He watched their movements and mannerisms with obsessive minuteness. No, they weren't narcs . . . it was OK.

'A glass of dry sherry, please. Thank you.' He gave the barmaid a small smile. Higher Executive Officer Nicholas Baker handcuffed himself to Howard's wrist.

They were not going to let him go this time. Early the next morning, a middle-aged Scotsman came into the detention room at Fetter Lane, where Howard had been issuing a stream of 'No comments' since dawn. 'Deputy Chief Officer McLeod, Drugs Group,' he said, and shook Howard, to his astonishment, by the hand. 'Well, Howard, you've been a fugitive from justice for seven years!'

'Justice,' said Howard. 'Injustice!'

He was not going to let them crack him this time either. Senior Investigator Byrne conducted the interrogation.

'Well, what do you do for a living?'

'My work is of a secret nature.' That was just about Howard's last perfectly truthful witticism.

As the newspapers blared on about 'Britain's largest ever cannabis haul,' and the sensational capture of Howard Marks, he hesitatingly, but deliberately, embarked on the biggest gamble of his career. The maximum stake was a 14-year prison sentence. The name of the game was 'perjury'.

Howard inspected the problem. Half a dozen others had been picked up at the same time as him. 'Crab' Prentiss, Goldsack, and five minor workers – Marty Langford, Nick Cole, Patrick Lane's old chum Hedley Morgan who was hired to count the money, Alan Grey at the Inverness store and Bob Keningale minding the Northamptonshire store. Peter Whitehead, after a grilling by Customs, was being put up as a prosecution witness. Howard had kept his head and not made an incriminating statement this time. He fell on the piles of evidence handed over at committal proceedings: 'What have they got on me?' he said.

The answer was alarming. Piles of paper, especially sets of rough accounts, had been seized all over the place. The team had been using the traditional dope-dealer's 'bottom-drawer' method. All the accounts were always kept handy for anyone to inspect. It avoided recriminations. There were three particularly damning pieces of evidence: Howard had clearly been doing Kerrera accounts. He had a large and unexplained amount of money – £20,000 – at one of his flats. And Whitehead was testifying that Howard was the prime organiser.

In his cell at Brixton, smoking a joint (it was easy enough to smuggle in, if you kept the bit of hash up your anus, and burnt orange peel to disguise the smell), Howard jotted down his problems.

(1) Justify possession of money
(2) Explain accounts
(3) Discredit Whitehead

His weapons were also threefold.

(1) Contacts in South America
(2) Time to think
(3) 1 million dollars (approx)

Judy was at her toughest and coolest.

'A message has been sent from your South American friends, Howard. They say a Brazilian film company will supply witnesses and documentation that they advanced you a large cash sum on your life story. That would be £200,000. Or a Mexican government official will fly over to testify he rewarded you for saving the life of his kid. Cost £150,000. Or, if you want to pursue the MI6 angle, there's another Mexican who runs a sort of arms and heroin police squad. He's prepared to testify, with backdated documents, that you worked for him, if it's any help. But that would be expensive.'

'Yeah. It all sounds pretty unreal. Maybe I'll be a cannabis martyr instead. Will you do the research for me to write a long paper on its medical uses, and how it was outlawed in a conspiracy between prohibitionists and the US synthetic textile industry? I could do a big statement from the dock. And then go to jail for ever, I suppose.

Listen, let's get married, as you're pregnant. We can give the baby a name this time. Mine. Marks.'

'That would be nice. Do they let you do that?'

'Only time they do is if you're pregnant. Order a wedding cake!'

At an upstairs room in the Basil St Hotel, near Harrods, Howard's friends and family gathered for the wedding reception, prepared to commiserate with the grass widow on her husband's immediate return to Brixton. Her white Cadillac drew up, and out stepped Judy in a beautiful long white dress. She was seven months' pregnant. Two sheepish prison officers followed her, and bounding up the stairs in a smart blue suit, and a red and blue diagonally striped tie, with a red carnation, was Howard Marks.

'Albi! How'd they let you come?'

'Aw, they like it. It's a day out and they wanted to ride from the church in the Caddy. They're good blokes really. Give them lots of champagne. Give *me* lots of champagne!'

The jailbird look well. Better than usual even.

'Yeah. I've become a Vegan. It's the only way to get round prison food. It's not easy. They make you apply to join the Vegan society and all sorts. Carrot. And onion. And soya pellets. I do yoga every morning too. I can do a full lotus.'

'Are you running Brixton already?'

'I've had a few bad experiences, actually. This bloke in the cell turns out to be grassing me up to Customs. One of the East Enders who shares a brief with him, tipped me off. So I fed him all this nonsense about 40 tons waiting to come over from Ireland. Exhaust the enemy!'

'Cheers. Every happiness.'

'Well, yeah. I tried to get bail, you know. But they wouldn't do it. Can't think why. I sent this bastard tea-boy in Brixton six grand because he said he could bung the Customs for me to get bail. It was just a rip-off. Ended all right though. He got transferred to Pentonville, and said I could inherit his job.'

'Tea-boy?'

'It's the best job in Brixton. Don't sneer. You make tea for all the screws all day. You get out of your cell. You get into the kitchens. You can do all kinds of scams. Eggs. And towels. They only give you one mangy little towel for everything. The art of it is to give all those screws a big smile. Cheerful and willing. They made their stupid little jokes and you think "Laugh you Welsh twat, laugh!"'

'Aren't they afraid you'll escape, letting you out like this?'

'Oh Jesus, I nearly did, I tell you. I was sitting in the back of the Cadillac with Jude. The screws in front. And we're crawling through these traffic jams. I'm whispering "Shall I, Jude, shall I?" And she's saying "It's up to you. There's money in my handbag." But I honestly didn't have the bottle. On the run again, never see your family. No, I've decided – I'm completely guilty, and I'm gonna get out of it!'

Later that year, one of Howard's friends drove out to Box Hill, in the countryside south of London. He dug up a parcel containing one of Howard's passports in the name of 'Tunnicliffe', and flew to Mexico with it. It came back with Mexican entry and exit stamps for 1976 neatly inserted. They looked almost genuine.

'Bernie, this business about me working for the Mexican government that you don't seem awfully interested in?'

'Yes Howard?'

'I think Judy might be able to lay her hands on one of my false passports which prove it. Would that be of any use to you?'

'Well, goodness, yes, *definitely*.'

An IOU in Spanish for $150,000 was smuggled into Brixton. Howard signed it 'Anthony Tunnicliffe' and smuggled it out again to Judy.

'Ta. Apparently the idea is that they'll go and over print your signature now with a date stamp in Tijuana, Mexico. Must have been signed before you were arrested, right? You couldn't have forged it while you're in jail. Right?'

He had a lawyer's visit. 'Bernie?'

'Uh-huh.'

'I don't believe in legal aid. I don't mind what the lawyer's fees are. The Mexican government will pay. It'll be laundered to protect the Mexican secret service, but the cheque will come from Mexico.' Two Mexicans arrived at Judy's house. They wanted to see Lord Hutchinson, Howard's tough, expensive QC, and they wanted to see his solicitor, Bernie Simons. They had already despatched some hotel receipts, proving Howard was in Mexico in 1979, at a period when the crown witness Peter Whitehead claimed Howard was in London.

Simons jotted down what happened. A good-looking one with the neat fingernails and the incongruous green throwaway lighter, produced an identity card in Spanish.

'As you see, it shows I am a member of the Mexican security police. May I have it back, please? I have a particular interest in anti-terrorist activities, and my base is in Tijuana, on the Mexican border with

California. My family own a cancer clinic there. It was there that this man Tunnicliffe appeared. He expressed an interest in cancer research and asked about our use of Laetrile as a cure. We formed an association, and as a result of his past intelligence experience, Tunnicliffe worked for several months in 1977 close to the border of San Diego, California, on our anti-terrorist activities. He also stayed for a while at the home of a police officer in Chulavista. We knew of his interest in drugs and heroin, and that he had stayed in Miami. There was someone called "Cantu" he appeared to be investigating.

'Suddenly, around 1980, he reappeared with a story of a conspiracy to import guns and narcotics into Mexico. He could arrange for the arrest of all concerned if he had 150,000 dollars to bait a trap. . . . A private loan was arranged through a Mexican bank, but he disappeared. We learned that he had been arrested, and had not run away with it, as we thought. We understand that HM Customs are now holding much of our money. He provided us with information which led to important arrests before. Yes, we can document all this, and I will come to court in September to testify.'

The morning the trial was due to open, Patrick Lane was safe near Vancouver. Normally his favourite reading was the heartless farces of Tom Sharpe. Today, however, he wrote a poem for Howard on his expensive electric typewriter:

Daybreak
Dear Brother: Five hundred days stand between us, and
All the distance I have managed to create
No word has passed, no smile exchanged, no touch of hand,
And yet, as Dawn intrudes, we still relate.
I cannot sleep whilst you, awake across the Globe, await
The turn of Fortune's wheel, and take her dare,
To chance your luck against the odds as they rotate
And play for both of us and all the precious 'ours' we share
In Time and Space and Circumstance we're Night and Day
Upon the circle, although the axis is the same.
But all around your friends and family hope that they
May share with you and help you play, and win, this game.
In one brief span, as the world turns, the sun's warm kiss
Touches many loving hearts that beat with yours: you will get this.

The Old Bailey is an impressive place. It has a gilt rooftop statue of

Justice, with her sword and scales; and bewigged judges, turnkeys, solicitors in dandruffy suits, policemen, barristers and flunkeys – all making a living out of crime. Howard stood in the high-railed dock almost alone. Only the bearded yachtsman, Prentiss, and the ingenuous Hedley Morgan who had been hired to count the money, were making a fight of it. They stood in the dock alongside him: Prentiss's defence was 'duress', and Morgan's was 'ignorance'.

All the others had confessed, and some had made long statements naming Howard as their leader. They were sitting in Brixton prison waiting to be sentenced when it was all over. Of course, the jury had no idea of that. Fortunately for Howard, their statements could not be used against him. Judge Peter Mason stared impassively down from his bench at the black-haired Welshman with the full lips and the reddened veins on his face that testified to years of cheery beer-drinking. He wasn't getting any younger, Howard was thinking to himself. He was dammed if he was going to spend the next ten years in jail for these men in fancy dress.

The lines of press benches below the jury seats were crammed. The tabloids always enjoyed writing in tones of self-conscious outrage about soft drugs. And the serious papers were looking foward to a good scandal about MI6, whose self-styled agents rarely turned up in a British dock in such lurid circumstances. Of course, to the remnants of the 'Underground press', and to the gossip columns, Howard had also become a figure of myth. He was the Balliol man on the run, a figure at smart parties, a friend of a friend at least of practically anyone who worked in the London media. Howard was a Name and it looked as though the truth about him was finally to come out.

Howard planned otherwise. He scanned the faces of the jurors anxiously as twelve were sworn in. He used his maximum allowance of three 'challenges', hoping to get young chicks. Unlike some of his new criminal friends in Brixton, he did not really have the connections to bribe jurors.

On the other hand, it was reasonable to assume some of the younger ones smoked dope themselves. He tried with the girls, one by one as he caught their eyes, a small, experimental, complicit smile.

John Rogers, the Director of Public Prosecution's counsel, started to lay out the case with all the authority of an outraged state behind him, and piles of incriminating evidence stacked in front of him on the tables. There were address-books, files, sheaves of statements, and of course, samples of the weed itself, tired and odourless in plastic bags.

271

'How is it, er, ingested?' asked the judge as he fingered the dried grass. Howard suppressed a giggle. His eyes shot to the jury, who were also examining the stuff.

'This was crime on the grand scale!' intoned Rogers sonorously. 'It was no surprise that a man of his background and intelligence set up the UK side of the organisation just like a high-powered business.' He warmed to his work. 'Mind-boggling quantities of cannabis and money! The whole of this smuggling operation was like a military operation under the code-name "Eagle"! An intricate web of bluff and counter-bluff and false names!

'It was the largest seizure of cannabis ever in the United Kingdom. Marks had so many identities one wonders how on earth he remembered who he was.

'The organisation had to be very slick, very smooth and carefully planned to succeed, and it will not surprise you to learn that those involved are extremely intelligent people.'

The papers loved it. All of them seized on the angle Rogers had so astutely fed the largely working-class jury – that here were a gang of expensively-educated smart alecs.

'EGGHEADS RAN £20M DRUGS RING' said the Murdoch paper, the *Sun*, speaking in its usual coarse tones.

'An Oxford graduate was the mastermind in a brainy gang' the *Daily Mail* told Mr and Mrs Suburbia. So did the *Daily Express*. 'A team of ex-university whizzkids', it said. 'The gang of super brains included a barrister, an accountant, and a farmer with an honours degree.'

The *Daily Telegraph*, expecting its readers in the managerial classes to have some pretensions, made a cinematic allusion. What was revealed, its Old Bailey reporter pronounced, was: 'The Graduate Connection'.

The next morning, Howard's nerve began to crack. He calculated rapidly: he had been locked up on remand for more than a year already. There was one-third remission, and parole from about half-way through. 'I'll change my plea to guilty if I can get away with 7 years,' he told Hutchinson. On a sentence like that, he would be likely to have to spend in practice barely another year in prison. Lord Hutchinson was eventually to go backstage, to see the judge.

He came back shaking his head.

'Judge Mason says it's a very serious case. It's clear he wants to jail you for a lot longer than 7 years.'

'Old bastard. I was offering him a really good deal.'

'You know what they all call him?' whispered the solicitor's clerk.

'No. What?'

'Penal Pete.'

'Oh, terrific.'

If plea-bargaining wasn't going to work, Howard steeled himself for perjury and perversion of the course of justice. Where the hell was the Mexican? He had promised to be here for the start of the trial.

Meanwhile, front of house, crown counsel and the judge were playing it for laughs.

'So it was,' said Rogers, 'that the Isle of Mull, which was once the scene of Sir Compton Mackenzie's great, hilarious novel *Whisky Galore*, once again hit the headlines. You can guess what the press did with it. They called it "Cannabis Galore".'

'I must interrupt you I am afraid, Mr Rogers,' said the judge. *Whisky Galore* was in fact set on the island of Barra.'

There was suppressed snickering from the press benches. Rogers was not going to have his jokes fall flat. 'And I must tell you the name of the place on the foreshore where most of the bales were washed up. It was called Grass Point.' He drew a gratifying cluster of giggles from the body of Court 6.

Now came a long stream of crown witnesses. Most of them were men in uniform. They had followed this car, seized that scrap of paper, kept observations on such-and-such a flat. But the key witness for Howard, at this stage of the game, was film-producer Peter Whitehead. He showed no sign of bearing Whitehead a grudge for co-operating with police in the way that he had done. That was life. But Howard had worked to discredit him. He had typed sheaves of notes. They raised the unsubstantiated idea of accusing Whitehead of tax evasion on a grand scale. His notes debated whether the keen falconer's sales of birds to Saudi Arabia, and his brush with the wildlife protection laws, might not prove embarrassing. Lord Hutchinson could certainly have a good try at showing that Whitehead must have been remarkably gullible to have taken Howard, as his long statement explained to police, entirely at face value. Hutchinson also had something else up his sleeve. The suave figure of Whitehead climbed into the witness-box. He had blondish hair and a moustache that was slightly reminiscent of Clark Gable. Rogers sat him down on a chair, and took him through the story of Whitehead's meeting with a man called 'Donald Nice'.

'Did you ever know him by a different name?'

'I knew him as "Donald Albertson", and then as Howard Marks.'

Whitehead explained laboriously that Nice-Albertson had paid Whitehead a lot of money, lived in a flat rented through Whitehead, and took over the house in the Highlands via Whitehead's company:

'Knowing I had a lot of experience filming in Scotland, he said he was having trouble with a similar project of his own.' He explained, even more elaborately, how he had lent Nice-Albertson a car, and installed a friend of Nice-Albertson as caretaker in his Northamptonshire falconry.

'A very large sum of money was found in the red filing cabinet by Customs officers who found it at Porters Lodge. . . . Has that anything to do with you?'

'Nothing whatever.'

The next morning, Lord Hutchinson started in, with a voice like ground glass.

'Well, Mr Whitehead, it is perfectly clear from what you were saying to the jury yesterday that, as far as you are concerned, the taking of this estate at Conaglen was purely for the purpose of film-making.'

'That's what I understood.'

'Is that *right*?'

'That's right.'

'You are quite an experienced person in business?'

'I would like to think so.'

'You have got your head screwed on?'

'I don't like that phrase, but it is clear that it is on my shoulders.'

'You are not an innocent abroad?'

'I am certainly not.'

Hutchinson ground on.

'You went up to Scotland, you negotiated the lease, you agreed the figure?. . . Your company rented Hans Court?. . . Porters Lodge, rented by Lorrimer films, your company?. . . premises where the cannabis was found, you had a tenancy of that cottage?. . . you took Mr Keningale up, you paid him, found him accommodation. And apparently when he was up there, he received large quantities of cannabis?'

'That I wouldn't know.'

'Were you arrested by Customs?'

'I don't know if arrest is the word. I was taken away for questioning.'

'For about how long?'

'Eight or nine hours.'

'Did you agree to give evidence for the prosecution?'

'I agreed to make a statement.'

'Yes I know that . . . there was quite a lot of explaining to be done by you?'

'Yes, the statement is quite long.'

'Was there a suggestion they would charge you with being in possession of a small amount of cannabis for your own use?'

'There was a small amount of cannabis found, in my wife's studio and the music studio . . . it was very old and had clearly been left there by people using my studio . . . I was subsequently conditionally discharged.'

Whitehead endured, and Howard watched this barrage – both with equanimity.

'You will appreciate that quite a lot of the things I am going to put to you are not quite the same as the account you gave yesterday?'

'I see no reason at all to suspect they should be any different.'

'You knew Mr Patrick Lane later on?'

'I don't know Mr Patrick Lane.'

'You never knew Mr Patrick Lane?'

'No.'

'Are you swearing that?'

'I am . . . what I did for Howard Marks is entirely consistent with the fact that I considered him to be a successful film-maker. It was quite natural and spontaneous.'

'And that is your explanation, of course, of being associated with all these things which are of importance in this case . . . you knew he represented "Overseas Investments" here in London on behalf of Patrick Lane?'

'I certainly knew nothing of that.'

'By 1980, he was, in fact, your best man at your marriage?'

'He was an intelligent person and I was delighted to find someone at that time to help me in my work. Considering I only decided to get married on Thursday and got married on Monday morning, he was the nearest man for the part.'

'He was just around,' said Hutchinson sarcastically. 'You just happened to assist him over the flat and the place where the cannabis was, and he just turned up conveniently for the marriage.'

Now Hutchinson lobbed in the weapon which Howard faintly hoped would reverse his dangerously low fortunes.

'In July 1979 you saw these newspaper reports bearing his photograph, indicating that he had been involved in drug-smuggling in 1971, *while working for British Intelligence?'*

On the press benches, a dozen idle pens suddenly began scratching.

'Obtaining information was the suggestion,' declared Hutchinson into the suddenly tense court. If there was one subject nobody had brought up so far, and with good reason, it was this. 'That money got by people involved in drug-smuggling was going to the IRA for the purpose of buying arms, and that he was giving this information to MI6, the Intelligence Service . . . he was Howard Marks, and he had been involved in this way with the British Intelligence, drug-running, and the IRA . . . and furthermore, he was, according to these articles, involved with an Irishman called James McCann, who had been arrested as a result of the information he had given?'

The icy quality of Whitehead's reply was probably lost on everyone at the Old Bailey except Howard himself.

'I believe', said Whitehead, 'that this is what we might call the Howard Marks political story.'

But Hutchinson was unquenchable:

'And it was suggested, was it not, that he had been charged in relation to this matter of the drug-smuggling, and had been kidnapped while awaiting the trial, kidnapped by the IRA it was suggested, or kidnapped by MI6? Anyway, forcibly taken away?'

Then Hutchinson darted off on to other topics. The jury brooded on this exciting information about MI6, as Whitehead started explaining about his falcons.

'You sell them to Arabs in the Middle East?'

'It is my private business, my Lord,' said Whitehead, appealing to the judge. 'I think it is rather cheap to mention details of my other business, which is a delicacy, both legally and ethically. I would prefer not to discuss it.'

'What you were telling him,' ploughed on Hutchinson 'involved a certain illegality about obtaining those eggs and selling them at a very substantial profit?'

Whitehead assumed an air of rage. 'Jimmy McCann complained of being assassinated by Howard Marks, and now I can complain of character assassination. I got the eggs and in 1974 the legislation came in which made it impossible . . . I don't want to discuss it. I am employed to help a Royal Family in the Middle East. It is a noble and expensive venture . . . I do think this is totally irrelevant and indiscreet!'

Eventually, Judge Mason wearied of this point-scoring, in which Hutchinson lost no chance to accuse Whitehead of script-writing and fabrication.

'This case', said the judge, 'is about cannabis, not falcons.'

'I agree, my lord,' said Hutchinson, smoothly.

But Judge Mason did appear to have begun to enjoy himself. The cross-examination turned to the caretaker of the remote Scottish mansion where Howard had landed so much dope in the dead of night. Had not the caretaker seen Whitehead himself with some of the film costumes Howard had imported to make his 'filming' cover look plausible?

Whitehead was contemptuous. 'People can make the wrong kind of judgment.'

'But it isn't the caretaker that lives in the fantasy world!'

'He watches television all the time. All he does is shoot crows and watch television. He must have drawn incredible conclusions.'

Judge Mason intervened. 'There are worse ways of spending your time!'

Did Judge Mason too shoot crows in his spare time? The jury were never to know. Hutchinson raced on to pour scorn on the theory that 'Donald Nice' introduced himself as a rich entrepreneur who would help finance Whitehead's film projects.

'You are the person with the knowledge, with the know-how, with the Aga Khan and the Princes in the Middle East. You are the person with the money!'

'I wish I was.'

'The lady you married very rapidly is the niece of one of the richest men in the country?'

Whitehead sprang to the bait of Sir James Goldsmith's as yet unmentioned name:

'Once again, your lack of discretion, I consider to be vulgar . . . it is true – but it is vulgar. This is a total misrepresentation, and in very bad taste.'

Hutchinson ran savagely through the flat leases, bank payments and film contracts Whitehead had signed, freely using phrases like 'bogus' and 'rubbish'. He wound up on a low, but dismissive note:

'Did you quite simply have this contract up your sleeve to be able to produce it to cover payments which were made to you from the sources we have seen?' Whitehead said, as stoutly as he could:

'Quite untrue.'

The prosecution case was over.

Howard went into the witness-box. He took the Oath, and lied like a trooper. He enjoyed it. He had read books on acting, which weren't much use, and a book on advocacy by the barrister Richard du Cann, which was quite helpful. It warned him for example, never to use the phrase 'I dare say', which a good cross-examiner could make much of. He had also spent his interminable months on remand learning by heart every page of the 12 volumes of evidence and exhibits. In the course of perjuring himself, Howard was strictly to maintain certain ethical standards. He would not denounce cannabis, for example. 'I am a fanatical proponent of the legalisation of cannabis. I feel it's essentially harmless, and its criminalisation causes terrorist groups to be able to make money out of it.'

Otherwise it was a piece of lying of which Jim McCann himself might have been proud:

'I smoked a lot of cannabis. . . . I went to Amsterdam and met a person called Jim O'Neill . . . yes, I discovered his real name was McCann, a leading Provisional. Then, in 1972 I went to Ireland concerning information about McCann . . . and discovered they were smuggling arms from Rotterdam. In Hamburg, McCann's girlfriend Anne McNulty was arrested in possession of a large quantity of arms and drugs. . . . I had passed on a good deal of information on McCann leading to this arrest. . . . Whilst on bail, there was a threatening phone call from McCann. . . . I was forcibly abducted and taken to Italy. . . . I finally escaped by breaking out of the slum in Genoa where I was being held by US organisers of the conspiracy. The publicity exposed MI6 connections, and that I was an informer of the IRA. I was in fear from the IRA. My cover had been blown.

'I was approached by someone concerning intelligence work. He wanted me to go back and find out more about McCann. I was asked to go abroad to track down McCann in Miami, with co-operation from Mexico. This was concerning heroin dealing and the money from it. . . . McCann was arrested in Vancouver as a result of my information. Yes, I was paid for this intelligence work: 10,000 dollars. I went to Mexico and spent 7-8 months under the auspices of Mexican government. The CIA have long used narcotics missions as covers for their operations. . . . Right-wing terrorists de-stabilising Mexico. . . .'

Judge Peter Mason and the jury, several of whom Howard was

convinced were smiling back at him, listened interestedly as Lord Hutchinson continued to extract from Howard his ludicrous story:

'In 1979 I went to Dublin. An old friend using the name Clarke revealed McCann was still using gun routes to import drugs from all over the world. In particular he told me 30 tons of cannabis would arrive from Latin American contacts. He agreed to help me in trapping McCann. McCann was arrested beside a van full of cannabis holding a revolver . . . the *New Statesman* article, about that time, revealed I was trying to trap McCann . . . yes on November 11, 1979, I went to Mexico.

'A month before, I had been contacted by my superior – No, I would prefer just to call him "Antonio" – in Mexico, to go over about a new project. This concerned the two-way traffic of arms for heroin and a right-wing terrorist group the September 23 Group. . .'

Howard gave the court one of his frank and ingenuous smiles.

'Why are you apparently smiling so often as you give your evidence?' said Judge Mason disagreeably.

'I am fully aware I must establish my innocence,' said Howard hastily, 'or I face many years imprisonment, with considerable distress to myself and my family.'

He assumed a solemn expression:

'But I still try to smile, although I have spent the last 18 months in prison. It is the only way of dealing with adversity, and is in no way smugness, or contempt.'

Judge Mason stared at him, unenthusiastically. He was well aware of Howard's wholesale perjury, but there was little he could do to stop it.

'I also saw Judy's sister Natasha and Patrick Lane; we went to Aviemore for a holiday. . . . Natasha told me Prentiss, the yachtsman she knew from Kerrera, was being sounded out by an American who was there with a view to importing 30 tons of cannabis. It was the same quantity as Clarke had told me about in Ireland. "Antonio" told me to bring it up with the Mexicans. It was connected with my 1977 work, with contacts of McCann. There was somebody called Cantu, a CIA agent sent to de-stabilise the Mexican regime. It was to do with heroin. . . . Well, the question was whether drug-smuggling was being used to finance the group. Much of the exporting was done by Cuban exiles, mostly former CIA agents . . . the interest of the Mexican side was regarding the financing of the operation in Colombia because their funds were held in Mexico. . . . When I was in Mexico, I was given

279

150,000 dollars as a loan . . . that is the way one gets paid there. No, I telexed some of the money to Lane to keep for me: the residue I brought back into the UK in a suitcase . . . I had been invited previously by Whitehead to Northamptonshire to see how the eaglets were getting on . . . "Alex" said he was responsible for the export of this cannabis load. He said, "Do the names Cantu and Desmond Quinlan mean anything to you? I know who you really are".'

Judge Mason was getting upset again. 'I have got lost in this mass of, this mass of detail. I find it extraordinarily difficult to follow, even with notes. How the jury copes, I just do not know!' He had interrupted Howard's hypnotic flow of glamorous espionage. But an encyclopaedic memory came to Howard's rescue.

'Let me put it this way. Quinlan was a friend of McCann, who was arrested in Colombia with 570 tons of cannabis. Because there were a great many disputes, Lacey and Lane had suggested I do their accounts. As an arbitrator. So I seized on this opportunity to try and find out more about them. The suggestion that McCann and the DEA were both involved confirmed my view that this was a direct link with the activities I had researched in Mexico.

'No, I did not have anything to do with importing this cannabis.'

Howard had given his evidence. It was a *tour de force* of untruthfulness. John Rogers rose for the Crown to demolish it. Unfortunately, he started from a dangerous admission. No matter how low-key was his concession, the jury were bound to be impressed. Yes, it was true about MI6, he conceded. Howard had been a spy. There was nothing else Rogers could say. The Fairweather report had been leaked to the world already.

'It is conceded that you worked for the Secret Service until March 1973. But then, after your arrest for drug offences, you were immediately dismissed.'

'No, that is not true. I carried on working for them.'

'Your connection with MI6 had nothing to do with drugs. As a result of that charge you were told in categorical terms that the Intelligence were dispensing with your services.'

'What you say is untrue in two ways. My involvement with British Intelligence *was* to do with drugs, and I have been involved with them since.'

'You were only involved in providing cover for the Intelligence. You are using a little bit of truth and then glossing it.'

'I was involved in cover work first, but then it became counter-IRA work involving drug-smuggling. It's not unusual for British Intelligence to make these denials.'

'You fanned the legend, didn't you? You encouraged the Marks religion to grow that you were a secret agent on the run from the police, and made as many smokescreens as you could, while indulging in very high-level drug-trafficking?'

'I deny that most strongly.'

'Let me challenge you to name this MI6 "controller" you say recruited you for the Mexicans.'

Quick as a flash, Howard replied: 'Anthony Woodhead'. Serve him right for ripping me off, he thought.

And then the mysterious secret policeman from Mexico – late in the day, sweating and shifty – finally turned up. Howard was overjoyed.

'I'll only testify in camera,' the Mexican told Simons, the solicitor. 'I won't do it in public. Secret matters.'

Judge Mason was prevailed on to have the court cleared. The jury were told this was because of the 'delicate nature' of the evidence.

'Do you understand English, Sir?' inquired Judge Mason, thoughtfully, once they were in secret session.

Hutchinson loudly and solemnly said to his secret policeman in the witness-box: 'The court has been cleared of the public and the press, do you understand?' He handed him a piece of paper.

'Is what is written on that piece of paper, as regards your name, correct?'

Mason broke in: 'Shouldn't the jury see it as well, as the court has been closed?'

'He would rather not,' said Hutchinson impressively.

Staring uneasily over the ledge of the witness-box, Howard's bribed secret policeman agreed that 'Anthony Tunnicliffe' had travelled to Mexico, both in 1977 and in November 1979, when the Great Big Monster was reaching a climax.

'Yes, sir,' agreed the Mexican. 'I was introduced to him by another person.'

'Called?'

'Anthony Woodhead.'

Howard beamed.

The Mexican gamely continued:

'Yes, I was interested in the activities of an individual out there, called Mario Cantu. It was contraband of arms and drugs.'

'Did Mr Tunnicliffe give you any information in relation to that man?'

'Yes, he did.'

'Was a sum of money handed over to him on the last occasion?'

'Yes, cash, US dollars.'

'And the amount was?'

'Er, 150,000 dollars.'

'And have you in your possession, but not here, a receipt for that amount?'

'Yes, Sir, I do.'

Roger's attempts at cross-examination did not get very far.

'What was the purpose of advancing the money?'

'I'm sorry, Sir, I'm not able to answer that. For *security reasons*.'

'Does the name Patrick Lane mean anything to you?'

'No, Sir.'

'You said you would be interested in exportations of cannabis from Colombia. To what – any part of the world?'

'Sorry, Sir, I'm not able to answer that.'

'So what opportunity will you afford me to check your credentials?'

'None.'

'Well, how am I to determine that you are who you claim to be?'

'You have no way to do it.'

Judge Mason broke in again, as the jury stared, intrigued, at the first Mexican secret policeman any of them had certainly ever seen. 'He is saying you might be *anyone*, you follow that?'

The Mexican shrugged: 'I know that.'

And Hutchinson bounced to his feet: 'Can I ask you, in view of that – Are you *ever* allowed to show your credentials?'

'No, Sir.'

'Thank you very much,' said Lord Hutchinson briskly. 'You are free to go.' The Mexican scuttled away, and headed for Heathrow Airport.

John Rogers made a closing speech based on the premise that Howard was the world's greatest liar, and therefore ought to be found guilty.

'Marks is the biggest-ever trafficker apprehended with a single consignment. His claims of being a secret agent are utter rubbish. It is conceded that Marks was recruited for three months in 1973 by someone who was indiscreet enough to ask for his assistance. The rest is a myth mounted by Marks in order to conceal his real activities. His cover story is that he was an intelligence agent. I invite you to treat that as a load of rubbish!'

Lord Hutchinson, a dry pugnacious figure in his wig and gown, made a much more interesting speech.

'He was used by MI6 to infiltrate the IRA. Three times he traced Jim McCann, but three times he managed to slip away. But British Intelligence would not come into this court and admit Howard Marks was working for them. He was left "out in the cold". It is the code of the intelligence services. They say: "You are out on your own, old boy". You may remember the cases of those Russian spies, not only Kim Philby, but Anthony Blunt. It appears that British Intelligence can grant immunity from prosecution to spies who have acted against this country. But not so, it would seem, when they have actually been acting on behalf of this country!'

The jury trooped out. They had been listening to the trial of Howard Marks for nearly two months. The hours ticked away, while Howard was locked in the gloomy tiled cells in the bowels of the Old Bailey. At the end of the afternoon, they came back.

'We can't agree.'

The four women and eight men retired to a hotel for the night as guests of Her Majesty. Howard, too, retired, with rather worse bedroom facilities, to Brixton prison. The next morning, the jury stayed out again, until well past lunch. When they came back, they finally announced a verdict.

It was 'Not Guilty'.

Howard, last public representative of the Spirit of the Sixties, had finally won. Was it because of the bribed witness; or the folly of British Intelligence; or was it the reluctance of a youthful jury to send down a friendly young millionaire for importing something so trivial to the 1980s as marijuana? No one will ever know.

# INTERLUDE

*Jim McCann*, 'His Nibbs', as he thought of himself, continues to be at large. He lives in a large house in France, the one country that still grants him asylum, occasionally surfaces to talk to journalists, and likes to be seen flying what he says is his private jet. He describes himself these days as an art dealer. Unkind people suspect he has taken up the newly fashionable trade of cocaine-smuggling.

*Stewart Prentiss*, the bearded yachtsman, was acquitted by Howard's jury. He explained that he had only landed cannabis under duress, because his family were being threatened by Mafioso types in America. He left the court without a stain on his character.

*Hedley Morgan*, who counted almost two million pounds in grubby banknotes, was acquitted also by Howard's jury. He explained that he had been in complete ignorance as to the origin of the money. Howard's jury certainly acquitted a guilty man in Howard's case. There is no reason, of course, to doubt the innocence of the other two.

*Alan Marcuson*, the underground journalist who edited *Friends*, later took over Plinston's abandoned carpet shop in West London. Disillusioned with the hippy press and the dope scene, he ran the shop for eight years, became something of an expert on Eastern textiles, and occasionally still appears on nostalgic TV shows as a spokesman for the Sixties. He still lives in London, and trades in antiques.

*Philip Fairweather*, the leaky policeman whose report into Howard's 1973 disappearance exposed the role of MI6, made a serious mistake.

After the unsavoury spectacle of Howard's trial, he went and confessed to his former police colleagues that he had been inadvertently to blame in letting a journalist have the report years before. They threatened to prosecute him in public, under the Official Secrets Act. The TV producer concerned, Stephen Scott, was also later arrested, but released. Fairweather went into his back garden and cut his throat with a kitchen knife. In keeping with the spirit of general furtiveness, his reasons for doing so were kept secret at the inquest on his death.

*Ilse Kadegis*, the vivacious Latvian who first married Howard at Oxford, later re-married. (Howard sent her divorce papers obligingly describing himself as a 'wastrel'.) Her husband, Michael Sissons, heads one of London's best-known literary agencies and she continues to lead a life of the utmost respectability.

*Charlie Radcliffe* went to jail with a five-year sentence for cannabis smuggling. He is now at liberty.

*Marty Langford* went to jail with a four-year sentence, after confessing his part in the Kerrera operation run by Howard. He is now living back home in Kenfig Hill.

*James Goldsack*, the judge's son-in-law, went to jail for six years, after pleading 'guilty' to helping Howard. His wife, Mr Justice Oliver's daughter, said indignantly afterwards 'What he did was no worse than selling cans of beans.' He is now free.

*Nick Cole, Robert Keningale and Alan Grey* went to jail for four years each, having admitted helping look after Howard's cannabis imports. They are all free now.

*Peter Whitehead*, the film-maker who married Sir James Goldsmith's niece and was a prosecution witness at Howard's trial, now lives in Saudi Arabia. He breeds falcons.

*Bernard Simons, Lord Hutchinson and Stephen Solly*, Howard's lawyers, divided up a total bill between them of £165,000. Of that, £70,000 was for counsels' fees during Howard's prolonged and complex court appearances. Howard arranged for it all to be paid with a cheque from Mexico. He regarded it as money well spent.

*Jim Morris*, whose adventures in the music business involved so many capacious loudspeaker cabinets, changed his name in 1973, and stayed in the US. He is thought to be still there.

*Graham Plinston*, the Oxford dope tycoon who first introduced Howard to smuggling, was never caught. He too, went to the West Coast of the US and changed his name.

*Anthony Woodhead*, who Howard so untruthfully named in public as his MI6 'controller', went to Nicaragua and stayed there.

*Hamilton McMillan*, 'Mac the spy', and Balliol man, quietly rose in the Secret Service. During Howard's years on the run, he was posted to Rome. (MI6 had pulled out of their unsavoury involvements in Ireland.) It is from Rome that MI6 attempts to conduct operations against the Soviet Union. When Howard was re-captured in a blaze of publicity, McMillan was posted a very long way away indeed – to Bangladesh. There he remains to this day.

*Mike Durrani* died in London of a heart attack.

*Dennis Irving* died in Sussex, crashing his hang-glider.

*Fanny Stein*, daughter of the Master of Balliol, Christopher Hill, still lives in north Oxford.

*Rosie Brindley*, the mother of Howard's first child, lives quietly in Sussex. 'I no longer think dope is the answer to society's problems – like I did in the Sixties,' she says. 'It takes away your will to do things.'

*Richard Lewis*, Howard's old friend when he was a student, still lectures in Mathematics at the University of Sussex. These days, it is a much quieter place.

*Julian Peto*, Howard's undergraduate colleague, now holds the Cancer Research Campaign chair of epidemiology at the Institute of Cancer Research. He is a major authority on the disease.

*Henry Hodge*, Balliol man and former friend of Howard, went on to make a reputation in his London law firm for work with the poor, the homeless and the deprived. He married Margaret Watson, who became Labour leader of Islington council.

*Belinda and Redmond O'Hanlon* are still flourishing in Oxfordshire. Annabelinda, Belinda's Oxford boutique, has now been selling nice clothes to debutantes for more than a decade. Redmond O'Hanlon has become something of a media figure: his long-awaited major work *Joseph Conrad and Charles Darwin: a study of the influence of scientific thought on Conrad's fiction* was published by the Salamander Press in Edinburgh in May 1984. His travels to Borneo with James Fenton, runner-up in 1984 for the post of Oxford Professor of Poetry, were chronicled in *The Times*, and published as 'A Journey into the Heart of Borneo' by the Salamander Press and Penguin. The London *Observer* profiled him in the same year, noting that a Hieronymous Bosch reproduction hung on his study wall. It was, said O'Hanlon, 'a reminder of my beatnik days'.

# Marco Polo's Grand Finale

The anarchistic Sixties may have finally faded away for many of the Marks generation, as they reached middle age. Not so for Howard. He intended to make the Eighties go with an even bigger bang.

The celebrity outlaw in the international swim took six months finally to saunter out of jail after his dazzling acquittal. This was because the authorities attempted rather lamely to fight back. HM Customs were particularly distressed by his cheating of justice, not least because he successfully claimed back afterwards the £30,000 they had seized among his belongings.

The Director of Public Prosecutions announced he would try Howard a second time – for the old ATA Carnets scam Howard had fled in 1973.

Howard told Lord Hutchinson he might plead 'Guilty', if Judge Miskin, the Recorder of London, did not want to give him more than four years. He hoped the offer to spare MI6 further embarrassment would be welcome. Hutchinson came back. 'You'll only get three.' Howard accepted with gratitude. In open court, Judge Miskin solemnly announced that an appropriate sentence was – three years. Howard showed, he added portentously: 'Greed and insensitivity to the misfortunes of the ultimate buyers.' He did not say what misfortunes these might be. Howard wondered if he meant the misfortune of being arrested. He had never observed any other misfortune to follow the smoking of cannabis.

As Miskin elaborated his justification for the sentence, Howard struggled not to snicker in the dock.

'I work on the basis that you were then young, and were full of remorse, and that you are even more full of it now: that you were a first offender . . . you spoke the truth. You agreed to come to England, and waive any rights you may have had to deportation. . . .

'If I thought you had disappeared without any understandable reason in an attempt just to avoid your trial, I would wholly ignore the passage of those years and the evidence I have that during them – save for the passport offences, you have led an honest and industrious life.

'But I cannot reject, on what I have heard, the live chance that you may have been got away by those anxious that your evidence should not, at that time, be heard – and that your adoption of an alias in England, and elsewhere, once you had escaped, was perhaps not so much the consequence of fear of trial, as of fear of those who might wish you ill: and do it if they learned of your whereabouts. . . .

'I can and do take into account in reduction, the evidence I have of your blameless life over these years.'

None of this rhetoric mattered in any event. As everyone knew, Howard would only serve three more months of his 'three-year' sentence. All the time he had so far spent locked up was to be deducted. Howard's sheet was clean barely two years after his arrest. It was a good bargain struck with Miskin.

The only problem came from an unexpected quarter: yet another government body whose existence was unknown to the general public. An ominous letter arrived from 'Special Office Ten' of the Inland Revenue. As they smoothly explained, their aim was to raise money from prostitutes, gangsters, pornographers and other stalwarts of the black economy. Now, if Howard could see his way to giving them, say quarter of a million pounds as a contribution to the estimated back tax on ten years of dope-smuggling . . .?

'But I was acquitted,' said Howard.

'Oh, don't worry about that,' said the man from Special Office Ten. 'Give us the money and you can make a fresh start.' He smiled faintly.

'You'll have a long job getting it,' said Howard.

Special Office Ten continued to chase Howard for two years. They quoted legal precedents for successfully taxing crime – in 1927 the Privy Council had upheld Canadian efforts to tax whisky bootleggers. In 1932 tax had been levied on illegal fruit machines. In the Scottish courts, they unearthed a declaration by a judge: 'The burglar and the swindler, who carry on a trade for business for profit, are as liable for tax as honest businessmen.'

Howard refused to pay and filed an appeal. He complained that the criminal courts had found he had led a blameless life. 'Ah,' said the Revenue, 'but they had to prove you guilty beyond reasonable doubt. In the civil courts, we only have to show you did it on the balance of probabilities.' The two SO10 investigators had yet another meeting with Howard and his lawyers. 'Look,' said one, 'if you want the freedom to enjoy your drug profits without us constantly looking over your shoulder, surely it would be sensible of you to negotiate a settlement.'

They offered a compromise. How about accepting a tax assessment that Howard had earned at least £300,000 over the previous seven years, no doubt quite honestly? They wrote wheedlingly:

> The Revenue, though remaining unconvinced that substantial profits had not been made from dealing in drugs, felt this to be the minimum acceptable, and were prepared to conclude its case largely to enable Mr Marks to put this unfortunate chapter of his life behind him.

'Nope,' said Howard. The Revenue broke off negotiations and issued an enormous new tax demand for almost £1 million. This was, they said, based on his estimated total gigantic income from drug-smuggling.

Shortly afterwards, the first edition of this book, Howard Marks's real life story, hit the streets. Entitled *High Time*, it was no sooner published than it was being rapidly emptied out of the shops by the intrigued policemen, taxmen and lawyers who had been bamboozled by Howard's previous fictions. Howard interrupted his latest hobby – playing at fighter pilots on the flight simulator of his expensive home computer – and studied the book reviews in his modestly affluent Chelsea basement flat. His children, Amber and Francesca, played on the patio. The *Guardian* said: 'For the first time it spells out a charge of perjury and perversion of justice . . . a fascinating read.'

Any prudent criminal would have decided to stop after becoming so notorious. But Howard Marks had rejected respectability long before when he treated Balliol, and its opportunities to become a minor member of the British establishment, with contempt. He was addicted – not to drugs, but to living by his wits and defying authority. He literally knew no other life than that of dope-smuggling.

What Howard concluded was that it was time to leave town. 'Look,' he said to Judy, 'I'll never smuggle dope into England again. It's too dangerous. Let's go and build a villa in Majorca. It's lovely there.'

Great numbers of Englishmen thought Spain was lovely at that time. It was such a warm country, with such ineffective extradition arrangements with Britain that its beaches were known to the popular press as the 'Costa del Crime'. Builders from Essex with tattoos and an abiding interest in the contents of bank vaults mingled on the streets in a classless way with errant financiers from the City of London. They all had millions.

Howard began to put it about that he was setting up small businesses – just as Mrs Thatcher told everyone they should. He understood there were grants available to boost the economy of his native Wales. Howard could be seen at meetings with men in suits and portfolios of documents under their arms. It rained a lot in Wales, he said, the biggest natural resource of the country was therefore water. He proposed to export the Welsh water surplus in tanker ships to parched areas of the world – Saudi Arabia, for example. Naturally, launching this venture would involve frequent trips to the Middle East.

Then there was the travel agency: Hong Kong International Travel, with an office in London. It was run there by a Chinaman, Chu Chuen Lo. Hong Kong was a location particularly well suited for tourism in the Far East. Thailand was a well-known popular holiday destination. One of Howard's long-standing friends, a cockney called Phil Sparrowhawk, was already living in Bangkok and seemed to find life rewarding in that colourful town. Howard had always been interested in travel. He was particularly fascinated by that part of a travel agent's duties which involved writing out large numbers of airline tickets in a variety of different names. It was well-known to aficionados, if not to the general public, that the CIA had a big computer into which they fed the passenger manifests of airlines throughout the world. It was reasonable to assume that they loaned their facilities to the drug enforcement agencies as well. This made air travel under one's own name into a goldfish-bowl.

Howard also developed a sudden interest in education. His wife's younger brother, George, was the beneficiary. Howard put him in charge of the 'International Language Centre', a school of English located, for no doubt sound commercial reasons, in Karachi, Pakistan. Meanwhile, contact was resumed with the elder Lane brother, Patrick, Howard's 'money-manager' for a decade. Patrick was living under the name 'Barry John Doyle' in the United States. Another old friend Howard looked up was Ernie Coombes, the lanky high-liver from California with the long-standing US distribution network, currently known as 'Nick Sims'. Clearly, Howard felt the commercial expertise of his old contacts might help him in his new business career.

All 'fronted up', Howard disappeared from England in 1984. Shortly afterwards, extremely large consignments of hashish and marijuana began to arrive, regularly as clockwork, once or twice a year, on the western seaboard of the United States. They came from the Far East. As

291

economic pundits had long been predicting, the 'Pacific Basin' was becoming one of the world's most dynamic growth areas.

Meanwhile, Howard and his family sat in the Mediterranean, peacefully furnishing his villa. They had another baby, a son. Howard was occasionally to be seen heading towards the airport, it was true, and there were occasional odd coincidences. Shortly before two tons of Pakistani hashish materialised in Alameda, California, for example, Howard had been noticed on 22 June 1984 in the region of Karachi. For some reason, he was delivering to the firm of Forbes, Campbell & Co., four large crates. They were labelled 'propellors'.

But who was interested? As Howard had correctly surmised, Scotland Yard lost interest in Howard once he left the country. He showed no sign of trying to smuggle dope into England. Whatever he was doing was someone else's problem.

The Spanish police were initially fascinated by the arrival on their holiday island of the famous British drug-smuggler. Howard knew that they knew. They knew Howard knew that they knew. Everyone did what was expected of them: the Spanish police tapped Howard's phone religiously, and he, equally religiously, made sure that he said nothing to upset them, and never smuggled dope on to the sacred soil of Spain.

He was a multi-national businessman – 'The Marco Polo of the drug world' as the US Drug Enforcement Agency indignantly called him. He lived on the Mediterranean, bought in Bangkok, freighted in Manila, banked in Hong Kong, and cleaned up in California. By 1988, he was larger than life and twice as prosperous. Each shipment brought him £1 million or even £2 million net profit. In Howard's professional career, as DEA men calculated – sourly thumbing through copies of 'High Time' – he had probably smuggled thousands of tons of dope. Laid end to end – as the statistics to which they were so attached would have it – his reefers would have girdled the globe in aromatic smoke.

Typically, Howard took with him on his travels a large number of copies of *High Time*, which he used to give as presents to people he met.

One of those new friends was a fat English peer, living in exile in the Philippines. His name was Lord Moynihan. Howard had started life as a dope-dealer twenty years before when he first came into contact with the degenerate English upper classes at Balliol, and realised he could beat them at their own game. Perhaps what was about to happen to him now was only fair.

'Sunshine after clouds' is Moynihan's family motto. Moynihan went to a public school – Stowe – and was in the Coldstream Guards. He was an

Oxford man – just like Howard. But he belonged to an older tradition: the portly young heir insisted on marrying an actress and one-time nude model. He was packed off by his family to work on a sheep farm in Australia. The young Moynihan promptly headed for the fleshpots of Sydney and returned to Britain with a hula-hula dancer on his arm.

His next marital adventure was with a Malayan fire-eater's assistant. She did a belly-dance routine, under the name Princess Amina, in a Beckenham coffee bar purchased by Moynihan for the purpose. Moynihan set off on a career as a night-club pianist and agent for cabaret artistes. By the time he was 30, that marriage was over: four men were named in the divorce.

He inherited the title, if not the depleted family fortune in 1965 from his father, a former stalwart of the Liberal party who died – wisely perhaps – shortly before his own scheduled trial for soliciting young men in the lavatories at Piccadilly Circus underground. Moynihan imported another exotic dancer from the Philippines, Luthgarda Maria Della Roza, and married her. The reception this time was – naturally – in the House of Lords. Moynihan described himself as a Liberal, like his father: 'I have every intention of shaking this place up,' he asserted as he took his seat. 'The sparks will fly.'

The elder Lord Moynihan's second wife, and their son Colin, did not strike it so rich: they had a modest home in a gardener's cottage. Colin Moynihan grew up to be unusual in his own way – he was last heard of as Sports Minister in one of Mrs Thatcher's Conservative governments.

Meanwhile, the new Lord Moynihan left Britain for Spain in 1969, slightly ahead of detectives with a fraud warrant, who described him, flatteringly, as the 'evil genius' in a swindle. Moynihan issued a statement saying there was 'a personal vendetta against him' by the British police, and he therefore thought he would stay away. By the time the warrant arrived through Interpol, he had disappeared from Spain. His colleagues were tried at the Old Bailey. 'This is Hamlet without the Prince,' the prosecution said, unoriginally. 'The prince figuring behind all these offences is Lord Moynihan, who is not subject to the jurisdiction of this court.' By then, dozens of firms were looking for him because of his debts. Among the bouncing cheques was one for a £4,000 Rolls-Royce.

It was in these circumstances that Lord Moynihan eventually surfaced in Manila. In a country dominated by the US, run by the corrupt dictator Ferdinand Marcos and his family, and without a British extradition treaty, the renegade peer flourished.

He set up a girlie bar, the Yellow Brick Road, in Manila's Ermita district – a tourist precinct of bars, massage parlours and strip clubs. In 1980, an Australian Royal Commission under Mr Justice Woodward, was set up to investigate drug-smuggling in the Far-East. It focused on Manila, saying that under the Marcos regime it was a haven for international criminals and a transhipment centre for drugs from Thailand, Burma and Cambodia. There was a group of Australians involved, known as 'the Double Bay mob'. An associate of the Australian drug traffickers was 'a shadowy figure' – none other than Lord Moynihan. The publicity did not trouble the exile peer, who later took to writing a restaurant column in the Manila *Business World*, although it did little for the blood-pressure of his half-brother, the rising Tory politician.

It was perhaps natural that Howard should seek out Lord Moynihan. A man with as good protection as he seemed to have acquired was worth knowing. After all, Howard very frequently had to do business with Philippines airline officials and the like. They met in 1985.

Howard had some sizeable consignments in mind. In May of that year, he was buying a boat, not that it had anything ostensibly to do with him. In June, in the US, a man called Gerald Wills offered to purchase the 187-ton crab boat AXEL-D for £675,000 dollars from its owner, Norman Ursin. A few weeks later, he opened a bank account for the purpose at the Bank of America. The name he gave was 'Gerald Livingstone' and the company on whose behalf he was acting was 'International Offshore Operators Inc' – something of a joke title. The years of international crime had not altogether eroded Howard's sense of humour.

Six days after the account was opened, £696,000 was put into it. It came from the Hong Kong head office of the Hong Kong and Shanghai Bank, and the boat was bought with the money. The moment the transaction was done, Phil Sparrowhawk, Howard's Cockney friend, flew from Bangkok into London.

Later that autumn, there was a certain amount of activity revolving around the Karachi language school. George Lane, Howard's brother-in-law, took time off from his educational work to drive two men to the airport in Pakistan, who promptly boarded a flight to Bangkok. They were Howard himself, and – rather incriminatingly – the selfsame George Wills who had bought the boat. He was Howard's transport manager, it was later said. From Bangkok, Howard went to Hong Kong. From Hong Kong, he went to Manila. Three days after he checked into the Mandarin Hotel, his friend Philip Sparrowhawk turned up in an adjoining room. Oddly, he was using the name 'Brian Meehan'.

As soon as Sparrowhawk arrived, the pair of them went to the genteel suburb of Baquio and knocked on Lord Moynihan's door.

It may have been the merest coincidence that, after these comings and goings, the following March nearly six tons of marijuana from Thailand was sailed across the Pacific and landed in California, to be efficiently distributed by Ernie Coombes and his friends. It may have been coincidence that Patrick Lane, the Lane family's money-manager, made a number of phone calls to Howard at his villa and that, come August, Gerald Wills and Phil Sparrowhawk assembled at Howard's Majorca villa for a bit of a party.

One man who didn't think so was the Drug Enforcement Agency's resident officer in Madrid. Craig Lovatu, a broken-nosed six-footer with a master's degree in politics, had been listening to Howard's Majorca telephone conversations for six months. The Spanish, intrigued, had asked him to translate, before losing interest and disconnecting the tap. Lovatu had picked up an inkling of the earlier Pakistani shipment. But neither the DEA on the West coast nor the British Customs could be stirred into giving priority to a pursuit of the charming and slippery boy from Balliol. Dope was not much of a glamour cause when cocaine and heroine were practically keeping the entire economies of South American statelets afloat.

Lovatu was recalled, low-spirited, to Miami, while Howard and friends celebrated in the Mediterranean sun. It was the book *High Time* which was the catalyst for Howard's eventual downfall. Lovatu lent the book to his wife, a Florida police officer, who happened to have it on her desk when some Scotland Yard detectives called in. They were trying to trace the laundered money from a £26-million Brinks-Mat security van robbery – the biggest armed raid in British criminal history – and were desperate to enlist the co-operation of the DEA.

When Lovatu's wife explained that her husband was preoccupied with this infuriating British Scarlet Pimpernel, a deal was rapidly done. The crucial cog in the wheel was Lord Moynihan, the renegade peer. Howard, disgusted, later said Moynihan had been 'a complete shit'. Indeed he had, for the peer changed sides when life became hot for him. After the overthrow of President Marcos and his family in February 1986, he no longer had 'protection'.

Moynihan put a brave face on the danger that he would be extradited after the diminutive Mrs Corazan Aquino seized power from Marcos. 'Don't be silly, old boy – all that was thirty years ago,' he said. Undaunted, he was going to open a new hotel for randy Australians called the House of Lords.

But he was placed under virtual house arrest and refused permission to leave the country after the murder of a business partner, Robert Walden. The two men had run 'girlie bars' together and were at the centre of allegations about brothels and 'massage parlours'.

For years Moynihan had been rumoured to be the kingpin of a number of hard-drug smuggling-rings. But now the Manila press gleefully started investigating him.

Then, suddenly, Moynihan's freedom to travel was restored. This followed a visit to Manila by Scotland Yard detectives. They seem likely to have offered him a way out of his troubles: in return for betraying Marks and working secretly for the DEA to entrap him, he might find a home in the US, or even back in London. He could be a 'protected witness' in the US, and be, for once in his life, depicted as the 'good guy', in continuous danger of assassination from the evil men of the drugs trade.

An enormous international police operation was organised. Operation ECLECTIC ultimately involved policemen from the DEA, the FBI, Scotland Yard, two regional British forces, the British Customs, Canada, Spain, Switzerland, Holland, Germany, Thailand, Singapore, Hong Kong and the Philippines. Lovatu took a technological, if humourless, pride in his work: 'In *High Time* Marks says he was way too smart for the then current law enforcement agencies. At the time I think he was right. Private industry is always ahead of the government . . . He is as dedicated to breaking the law as I am to enforcing it.'

From now on, Howard was to face the really big battalions. His next run was doomed. This project, in 1987, was to ship nearly seven tons of marijuana into the US, via Vancouver. The DEA carefully watched the enterprise take shape. They knew the shipment was coming although Moynihan did not have all the details. Its seizure in Vancouver was, the DEA says, 'a lucky find'. Marks's alleged operations manager in the field, John Denbigh, a Briton nicknamed 'The Vicar', was arrested along with two other people as he flew into Canada.

DEA evidence had already mounted against the smaller fish of the Marks syndicate. For example, in April 1986, at the Beverley Pavilion Hotel in Los Angeles, DEA officers watched an American, Rick Brown, pass a bag, apparently a payment, to Ernie Coombes and a woman friend, Pattie Hayes.

Concrete evidence against the Welshman with the infectious grin sitting in the sunshine of Majorca with his three children, was much harder to get. But, by october 1987, Howard Marks had been thoroughly betrayed. In the Sofitel hotel in Miami, there was a swift but incriminating exchange of notes – $5,000 in cash – between his 'money-manager' Patrick Lane, and the twice-renegade Lord Moynihan.

The incident in the Sofitel Hotel was a small transaction, but a significant one. Altogether, some half-dozen meetings between Moynihan and the dope-traders, in the Philippines, and in Miami, are docketed on the DEA indictment. So too is the personal cable on 11 July 1987 from Howard Marks inviting Moynihan to the Majorca villa.

Lucki did not finally run out until the summer of 1988 for one of the most remarkable young entrepreneurs Britain has ever produced.

Two years of DEA planning came to fruition as squads of local drug enforcement officers started a series of raids in Majorca, New York, Miami, Vancouver, Bangkok, London and Manila, and arrested 14 of the 22 people named in the indictment. One allegedly involved in the procuring of false passports was a London solicitor, James Newton. Ernie Coombes from California was another arrested, along with Phil Sparrowhawk. William Reaves, a US agronomist allegedly expert at dope quality control, was picked up along with Howard in Majorca. Patrick Lane was handcuffed in Miami, and Chien Chun Lo, the Hong Kong travel agent, in London. It was a round-up on a global scale.

Howard was bundled at gunpoint out of his Majorca villa in front of his screaming children and into a Spanish jail. The world's biggest and longest-practising professional dope-smuggler was at last to meet his just deserts. Or so the US Drug Enforcement Agency boasted, after their complicated coup.

It remained to be seen whether the Americans would eventually succeed in extraditing a figure who had become, to his own delight, one of the few surviving celebrities of the Sixties.

No one was forgetting that Howard Marks had charmed, bluffed, bribed and perjured his way to freedom many times in the past, making fools along the way of the members of some hallowed British institutions, including MI6, the judiciary, Balliol College and an Old Bailey jury.

There are those who suspect he might yet return in triumph to the undercover trade he has organised almost uninterrupted for 18 years, ever since he graduated from Balliol at the height of the 'pot-smoking' craze of the 1960s – those almost forgotten days of the Vietnam War, Harold Wilson, and the 'alternative society'.

The Sixties' fashion for cannabis had grown into an unstoppable – and, some say, relatively harmless – worldwide commercial black market. On the day Howard was arrested, as if to mock the DEA's excited claims that they had imprisoned the biggest dope-smuggler in the world, 15 tons of hashish was discovered further up the Spanish coast, at Lloret del Mar. Whoever had smuggled it, it was not Howard. It was probably the Mafia.

But all the policemen in the case seemed obsessed by the disclosures in *High Time*. DEA man Jack Hook repeated in Miami, after his agency targeted the internationally co-ordinated hit-list of 22 names in the Marks conspiracy, that 'Marks said in the book that he was too smart for us. We are very pleased to have the chance to make him eat his words.'

Howard, too, blamed the book for his downfall in an impromptu press conference after his arrest by Spanish police. Dishevelled and chain-smoking, while his wife Judy sobbed noisily in the background, distraught that she had been taken away from her children, he said ruefully that the DEA had been misled by *High Time*'s 'silly' contents into hounding an innocent man, long retired from crime.

The scholarship boy from the Welsh valleys always described dope-smuggling as 'the victimless crime': he himself invariably and continuously smoked joints of extremely potent Thai 'weed', which clearly did little to cloud his business ingenuity. There is no evidence that he ever engaged in the violence that sometimes goes hand in hand with the drugs trade. Yet where was he to find sympathisers in the harsh world of 1988?

Howard spoke bitterly of Moynihan's behaviour at his police cell press-conference. But behind his wife's no doubt genuine tears, and behind Marks's air of outrage, connoisseurs of his Scarlet Pimpernel reputation could see the glimmerings of a defence being constructed.

Yes, he had met Moynihan in the Philippines. In the interests of his travel agency, he thought he could be influential in getting him business connections. Yes, many of his friends were marijuana-smugglers and did come and see him: he did not mind their company and he smoked a lot of dope himself. He had always thought it harmless.

So Howard had met a lot of shady people. So what? The legal problem for the DEA was demonstrated by their use of the extraordinarily powerful RICO statute (Racketeering-Influenced Corrupt Organisations) to charge Howard and seek his extradition to the US. Targeted primarily at the Mafia, this statute aims to lop off the heads of organised crime syndicates by showing they are at the helm of 'an unlawful enterprise'.

But all the DEA had was a sporadic pattern of meetings, phone-calls and contacts across the globe. As a stool-pigeon, Moynihan did not exactly have a reputation for stainless honesty that would easily convince a jury. Howard Marks was far too skilled after 18 years in the dope trade to leave his fingerprints on a single lump of hashish. So the charming self-made millionaire from the Welsh valleys may not have been completely out for the count.

Is the story of the biggest dope-smuggler in the world over yet?

# Index

Marks visit 233